Autonomic Computing

ON DEMAND COMPUTING BOOKS

On Demand Computing
Fellenstein

Grid Computing
Joseph and Fellenstein

Autonomic Computing
Murch

Business Intelligence for the Enterprise
Biere

DB2 BOOKS

DB2 Universal Database v8.1 Certification Exam 700 Study Guide
Sanders

DB2 Universal Database v8.1 Certification Exams 701 and 706 Study Guide
Sanders

DB2 for Solaris: The Official Guide
Bauch and Wilding

DB2 Universal Database v8 for Linux, UNIX, and Windows Database Administration Certification Guide, Fifth Edition
Baklarz and Wong

Advanced DBA Certification Guide and Reference for DB2 Universal Database v8 for Linux, UNIX, and Windows
Snow and Phan

DB2 Universal Database v8 Application Development Certification Guide, Second Edition
Martineau, Sanyal, Gashyna, and Kyprianou

DB2 Version 8: The Official Guide
Zikopoulos, Baklarz, deRoos, and Melnyk

Teach Yourself DB2 Universal Database in 21 Days
Visser and Wong

DB2 UDB for OS/390 v7.1 Application Certification Guide
Lawson

DB2 SQL Procedural Language for Linux, UNIX, and Windows
Yip, Bradstock, Curtis, Gao, Janmohamed, Liu, and McArthur

DB2 Universal Database v8 Handbook for Windows, UNIX, and Linux
Gunning

Integrated Solutions with DB2
Cutlip and Medicke

DB2 Universal Database for OS/390 Version 7.1 Certification Guide
Lawson and Yevich

DB2 Universal Database v7.1 for UNIX, Linux, Windows and OS/2—Database Administration Certification Guide, Fourth Edition
Baklarz and Wong

DB2 Universal Database v7.1 Application Development Certification Guide
Sanyal, Martineau, Gashyna, and Kyprianou

DB2 UDB for OS/390: An Introduction to DB2 OS/390
Sloan and Hernandez

MORE BOOKS FROM IBM PRESS

Enterprise Messaging Using JMS and IBM WebSphere
Yusuf

Enterprise Java Programming with IBM WebSphere, Second Edition
Brown, Craig, Hester, Stinehour, Pitt, Weitzel, Amsden, Jakab, and Berg

IBM Press

Autonomic Computing

On Demand Series

Richard Murch

PRENTICE HALL
Professional Technical Reference
Upper Saddle River, New Jersey 07458
www.phptr.com

Editorial/production supervision: *Donna Cullen-Dolce*
Cover design director: *Jerry Votta*
Cover design: *IBM Corporation*
Manufacturing manager: *Alexis Heydt-Long*
Publisher: *Jeffrey Pepper*
Editorial assistant: *Linda Ramagnano*
Marketing manager: *Debby vanDijk*
IBM Consulting Editor: *Susan Visser*

Published by Pearson Education, Inc.
Publishing as Prentice Hall Professional Technical Reference
Upper Saddle River, NJ 07458

Printed in the United States of America

First Printing

ISBN   0-13-144025-X

Pearson Education LTD.
Pearson Education Australia PTY, Limited
Pearson Education Singapore, Pte. Ltd.
Pearson Education North Asia Ltd.
Pearson Education Canada, Ltd.
Pearson Educación de Mexico, S.A. de C.V.
Pearson Education — Japan
Pearson Education Malaysia, Pte. Ltd.

To all IBM Employees—Past, Present and Future

May you continue to innovate and prosper.

CONTENTS

CHAPTER 2   **COMPLEXITY—IN ALL ITS FORMS**   **23**

CHAPTER 3   **AUTONOMIC PRODUCTS
AND APPLICATIONS**   **43**

PART 2 Industry Demand   57

CHAPTER 4 THE IT INDUSTRY—AN ENGINE OF GROWTH AND OPPORTUNITY   59

PART 3 Autonomic Computing—More Detail   117

CHAPTER 8   AC ARCHITECTURES   119

CHAPTER 9   AUTONOMIC COMPUTING AND OPEN STANDARDS   133

CHAPTER 10 AUTONOMIC IMPLEMENTATION CONSIDERATIONS   159

CHAPTER 11 GRID COMPUTING—AN ENABLING TECHNOLOGY   173

CHAPTER 12   **AUTONOMIC DEVELOPMENT
TOOLS**   **185**

CHAPTER 17 **AUTONOMIC RESEARCH CHALLENGES**   **271**

ACKNOWLEDGMENTS

Writing a book of the present scope and the direction of a new technology can be a daunting task. However I was very fortunate to have the cooperation and help from numerous sources. From within IBM I am grateful to Alan Ganek, Ric Telford, Veronica Tseng, Sam Lightstone, Miles Barrel, Mike Loughran, and Susan Visser who helped with my persistent questions and cajoling requests for information. Particular thanks goes to Peter Andrews of IBM who helped me reconstruct my early drafts as we threw out the original book organization and rearranged the table of contents to make it more legible and understandable.

Special thanks to my editor Jeff Pepper at Pearson Prentice Hall for his inspiration and patience as the book developed and helped by Linda Ramagnano who arranged the administration. Thanks to Jaclyn Vassallo for her copy editing. Also thanks to Donna Cullen-Dolce for the management of the book's production. And thanks to my many IT industry associates, among them Tony Johnson in Trinidad who helped with questions on the scale, impact and scope of autonomic computing.

Lastly, I would like to thank my wife Annette, who has always given me encouragement in anything that I do or projects that I attempt.

PREFACE

he term and technology of autonomic computing is unfamiliar to most IT people. However, it will become familiar and understood after reading this book. Today, IT organizations are faced with the growing challenge of supporting the needs of the corporate enterprise with a reduced budgets and persistent or growing computing demands. For many enterprises, the challenge is compounded by complex architectures and distributed computing infrastructures that were developed over the last 20 years. This situation has caused system management costs to escalate while budgets and corporate spending are shrinking.

CIOs and CTOs everywhere are now tasked with reducing the costs of the IT organization while continuing to support the ongoing and growing computing needs of the enterprise. To succeed, the CIO must find new ways to operate the computing infrastructure of the company more efficiently. Solving this problem requires a new computing model—one that allows for efficiencies in IT infrastructure and resources. Indeed one such model is now emerging. IBM calls it autonomic computing. This is a new methodology for managing enterprise computing environments. Autonomic computing is a new approach that enables software to operate intelligently and dynamically, basing decisions on IT policies and service requirements. Top hardware vendors, such as IBM, Microsoft, Hewlett Packard and others are looking at how to develop servers, operating systems and system management tools and services that encompass the fundamental requirements of autonomic computing.

WHAT IS AUTONOMIC COMPUTING?

The word "autonomic" means acting or occurring involuntarily. Autonomics is used to describe an action or response that occurs without conscious control. In physiology, it relates to the activities controlled by the autonomic nervous system (ANS).

Autonomic computing is the ability to manage your computing enterprise through hardware and software that automatically and dynamically responds to the requirements of your business. This means self-healing, self-configuring, self-optimizing, and self-protecting hardware and software that behaves in accordance to defined service levels and policies. Just like the autonomic nervous system responds to the needs of the body, the autonomic computing system responds to the needs of the business.

GOALS OF AUTONOMIC COMPUTING

Autonomic computing is a new approach to computer and systems management. The purpose is to reduce the cost of managing the IT infrastructure, and at the same time, increase service.

The goals autonomic computing is to reduce the cost of service through far more automated and efficient use of available resources and capacity. This includes dynamic resource allocation, self-healing hardware and software, and setting service-level agreements according to business needs. Autonomic computing have four basic value propositions that can be stated as business goals:

- *Reduced costs*—achieved by better and more efficient resource usage, and by reduced system-management (labor) costs.
- *Improved service levels*—achieved by dynamic adjustments or tuning of IT services.
- Increased agility—achieved by rapid provisioning of new services or resources and scaling of established services.
- *Less complexity*—by self-managing and intelligent decision making in IT operations much of the complexity is managed without human intervention.

There are eight key elements of an autonomic-computing system:

1. *Knowledge of itself, in terms of resources and capabilities*
   An autonomic system has knowledge of its components, status, capacity and connections with other systems to govern itself.
2. *The ability to configure and reconfigure itself*
   The autonomic system is capable of configuring itself and making dynamic adjustments to that configuration as its environment changes.
3. *The ability to continuously self-optimize itself*
   The autonomic system monitors its constituent parts and fine-tunes workflow to achieve established system goals.
4. *Self-healing capabilities*
   The autonomic system must be able to discover problems or potential problems and find alternate ways of using resources or reconfigure the system to keep functioning smoothly.

5. *Self-protection capabilities*

   The autonomic system must be able to protect itself from various types of internal/external attacks and failures to maintain overall system security and integrity.

6. *The ability to discover knowledge of its environment and context—and to adapt accordingly*

   The autonomic system must be able to understand how to best interact with neighboring systems, using available resources and adapting to its environment.

7. *The ability to function in a heterogeneous computing environment*

   The autonomic system must be able to function in a heterogeneous world—in other words, it cannot be a proprietary solution.

8. *The ability to anticipate and adapt to user needs*

   The autonomic system must be able to meet the goals of the business without involving the user for data collection, analysis, and decision-making.

The fundamental process is to have autonomic systems that can enforce your computing policies and service-level agreements through the use of intelligent hardware and software. Maintenance and processing tasks are automated and computing resources are dynamically allocated for maximum efficiencies.

SUMMARY

With the continuos and unrelenting demands for cost reduction and economies of scale that are placed on IT organizations today, new methods for managing the computing enterprise are essential. IT organizations must operate as efficient service centers or contend with the choice of being outsourced. Service centers must operate efficiently and keep costs low to sustain their business. This requires IT organizations to operate differently—using new methods. Automating work, using intelligent software, and managing the enterprise with a holistic view are essential today. Autonomic solutions are required for cost-efficient operations—and must be based on the policies and service-level agreements of the enterprise. The major hardware vendors have initiatives underway to deliver servers, operating systems, and utilities that are self-configuring, self-optimizing, and self-healing. The ISVs must deliver software that not only meets those requirements but add additional value. This leads the major hardware vendors to strive for automatically adjusting servers and dynamically managing workload. It also forces independent software vendors (ISVs) of enterprise management tools to develop autonomic solutions that not only meet the same requirements, but also take advantage of this important technology.

The intent of this book is to provide all readers with and understanding of the scope, issues, elements and examples of autonomic computing and prepare IT for the benefits that can be achieved.

—Richard Murch
Columbus, OH

AUTONOMIC BEGINNINGS

- Autonomic Attributes and the Grand Challenge
- Complexity—In All Its Forms
- Autonomic Products and Applications

AUTONOMIC ATTRIBUTES AND THE GRAND CHALLENGE

INTRODUCTION

In March 2001, IBM Senior Vice President and Director of Research Dr. Paul Horn spoke about the importance and direction of autonomic computing before the National Academy of Engineering conference at Harvard University. He had a very direct message:

> "The information technology industry loves to prove the impossible possible. We obliterate barriers and set records with astonishing regularity. But now we face a problem springing from the very core of our success—and too few of us are focused on solving it. More that any other IT problem, this one—if it remains unsolved—will actually prevent us from moving to the next era of computing. The obstacle is complexity . . . . Dealing with the single most important challenge facing the IT industry."[1]

This was the first time the world was told of IBM's autonomic computing program. Shortly after, Mr. Irving Wladawsky Berger, the IBM Vice President of Strategy and Technology for the IBM Server Group, introduced the Server's Group project (known then by the internal IBM codename eLiza). He stated goal was to provide "self-managing systems." This was expanded to many other divisions and business units within IBM. It was and remains a company-wide project. Project eLiza would eventually become known as the autonomic computing project. Thus began the autonomic computing journey within IBM. Dr. Paul Horn's presentation was released as a manifesto, and as many as 75,000 copies were reportedly distributed to customers, press, media, and researchers worldwide. In the manifesto, Paul Horn invites customers, competitors, and colleagues alike to accept the "Grand Challenge of building computing systems that regulate themselves."

The term Autonomic Computing derives from the human autonomic nervous system (ANS). The same way we take for granted the human body's management of breathing, digestion, and fending off germs and viruses, shown in Figure 1.1, we will take for granted the computer's ability to manage, repair, and protect itself. That process has begun with autonomic computing.

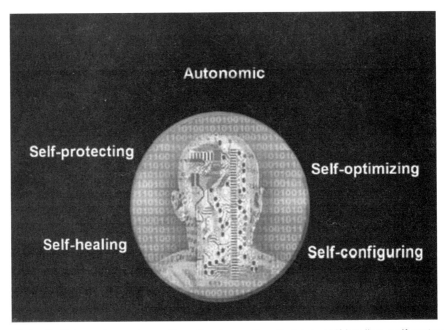

Figure 1.1   Defining autonomic—self-configuring, self-optimizing, self-healing, self-protecting.

We can learn much from how the human body manages itself and apply those same techniques to software to create system management functions for commercial corporations. This is the fundamental purpose of autonomic computing.

The grand challenge of autonomic computing is not just about one company. It is bigger than IBM. To be successful, it must be a joint effort of the entire technology industry, involving software and hardware vendors of all sizes. In addition, it will require the involvement of the academic and university community, as well as customers, who will be the ultimate users of this technology.

The Information Technology (IT) industry today faces the biggest threat to its continuing success. That threat is *complexity*. The systems that we have developed and installed are becoming so complex that they verge on becoming unmanageable. Complexity is everywhere—in architectures, networks, programming languages, and applications and software packages. The IT industry is a victim of its own success. The complexity now facing most CIOs is a direct result of internal and external pressures—management, economic, market—to make everything *cheaper, faster, and smaller.* Now IT staff are succumbing to the effects of this complexity. Data center staff, network administrators, and IT support staff are wrestling daily with major problems of incompatibility and software failures, and they must deal with these problems manually. The situation is further convoluted by computers from multiple vendors—each with their own proprietary software, data protocols, transmission standards, and so on. This presents challenges and makes it difficult for IT personnel to manage an environment containing diverse and heterogeneous infrastructures. Often, IT personnel can't integrate different systems. Even when they can, IT personnel still face difficulties adding new systems to existing environments and then configuring and managing them. Thus, most organizations now spend about three-fourths of their application deployment time and costs on the integration of different systems. They must also deliver services across geographical and business boundaries. This means organizations, in addition to managing heterogeneous vendor and technical environments, also have to put extensive efforts into customizing technologies to meet the requirements of different IT policies, while delivering unique services to customers. This complexity keeps the cost of managing IT infrastructure high. At times, the complexity causes overruns in IT cost and delays in implementation. This, in turn, translates into losses in productivity and missed business opportunities.

The second complexity factor is the increased size of IT infrastructures. The accelerating pace by which myriad devices are being added to almost all IT networks (especially the Internet) further complicates the already sophisticated technological environment. Rapid advances in technology have led to significant improvements in price/performance ratios, thus making technology accessible to many. Today, corporations are no longer dealing with one person accessing one application on a local PC or on a network server. Instead, organizations are seeing thousands, and eventually even millions, of users accessing the same service hosted on one or more servers, potentially at the same time. Relying on human intervention to manage this complexity bears a steadily increasing risk of as the scale and level of complexity extend beyond the comprehension of even highly skilled IT personnel.

The third complexity factor is the escalating costs of systems. The increasing complexity of integrated systems makes the job of maintaining and fixing systems more challenging than ever. In today's competitive world, where customers expect uninterrupted services, even a short breakdown can cost organizations millions of dollars in lost business. In fact, it has been reported that one-third to one-half of typical IT budgets are spent on preventing or recovering from crashes.

The fourth complexity factor is the shortage of skilled labor. Workers who have the knowledge to manage complex IT infrastructures are expensive and remain in short supply, even in today's depressed economy. According to a study by researchers at the University of Berkeley, depending on the type of system, labor costs could surpass infrastructure costs by a factor of 3 to 18. Therefore, the strategy of relying on human intervention to manage IT infrastructure might not be a favorable strategy in the long run, as there might come a point where existing skilled labor and manpower will not be enough to supply e-business on demand. Complexity is discussed in more detail in Chapter 2.

The challenge is to simplify IT. The sheer size and complexity of current computing environments has hindered efforts to integrate systems, databases, applications, and business processes, and has substantially decreased management and operational efficiency. Making IT infrastructures flexible enough to respond quickly and effectively to dynamic customer requirements, marketplace shifts, and competitive demands remains a challenge. Autonomic computing can meet that challenge.

DEFINITIONS

The strict and formal definitions of autonomic and autonomous are as follows:[2]

AUTONOMIC
SYLLABICATION: au·to·nom·ic ADJECTIVE: 1. Physiology a. Of, relating to, or controlled by the autonomic nervous system. b. Occurring involuntarily; automatic: an autonomic reflex. 2. Resulting from internal stimuli; spontaneous. OTHER FORMS: auto·nomi·cal·ly —ADVERB

ATONOMOUS
SYLLABICATION: au·ton·o·mous ADJECTIVE: 1. Not controlled by others or by outside forces; independent: an autonomous judiciary; an autonomous division of a corporate conglomerate. 2. Independent in mind or judgment; self-directed. 3a. Independent of the laws of another state or government; self-governing. b. Of or relating to a self-governing entity: an autonomous legislature. c. Self-governing with respect to local or internal affairs: an autonomous region of a country. 4. Autonomic. ETYMOLOGY: From Greek autonomos: auto-, auto- + nomos, law; OTHER FORMS: au·tono·mous·ly —ADVERB

A QUICK GUIDE TO THE HUMAN AUTONOMIC NERVOUS SYSTEM

IBM chose well when naming their new initiative of self-healing, self-configuring, and self-protecting systems. We would not be able to live healthy normal lives if it were not for our internal autonomic nervous system (ANS). This silent guardian is working constantly to ensure that the body is stable and performing at optimum levels. The human nervous system is divided into the voluntary and involuntary systems. You control the voluntary system. For example, when you feel something uncomfortable, such as pain, heat or bright light, you can choose to move away from it or react to it in some fashion, normally defensive. The involuntary system—which is the autonomic nervous system—handles actions over which you have no control, such as heartbeat, digestion, circulation, and glandular function.

Although it is located in your physical body, the ANS is affected by everyday emotions. For example, when you feel fear, that emotion will be translated into a physical response—the release of the hormone adrenaline—that will increase your heart rate, blood pressure, and digestive processes. This process is managed and controlled by your ANS.

The ANS is very complex. In keeping with the goals of this book, however, we are going to present it as simply as possible. The ANS runs throughout the entire body. It originates from the spinal column and is connected to every gland and organ. See Figure 1.2.

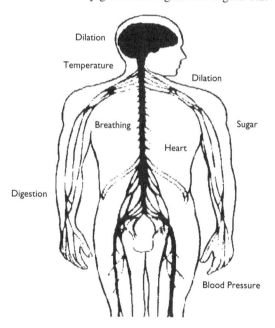

Figure 1.2 An illustration of the human ANS and some of the features automatically regulated by this system. Note that everything originates at the spine.

The ANS is divided into further subsystems: the sympathetic nervous system (SNS) and the parasympathetic nervous system (PNS). A third division, the metasympathetic system (MNS) is related to the central nervous system in the brain. Put very simply, the SNS tends to speed up responses in our muscles and organs to help us adapt to stress, while the PNS slows down those responses. When these systems are in balance, after a high stress response, the PNS will help to calm you down. It is known in modern terms as the "flight or fight" response.

Under conditions of balance, the SNS turns on organ responses to high levels of environmental stress. When the stressful conditions are removed, the PNS turns on to restore balance within your organ systems. Under conditions of imbalance, the SNS may be turned on for long periods of time, and the PNS may be turned on as well. This is like having your foot on the accelerator pedal and the brake at the same time.

The ANS system is a marvel of bodily management. If it is running well, you will feel well. The autonomic nervous system is always working, never resting or going offline. Even when you are sleeping, it continues to manage bodily functions. It is NOT only active during "fight or flight" or "rest and digest" situations. Rather, the ANS acts to maintain normal internal functions and works with the rest of the nervous system. Most important of all, the ANS does its work without any conscious recognition. This allows you to think and act the way you want. It simply says:

"Don't worry about it. I've got it covered."

This is precisely the approach we need to build future business computing systems.

E-BUSINESS ON DEMAND

IBM has announced their vision for the next major strategy of business adoption. They call it *e-business on demand*™. It is a statement of IBM's belief of how businesses will need to transform themselves to be successful. Businesses will have to adapt to cope with ever-increasing pressures from competition and other factors associated with the global economy. The modern business will require full integration across people, processes, and information, including suppliers, distributors, customers, and employees.

Autonomic computing is a fundamental aspect of IBM's e-business on demand strategy. E-business on demand is designed to address the growing dynamic between IT solutions and business strategies. Corporations and their management regard technology as a means to power business evolution to the next competitive level. To compete and win in today's markets, companies must be agile and responsive to customer demands, marketplace shifts, and competitive pressure.

The ability of e-business on demand solutions to leverage existing IT infrastructures with additional integrated services and capacities has implications for corporations of every size. Small- to medium-sized businesses can use e-business on demand solutions to gain the economic scale of large companies. Large corporations can use e-business on demand to become as nimble as small businesses. At its heart, IBM's e-business on demand offers corporate IT environments where every single employee, customer, partner, application, and process has seamless access to any and all necessary business assets, information, and resources.

IBM defines an e-business on demand business as a corporation whose business processes, integrated end-to-end across the company and with key partners, suppliers, and customers, can respond with speed to any customer demand, market opportunity, or external threat.

There are four key attributes of an e-business on demand business:

- **Response**—The ability to sense and respond to dynamic, unpredictable changes in demand, supply, pricing, labor, competition, capital markets, and the needs of its customers, partners suppliers, and employees.
- **Variability**—The ability to adapt processes and cost structures to reduce risk while maintaining high productivity and financial predictability.
- **Focus**—The ability to concentrate on its core competencies and differentiating capabilities.
- **Resiliency**—The ability to manage changes and external threats while consistently meeting the needs of all of its constituents.

These attributes define the business itself. For a business to successfully attain and maintain these attributes, it must build an IT infrastructure that is designed to specifically support the goals of the business. An entirely new kind of IT infrastructure must be put in place to support an e-business on demand business. IBM calls this infrastructure the e-business on demand operating environment.

To achieve this vision, IBM believes that information resources must be:

- **Virtualized**—allowing business assets, including data, applications and resources, to flow freely wherever and whenever they are needed;
- **Integrated**—enabling the efficient movement of information between systems, applications, databases, and business processes;
- **Open**—assuring the free integration and flow of business assets in an IT world that is both practically and philosophically heterogeneous; and
- **Autonomic**—empowering the stability and reliability of solutions in endemically complex corporate IT environments.

There are many technologies, both new and evolving, that can make this environment a reality. An e-business on demand operating environment is about a broad set of standards working together to provide a consistent and comprehensive set of services and deliverables, as illustrated by Figure 1.3.

An e-business on demand business is responsive, variable, focused, and resilient. To attain these business attributes, an information technology infrastructure must be put in place that supports the business and provides true business value. An e-business on demand operating environment supports the e-business on demand business by providing the capability to integrate, virtualize, and automate systems and processes.

Based on open standards
- XML
- Web services
- J2EE
- Open Grid Services
  Architecture
- Common Information
  Model

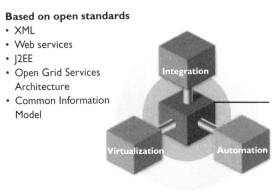

Shared components
- Integrated system console
- Security and identity
- Choreography
- Transaction coordination
- Data persistence
- Workload management
- Collaboration
- Application connectivity
- Configuration tool

Figure 1.3 The e-business on demand environment based on open standards and shared components.

AUTONOMIC COMPUTING ELEMENTS

To be truly autonomic, a computing system needs to "know and understand itself"—and comprise components that also possess a system identity. Since a "system" can exist at many levels, an autonomic system will need detailed knowledge of its components, current status, operating environment, and ultimate capacity, and of all connections with other systems. It will need to know the extent of its "owned" resources, those it can borrow, buy, or lend, and which ones can be shared or should be isolated. As shown in Figure 1.4, autonomic computing has four basic elements: self-configuring, self-healing, self-optimizing, and self-protecting.

SELF-CONFIGURING

An autonomous computing system must be able to install and set up software automatically. To do so, it will utilize dynamic software configuration techniques, which means applying technical and administrative direction and surveillance to identify and document the functional and physical characteristics of a configurable item. Also to control changes to those characteristics, to record and report change processing and implementation status, and to verify compliance with specified service levels.

Also, downloading new versions of software and installing regular service packs are required. When working with other autonomous components, an autonomous system will update new signatures for virus protection and security levels. Self-configuration will use adaptive algorithms to determine the optimum configurations.

Figure 1.4 The four aspects of autonomic computing: self-configuring, self-healing, self-optimizing, and self-protecting.

Examples:

1. Updating Web pages dynamically with software changes, testing those changes, analyzing the results, releasing the system back into production, and reporting back to self-management whether the procedure was successful.
2. Installation, testing, and release of regular vendor service packs.
3. Installation of vendor patches, corrections, and modifications together with the necessary testing and release.
4. Installation of new software releases—automatically and seamlessly.

SELF-OPTIMIZING

An autonomous system will never settle for the status quo. It will be constantly monitoring predefined system goals or performance levels to ensure that all systems are running at optimum levels. With the business constantly changing and demands from customers and suppliers changing equally fast, self-adapting requirements will be needed.

Self-optimization will be the key to allocating e-utility-type resources—detemining when an increase in processing cycles is needed, how much in needed, where they are needed, and for how long. To be effective, autonomous self-optimization will need advanced data and feedback. The metrics need to be in a form where rapid analysis can take place. Many new and innovative techniques are needed for optimization to be successful—for example, control theory is needed in new autonomous infrastructures. New algorithms to process control decisions will be needed.

Examples:

1. Calling for additional processing power from the e-utility when needed. Releasing those additional cycles when peaks are over.
2. Working with outside vendor software.
3. Interfacing with other autonomic modules to exchange data and files.
4. Optimum sub-second response times for all types of access devices, such as personal computers, handheld devices, and media phones.

SELF-HEALING

Present computer systems are very brittle. They fail at the slightest problem. If a period, a comma, or a bracket is not correct, the software will fail. We still have much to do in designing forgiving systems. Autonomous computing systems will have the ability to discover and repair potential problems to ensure that the systems run smoothly.

With today's complex IT architectures, it can be hours before a problem is identified at the root cause level. System staff members need to pore over listings of error logs and memory dumps, tracing step-by-step back to the point of failure. The cost of downtime to the business is prohibitive. For example, in large-scale banking networks, the cost can be as much as $2,600,000 per hour. Self-healing systems will be able to take immediate action to resolve the issue, even if further analysis is required. Rules for self-healing will need to be defined and applied. As autonomous systems become more sophisticated, embedded intelligence will be applied to discover new rules and objectives. For example, IBM will be building SMART (Self-Managing and Resource Tuning) databases into upcoming versions of their DB2 database product. This database is designed to run with less need for human intervention. For example, the user can opt not to be involved, and the database will automatically detect failures when they occur (and correct them) and configure itself by installing operating systems and data automatically to cope with the changing demands of e-business and the Internet.

Examples:

1. Self-correcting Job Control Language (JCL): when a job fails, the errors or problems are identified and jobs rerun without human intervention.
2. An application error forces the entire system to halt. After root cause analysis, the error is corrected, recompiled, tested, and moved back into production.
3. A database index fails. The files are automatically re-indexed, tested, and loaded back into production.
4. Automatically extend file space and database storage, according to previous data on growth and expansion.

SELF-PROTECTING

In an increasingly hostile corporate world, autonomous systems must identify, detect, and protect valuable corporate assets from numerous threats. They must maintain integrity and accuracy and be responsible for overall system security. For years before the Internet, each corporation was an isolated island where threats usually came from within.

Now, outside threats come daily, and security and protection are paramount. Threats must be identified quickly and protective action taken.

Autonomic system solutions must address all aspects of system security at the platform, operating system, network, application, Internet, and infrastructure levels. This involves developing new cryptographic techniques and algorithms, their secure implementation, and designing secure networking protocols, operating environments, and mechanisms to monitor and maintain overall system integrity. Such security solutions need to be standardized to provide/preserve interoperability and to ensure that these techniques are used in a correct way.

To achieve this will require continuous sensors feeding data to a protection center. A log of events will be written and accessed when appropriate for audit purposes. To manage the threat levels, we might expect a tiered level. Threats can be escalated through the tiers for increasing action and priority.

Examples:

1. Confirm the ability of backup and recovery resources that may be needed.
2. Implement tiered security levels.
3. Focus resources on network monitoring and immediately disconnect computer systems with suspicious network traffic.
4. Verify that network configurations inventories are correct and, if not, take action.
5. Contact system administrators outside of autonomous system and other offices that may be affected by the increasing threat levels.
6. Have the system verify that all computer systems are at the appropriate version levels, including "patches." Update automatically as needed.
7. Resolve any open security concerns.
8. Implement any special software for additional security protection according to the threat level.
9. Contact offsite vendors to determine if any preventive measures (patches, etc.) to be applied to both hardware and software.

OPEN STANDARDS

We have already identified that the IT industry is going through major changes. New technology—such as autonomic computing, Web services, and grid computing—is creating tremendous opportunities to massively increase business profitability. The potential of these technologies to transform business is amazing, and open standards will play a critical role in this new e-business on demand world. Just as open standards were critical to the emergence of the Internet and the first generation of e-business, they will play a critical role in the e-business on demand generation.

We can define open standards as interfaces or formats that are openly documented and have been accepted in the industry through either formal or *de facto* processes, and are freely available for adoption by the industry. Examples include HTTP, HTML, WAP, TCP/IP, VoiceXML, XML, and SQL. They are typically built by software engineers and programmers working for software companies that collaborate under known industry standards-based organizations such as the W3C, OASIS, OMA, and IETF.

Figure 1.5 illustrates the variety of different standards organizations.

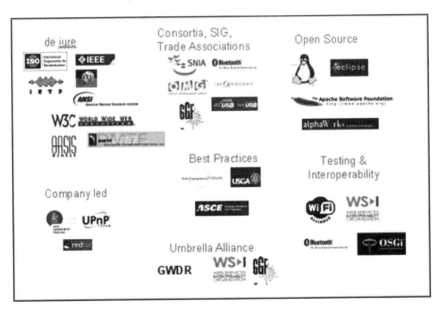

Figure 1.5   The landscape of standards organizations.

The open standards community counts major vendors such as IBM, HP, Sun, Microsoft, Cisco, and Oracle among its active contributors. Other members include Red Hat, Apple, and Intel. These examples are, of course, only a drop among the thousands of other companies involved in these initiatives. Their members also include contributors from the academic and university world, such as Stanford, Berkeley, and MIT.

Why are major IT vendors and software companies increasingly interested in open standards? Primarily because investing in these communities makes good business sense. The global computer industry must cooperate in developing the necessary open standards and interfaces to make future technology work and to establish standards that will support an autonomic computing environment.

Therefore autonomic computing needs open standards to be successful. IBM strongly agrees that open standards are *imperative* for the whole e-business on demand strategy. We define open standards as:

> The specifications that enable the construction of the universal building blocks for the development of software and solutions.

The adoption of open standards for autonomic computing may appear a daunting task, as each component of autonomic computing will need to "describe" itself to other software, their resources, and most importantly, their requirements. For example, the self-protection component will need to contact a virus signature vendor and state, "Send me the latest signature file to interface with adaptive algorithms."

A final comment on open standards:

> The days of developing and selling proprietary systems are over and we must go forward together with strategies that will benefit our future industry. Our customers deserve better.

AUTONOMIC COMPUTING—WHY NOW?

There are four answers to the question of how we know the time of autonomic computing has come:

1. Computing infrastructure and system complexity demands it.
2. The current business climate demands it.
3. The technology has evolved enough to deliver it.
4. We must act to prevent the situation becoming any worse.

First, computing systems continue to evolve to meet changing business needs. But process-based computing systems are more complex than any of the preceding paradigms. Dynamic process-based computing systems give corporations the ability to automate business processes and the flexibility to optimize and adapt processes according to their business needs. These systems interconnect all aspects of doing business and integrate multiple business applications. Integration results in computing infrastructures that are both interconnected, because multiple technologies are involved in delivering business services and processes, and dynamic, because new application modules and functions can be added at a faster rate. Technology interconnection and dynamism breed maintenance difficulties for three reasons:

1. It becomes impossible for manual-user administration, technology maintenance, and management processes to keep pace with the rate of infrastructure change.
2. Management of individual technologies and software modules does not guarantee the availability and performance of the end-to-end service or process.
3. Inter-relationships between individual technologies and software modules increase the complexity of configuration, performance, and security problems that need to be resolved.

Second, almost every Total Cost of Ownership (TCO) study shows that the more moving parts a system has, the more expensive it is to maintain in good working order. Indeed, the current rule of thumb is that for every dollar spent on computing infrastructure, another ten are spent for ongoing management. This ratio increases as system complexity grows. Eventually the growing cost structure becomes too much for the corporation to bear, even when the economy as a whole is performing well. The current weak spending environment places enormous pressure on IT departments to lower costs and increase the returns delivered by existing infrastructure. There is only one way to do that in an IT operations center. That is to automate tasks that are normally handled by people. The autonomic computing technology provides executives a blueprint for increasing the cost-effectiveness of their IT departments.

Finally, IT management technology has been evolving to deliver true "lights out operations," a concept for computing infrastructures having distributed processing power, modular software architectures, accessibility over public networks, and frequent configuration changes. Until now, these trends have been developing separately, related only by the basic concept of increasing the intelligence of management tools. The time to act is NOW.

IS AUTONOMIC COMPUTING NEW?

The phrase autonomic computing is new to many IT staff and is used to define the new technology of self-managing systems. However, the practice of designing and implementing self-managing systems has long been a goal and objective of IBM. Numerous examples exist within the IBM portfolio of products in hardware and software, some of which go back over twenty years or more.

A few examples:

1. The IBM 4300 series of mainframe computers were introduced in 1982. This line was a forerunner of the newer range of mainframes in use today, such as the OS/390 series. A feature was introduced with the 4300 that included internal self-diagnostics. Moreover, it contained a feature to transmit findings, logs, memory dumps, and return codes to remote IBM system engineers, who could then provide customers with quicker solutions.

2. More recently, personal computers now have some self-configuration abilities and can receive updates from the Internet, such as critical updates to operating systems. They also have the power to allocate memory.

3. The IBM Tivoli suite of software products has many autonomic capabilities. The IBM Tivoli Storage Manager has self-configuration features, such as automatic domain configuration and file identification; self-correction features, such as storage pool, restoration, and correction; self-protection features, such as automated backup to protect data and files when needed; and policy-based systems that optimize disk and tape storage systems.

4. RAID (Redundant Array of Independent Disks) systems are another example. These systems connect multiple disk arrays into one logical unit. If errors or problems arise in read/write functions, data is switched automatically to another part of the array.

So, the processes of self-managing systems have existed for some time. While these technologies move in the right direction, they are a precursor to fully autonomic computing. Autonomic computing enhances and builds on the base of existing IBM portfolio products and brings better levels of automation through the five level processes.

WHAT HAPPENS IF IT DOES NOT CHANGE?

What if the unthinkable happens, and we do not adopt autonomic computing or similar technology? This nightmarish scenario hardly bears consideration.

Mixtures of the following events will happen with different severity.

1. Complexity will continue to increase, reaching unmanageable proportions.
2. Further pressures will increase on IT staff to fix unfixable problems.
3. Reliability of systems and performance will deteriorate. Businesses will suffer.
4. Corporations will lose their competitive edge and lose substantial markets and profits.
5. Corporations will be required to increase their IT budgets to astronomical proportions.
6. Senior management will reject these astronomical budget requests—the cycle of problems will continue.
7. More and more skilled IT staff will be needed at substantial costs.
8. The health of many IT staff will suffer.
9. Chaos.

The IT industry has lingered too long in the religion of overspecialization, in which integration was just another specialty. The IT industry has made spectacular progress in almost every aspect of computing. But it has not made enough in the one area that now counts most: dealing with the complexity generated by all the systems we have installed so far. In this heady rush, there is a danger of losing sight of the very people who use IT and who have come to depend on us for increased productivity and improvement in many aspects of their daily lives. We've made it unnecessarily difficult for them to tap the potential we've promised them. *It's time for this to change. It must change.* Chaos is not an option.

This next era of computing will enable progress and abilities we can barely envision today. But the best measure of our success will be when our customers do not think about the functioning of computing systems.

CREATING THE AUTONOMIC CULTURE

Managing an increasingly diverse IT population requires cross-cultural competencies. A global, agile, virtual, matrixed, e-business on demand organization should be able to build effectiveness across national, organizational, team, and interpersonal barriers. Successful cross-cultural IT managers typically are flexible and possess a broad behavioral repertoire.

Culture is the complex pattern of ideas, emotions and observable behaviors that tend to be expected, reinforced, and rewarded by and within a particular group. You can most easily understand and observe culture at four levels:

- National
- Individual
- Team
- Organizational

Culture is not an inherited characteristic. It is shaped by what we learn in the context of our social group or category. Culture goes beyond narrow nationalistic definitions.

WHY IS A CULTURE IMPORTANT?

As an IT person, culture can be important to you. There are thousands of examples where cultural misunderstandings have killed deals, harmed working relationships, inhibited sales, or increased costs. You must be able to succeed everywhere. Understanding culture is part of success. When you become aware of potential cultural differences and realize their implications, you dramatically increase your ability to work with people across the globe. You will also enhance your competitive advantage by building stronger, more sustainable relationships. If you remain unaware of cultural differences, you can jeopardize business relationships and entire projects. Regrettably, IT culture is a subject that has been avoided.

IBM uses the COM (Cultural Orientation Model) developed by TMC of Princeton, NJ. This model is based on common tendencies of people on a number of dimensions, or values, and has identified the dimensions as:

1. **Environment:** How individuals view and relate to the people, objects, and issues in their sphere of influence.
2. **Time:** How individuals perceive the nature of time and its use.

3. **Action:** How individuals conceptualize actions and interactions.

4. **Communication:** How individuals express themselves.

5. **Space:** How individuals demarcate their physical and psychological space.

6. **Power**: How individuals view differential power relationships.

7. **Individualism:** How individuals define their identity.

8. **Competitiveness:** How individuals are motivated.

9. **Structure:** How individuals approach change, risk, ambiguity, and uncertainty.

10. **Thinking:** How individuals conceptualize.

Figure 1.6 illustrates this model.

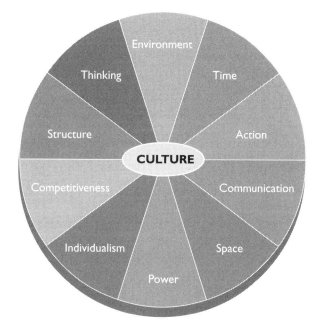

Figure 1.6   The Cultural Orientation Model.

This approach will be valuable for corporations and IT departments as one of the first steps towards autonomic computing transition. What is needed is an *autonomic cultural transition plan* based on the elements described above.

IS AUTONOMIC COMPUTING WORKING TODAY?

Autonomic computing is real. IBM customers are using it TODAY, and they are beginning to reap the rewards and benefits of this technology.

A few brief examples follow.

Efes Pilsen

This European brewer Efes Pilsen taps into increased productivity and sales with a high-availability data warehouse solution offering self-managing autonomic functions.

Santix

This systems integrator reduces the workload on administrators with self-optimizing, predictive software using IBM's Tivoli management suite to help prevent breaches in its service level agreements with its clients.

Bankdata

This bank uses autonomic hardware and software to help transform numbers into meaningful knowledge, allowing its management to understand customer habits, preferences, and profitability potential.

Below are two quotes and observations from IBM customers of autonomic technology that sum up the feeling of success that has been achieved.

> "People make mistakes when they are under pressure. Autonomic computing holds the promise in helping administrators reduce human error and improve data integrity. Our users can take advantage of the autonomic, self-managing features that IBM delivers."

> —Andrew Hall, President, ETI-NET[3]

> "We have derived great benefit from IBM's autonomic features—including self-configuration features, such as automatic hardware detection, as well as self-healing 'call home' functionality that alerts support staff in the event of a failure."

> —Frank Buthler, System Programming Manager, Bankdata[4]

SAME SOUP—DIFFERENT FLAVOR

True to its technological roots, the new self-managing industry, press and vendors have come up with a plethora of different names for autonomic computing and related technologies. This is likely to cause confusion to management and end users alike. There is a case for standardization here before the industry becomes mature. Below are a few examples.

- **Adaptive Enterprise**—Cap Gemini Ernst & Young
- **Dynamic Systems Initiative**—Microsoft

- **e-Business on Demand**—IBM
- **Autonomic Computing**—IBM
- **N1**—Sun Microsystems
- **On-Demand Computing**—EDS
- **Organic IT**—Forrester Research
- **Policy-Based Computing**—Gartner
- **Real-Time Enterprise**—Gartner
- **Utility Data Center (UDC)**—Hewlett-Packard

SUMMARY AND CONCLUSIONS

Today's competitive business landscape is bristling with innovation and change. Tomorrow will be different—it will be heightened and even more forceful. Therefore only the most durable and robust business models will survive. In this brutal environment, the IT strategy must be vigorous enough to stand out, yet flexible enough to evolve in an e-business on demand world. CIOs and IT management must be attuned to this shifting reality and aim to implement the technologies that directly address this actuality.

New technologies are rapidly emerging, and new versions of existing technologies will continue to be released. To keep pace, businesses need to quickly adapt their existing applications to new technologies and business requirements without losing their investments in current systems.

The ultimate scope of autonomic computing will go beyond just the corporate world. The technology of autonomic computing is based on sensors and effectors. (See Chapter 8 for more explanation.) When sensors are embedded in other devices, exciting things can happen. For example, Chrysler has long been perfecting Antilock Braking Systems (ABS) to ensure driver and passenger safety. The ABS is comprised of electronic sensors and solenoid valves in the wheel hubs. These sensors and valves use the concept of autonomic systems to prevent the wheels from locking when cars go into a skid. Goodyear and Michelin have created "Run-Flat" tires that allow drivers to drive safely for a few more miles after a tire puncture. Besides having a reinforced sidewall in the tire that acts to maintain the chassis level when a tire is deflated, Run-Flat tires also have sensors that relay information about the air pressure to the dashboard of the car so that drivers can monitor the pressure levels and act accordingly.

Sensors and embedded computers already exist in most industrial environments, but they are typically reserved for use on small numbers of expensive pieces of equipment. What happens when these devices make their way from the few mission-critical components to the multitude of equipment all around you? Just one benefit alone, such as real-time awareness of potential component failure, can save a utility from costly downtime, which in some cases can cost up to $1 million each hour.

Prototypes of smart homes are being built and tested. Smart homes are equipped with a network of sensors that track and monitor everything from cooking habits to purchasing activities to level and quality of physical movement. One potential outcome of this research is the early detection of the onset of dementia by monitoring changes in activity patterns and levels. A broader goal is to use the sensor data to build technologies that support and enhance people's ability to conduct normal daily activities, by providing an appropriate level of support without making people prematurely dependent on technology-based assistance.

Once sensors are placed in everything, computing will be truly pervasive. Already we have sensors and chips in cell phones to refrigerators and toasters. In the future, sensors in shopping malls will pick up your preferences as you enter the mall. This trend will run in parallel with the adoption of autonomic computing in the corporate world.

Autonomic computing in the corporate world is needed. There is not much of an alternative.

NOTES

1. Dr. Paul Horn, *Autonomic Computing, IBM's Perspective on the State of Information Technology, IBM Corporation*. October 15, 2001.
2. *The American Heritage® Dictionary of the English Language*: Fourth Edition. 2000.
3. See *www.306.ibm.com/autonomic/success_stories.shtml*.
4. See *www.ibm.com/software/data/solutions/pdf2/bankdata.pdf*.

CHAPTER 2

COMPLEXITY—IN ALL ITS FORMS

INTRODUCTION

T he very positive landscape that we described in the first chapter is clouded by a significant threat to progress—the threat of complexity. Complexity threatens to overwhelming our workplaces and our society. The reality in which we are living at the beginning of the third millennium is characterized by a drastic rise in complexity, which has caused rapid changes in corporate and human behavior. Complexity is an inherently subjective concept; what is considered complex depends on the point of view of a given individual or organization. When we term something complex, what we are doing is using everyday language to express a feeling or impression that we dignify with the label complex.

Every time a decision is made to significantly change an aspect of your business, you are starting a new battle between complexity and simplicity. This battle is fought on many fronts, and most of the time complexity wins. The first front is the analytical one, of which financial justification is the major part. Complexity usually sneaks across this front unseen. The cost of complexity is hard to quantify, so it is generally not considered.

"Clarity" is one of those rare words in the English language that is so basic, so fundamental, that it virtually defines itself. We know when we have clarity, but it can be very elusive. More importantly, it is something we need—in our lives and our businesses—if we wish to move forward. It is critical to have clarity. Questions in business need to be asked routinely, such as "Is there a more simple way?" and "What will the impact of this decision be on the business in terms of added complexity?" Simplicity won't always win the war against complexity. However, it has a much better chance of doing so if you take the first step and make the commitment to simplicity as a value. One small step for you, one giant step for your business.

There are numerous examples in our public, organizational, and private lives that illustrate the urgent need to create awareness of this critical problem and to seek clarity and, ultimately, simpler processes.

SOME EXAMPLES OF OUR COMPLEX SOCIETY

- In the Netherlands, an elderly woman spent a week in a shopping mall. She could not find the exit. She bought food during the day and slept on a bench at night. She could not find anyone to ask where the exit was.
- In France farmers rioted because they could not understand the new laws they were supposed to obey. They blocked the roads for days with tractors and farm equipment, almost paralyzing the country. The laws were too complicated.
- Industry research suggests that, unless they have an adolescent at home, over 90 percent of consumers do not use 95 percent of the features of their video recorders because they are too difficult to use.
- When we shop at a large mall, we frequently forget where the car was parked. Mall owners employ staff to help customers find their lost cars.
- Each year, millions of Americans wrestle with their income tax returns. The laws are so complicated that one in five of the nation's taxpayers wait until the final week to file their taxes by the deadline. In 2002, 27.1 million taxpayers—more than 20 percent—waited until the last minute to submit their income tax return. Generating maximum tax refunds is now a national pastime.
- Programmers and technicians write computer manuals, as they are responsible for creating the software. Know the computer systems as well as they do, they cannot understand the problems facing users who do not know the systems. The result is confusion due to complexity.
- After NASA first started sending astronauts into space, they quickly discovered that ballpoint pens wouldn't work in zero gravity. To combat the problem, NASA scientists spent a decade and several million dollars developing a pen that writes in zero gravity, upside down, underwater, on almost any surface, including glass, and at temperatures ranging from below freezing to 300°C. Cost to the taxpayer? Don't ask.

The Russians were faced with the same problem; they used a pencil.

CARTOONS ARE SIMPLE

We should admire the profession of cartooning. Cartoonists are daily faced with the challenge of making all sorts of readers smile and laugh by delivering an image and text in a simple, direct fashion. I suggest that they do this by using a simplified approach.

1. **Cartoonists use simple language and images.** Through its use of parable, a cartoon must speak to a wide audience.

2. **Cartoonists focus on the basics.** A cartoon strips the topic down to its bare essentials without clouding them in detail. The philosophy is that while the details may be important, they can always come later by reading about it elsewhere. Nonetheless, they won't be worth anything if the fundamentals are not understood first.

3. **Cartoonists do not think for us.** A cartoon should encourage us to interpret its message for ourselves. In this way, our conclusions are much more powerful and much more likely to stay with us.

Perhaps most powerful of all, is that cartoonists' results are **concepts** that can be easily shared. Readers of "cartoons" become members of an informal "club." They might share a new "language" and can readily compare each other's individual approaches to change using the simple cartoons. Cartoonists have to make the complex simple and direct. There are no second chances.

SOFTWARE COMPLEXITY AND DISASTERS

There is a long history of software problems that have led to serious disasters. The cost has been astronomical. Below is a list of some of the better-known failures. The figures in brackets are the estimated costs of the project. As you read through this list, a recurring theme is that these large projects were extremely complex—to design, test, construct, and implement, as well as manage.

- 1960—The first successful U.S. Corona spy satellite mission was launched after 12 previous failures due to software problems. (Cost too large to calculate)
- 1962—The United States launched Ranger 3 to land scientific instruments on the Moon, but the probe missed its target by some 22,000 miles due to software problems. ($14 million)
- 1962—Mariner I was launched for Venus, veered off course within seconds, and was ordered destroyed. It was later found that a single hyphen from the computer launch code was missing. ($16 million)
- 1981—U.S. Air Force Communications and Control Software exceeded estimated development costs by a factor of 10. ($3.2 million)
- 1987–1993—Attempt to build an integrated car and license software management system in California failed. ($44 million)
- 1992—The London Ambulance system had to be scrapped due to the system not being tested sufficiently before introduction. Lost emergency calls and duplicate dispatches were just a few of the problems encountered. ($50 million)
- 1993—Integration of SABRE reservation system with other online systems failed. ($162 million)
- 1995—The new Denver International airport was delayed for over nine months due to the software problems of the baggage handling system. (Cost not disclosed)
- 1997—All development on California's SACSS system was stopped after exceeding budgets. Eight alternative solutions were later considered. ($312 million)

- 1999—The Ariane Rocket—launched by the European Space Agency—was destroyed shortly after takeoff. The cause? Failure in the ADA launch codes. ($500 million)
- 2000—The Mars Polar Lander had software problems with metrics conversion that lead to the total loss of the spacecraft. It crashed into the surface of Mars. ($165 million)

It is estimated that software failures cost industry over $100 billion in the year 2000. Some observers say that figure is conservative and the actual is much higher.

Software that is used in critical life-supporting equipment should always be critically tested before release. On occasion, failures can have dire consequences. Take the case of the Panamanian x-ray disaster that happened in 2001. An x-ray machine was incorrectly computing the dosage rates and exposure on patients. Twenty-eight people were overexposed, and three died. The remaining survivors are likely to develop "serious complications, which in some cases may ultimately prove fatal," according to the FDA.[1]

There have also been several near misses. For example, in March 1997, the three-man Soyuz TM-24 barely evaded two potential catastrophic software flaws during its return to Earth. First, after separating from its propulsion module, the command module was nearly rammed by the jettisoned unit when its control computer fired the wrong set of pointing rockets. Moments later, the command module's autopilot lined it up for atmospheric entry—but in precisely the wrong direction, nose first rather than heat shield first. Manual intervention fixed that problem—but even at the height of the shuttle-Mir U.S.-Russian space partnership, there's no indication the Russians shared news of either of these flaws with NASA.

The rest of the descent appeared to go as planned, and the parachutes and soft-landing engines did their job. As in about half of all Soyuz landings, the landing module wound up on its side, probably pulled over by a gust of wind in its parachute just at touchdown.

The three men, who knew they were far off course, were able to open the hatch themselves and get out, as it's a much easier drop to the ground when the capsule is on its side. They then waited two hours to be spotted by a search plane, and several hours more for the arrival of the first helicopter. This is not what you would call a smooth and predictable landing.

The complexity of large software systems cannot be overemphasized. We simply do not have the rigorous testing and deployment mechanisms that can manage this complex environment. More efficient automated tools are needed to break down the complexity and manage it. Where automated tools do not exist, we need to manage the complexity with self-managing systems.

One would hope that we would have learned our lessons already, but it appears that we have not. Until we do, software disasters will continue to haunt us.

WHAT IS COMPLEXITY?

There are numerous definitions, interpretations, and academic theories associated with the study of organizational complexity. In this book and for simplicity's sake, we shall define complexity as arising from the inter-relationship, interaction, and interconnectivity of elements or processes within an organization or system and between a system and its environment.

Complexity is the opposite of simplicity. Complexity is simplicity that has failed. There is a simpler way of doing most things if there is a desire and motivation to look for it. But simplicity rarely happens on its own. There is always the possibility that there is no simple way of doing something. Even if there isn't, it is always worth the effort to find out. However, the simpler method is not easy. It requires creative thinking, effort, and analysis. It is always difficult to find a simpler method. But when organizations provide the tools to conduct business in a simpler fashion, there is always recognition that a substantial event has occurred.

Below is a set of eight general rules that define a process for reducing complexity in business.

1. **Management must support the initiative.**
   This is an obvious rule, but senior management must support and provide adequate resources, personnel, and time to make the project a success. Complexity reduction is a new process that may be unfamiliar to management. Therefore it will need a senior person as its champion.
2. **Determination to succeed.**
   The project team and the individuals on that team must be motivated to succeed. Clear guidelines for expectations, roles, milestones, and recommendations must be identified and agreed upon.
3. **Understanding and knowledge.**
   The team of individuals needs to be selected on the basis of their knowledge of and experience in the areas or processes under review for complexity reduction. If a process is to undergo complexity reduction, the team must be knowledgeable about the process to be successful. But they must have the motivation to make things simpler.
4. **Flexibility, options, and design.**
   The keyword for this rule is design. In order to make simpler and more effective business processes, analysis of the options and alternatives is required to reduce the stated complexity. Teams should present several options that provide flexibility in the solution.
5. **Challenge everything.**
   There is a rule that everything needs to be challenged. Teams need to dig deep in the pile and evaluate the need for every process or business area. This can often be difficult, as other managers will offer significant resistance to any challenge. Turf battles often result from the quest for simplicity. Systems have a tendency to grow increasingly complicated, and there is no effort to simplify them.

6. Decomposition.

Complexity can be effectively understood and often reduced when processes are broken down in to smaller, more manageable segments. This is the process of decomposition. Decomposition also clarifies thinking and will illustrate the complexity already in place.

7. Best of breed solution.

Teams need to recommend the best and simplest solution that will work for the business process. In presenting such a solution, the process by which it was arrived at must be documented, and a business case must be created, explaining potential reductions in costs, reduced timescales, and the like. The solution needs to be "defensible," as many managers will wish to see it fail. Determination and preparation for this event will help it to succeed through to implementation.

8. Continuous effort in reducing complexity.

Reducing business complexity is not just a one-time effort. There is a defined need to make it a continuous program with the resources and necessary funding to take on future projects. If this does not happen, complexity will creep back into the enterprise, and soon everything will be back to square one. Future new projects should undergo a simplicity review and have representatives that can assist other project teams to be successful. Spread the word on simplicity, and make complexity reduction a part of corporate culture.

Consider Figure 2.1. This structure can be described as follows:

- *Simple work management and coordination:* Business processes, project tasks, and technology are not new to the organization. Decision maker is known and has authority. Work is mainly coordinating resources and communicating progress.
- *Complex work management and coordination:* Business process design is nontrivial, or new project management methods or technology are in use. Project requires multidisciplined resources with multiple work assignments. Secondary levels of managers are needed to oversee complex business process designs, technology platforms, or workgroups.
- *Complex work and relationship management:* Project requires coordination and relationship management (negotiation of common understandings, agendas, and decisions among business process owners or unit managers). This style also is required when contractors do complex work.
- *All frontier projects:* Work is targeted at a new business domain or a new technology area where the methodologies are unknown and unproven. Project management must be developed, monitored, and adjusted as the project is being conducted.

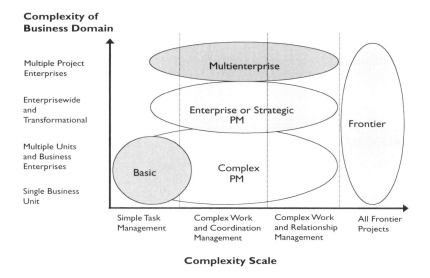

Figure 2.1 A diagram to illustrate the different work domains and their associated complexity levels.

A COMPLEXITY CASE STUDY—IBM

Consider IBM's experience with complexity when it hired Lou Gerstner as CEO in 1993. IBM's market share and profitability were eroding due to its difficulty in adjusting to the growth of new technology, such as PCs. IBM chose Gerstner, its first CEO from outside the company and outside the computer industry, to right the ship.

Why did IBM select Gerstner? The company recognized that, above all, it needed a strategist to determine what customers really wanted and a change agent to transform a complex engineering-oriented culture to a customer-driven culture. In this light, Gerstner's track record as a McKinsey strategy consultant, a turnaround specialist at Nabisco, and a builder of financial-service product lines at American Express was a great fit.

Gerstner was, by most accounts, highly successful. He changed IBM's culture to that of an eclectic technology services company. IBM's market value rose from about $29 billion, when he took over in 1993, to $181 billion when he resigned as CEO in March 2002.

Gerstner said shortly after joining the company in 1993 that, first and foremost, IBM was losing its way with regard to the customer. And, secondly, the need to integrate of IBM as a company. This was the biggest value it could bring to its customers. If the first point above isn't the definition of complexity, the second point certainly is. IBM had too much and too many of just about everything—data centers, commerce engines, network providers, client desktop configurations, and so on.

When Gerstner started at IBM, it had 24 different business units, and they did not share services across the company. Every unit had its full complement of everything—services, purchasing, and manufacturing, to name just a few. But after an internal effort to reduce the complexity, IBM went from 55 data centers down to 12. It had 31 different network providers; now it is has one. IBM had over 100 CIOs; today there is one. On the product lines, for example, IBM had over 100 different desktop configurations; today it has four. The effect on the company was dramatic and can be seen by its performance—for example, at the 2001 shareholders meeting IBM presented the following results:

- IBM had record earnings and revenue.
- IBM made significant investments to strengthen their portfolio: $5.6 billion invested in research and development; another $5.6 billion in capital expenditures, and half a billion dollars on strategic acquisitions.
- The IBM cash position was still strong enough to allow them to buy back $6.7 billion of common stock.
- On the technology front, IBM had the most U.S. patent awards for the eighth straight year.
- IBM had $85 billion in services backlog, which is basically future revenue already under contract.

Complexity was an issue at IBM as far back as the 1960's. An IBM employee at the time, Frederick P. Brooks Jr., one of the architects of the IBM 360 mainframe, and author observed, *"Complexity is the business we are in, and complexity is what limits us."*[2] That is changing at IBM, and with its autonomic computing initiative, so it will for IBM customers who embrace it.

IBM TRANSFORMATION—A SUMMARY OF RESULTS

IBM was on the verge of breakup: Bureaucracy, complexity, and silos was slowing IBM down—costing money and keeping the organization too opaque to function decisively. Stock prices were at a 20-year low, and the company had posted an $8.1 billion loss.

IBM drove common processes across lines of business: IBM began by breaking down barriers between lines of business, implementing enterprise-wide standards for five core processes:

- Market planning
- Product development
- Procurement
- CRM
- Fulfillment

Table 2.1   IBM Simplified Infrastructure and Governance

	Then	Now
Number of CIOs	128	1
Host data centers	55	12
Web hosting centers	80	11
Networks	31	1
Applications	16,000	5,200

Results: IT spending was reduced by 31 percent over the past decade—even as the IT infrastructure grew to support new applications and processes, higher volume, and enhanced functionality.

- Total savings: More than $9B
- Time to market: 75 percent faster
- Customer satisfaction: Up 5.5 percent

Simplification was not enough: Standardized processes stopped the tide of red ink. But IBM was still not fully leveraging the size, scope, and power to reach their customers and differentiate them in the marketplace.

Integrated across the value net: They reorganized to deliver unified processes across the value net—from suppliers to partners to employees to customers. This further increased efficiency, especially for cross-business initiatives like SCM and CRM.

Results:

- E-commerce:
  - $26.4 billion in 2002, up 4 percent YTY
  - $11.6 billion from IBM.com, up 3 percent
- CRM:
  - Cost avoidance from e-support in 2002: ~$600 million, up 17 percent YTY
  - 60 percent of phone contacts result in sales
- Fulfillment:
  - Applications reduced by 42 percent
  - 70 percent of PC orders "touchless"
- Procurement:
  - 90 percent of orders "hands-free"
  - Cost avoidance from e-procurement in 2002: ~$450 million, up 8 percent YTY

- IBM's e-business transformation efforts to date have realized:

  ○ $16.5 billion in benefits from $5.6 billion of investment

To stay competitive as the business environment grows faster, less predictable, and increasingly customer-driven, e-business on demand will allow IBM to respond quickly to changes and market opportunities.

Six key initiatives: IBM is still in the early stages of implementing e-business on demand. There are six key areas where they feel they are getting closest:

1. An integrated supply chain
2. New semiconductor manufacturing facility
3. Implementation of the on demand workplace at IBM
4. Grid computing
5. The build the next generation of infrastructure
6. E-business worldwide centers

IBM came back from the brink. To reach this stage, IBM has transformed its business processes, technology, and most importantly, its *culture*. This has involved a great deal of planning and effort, but the story is proof that it can be done—and that the rewards are enormous.

The organizations that move first will have an enormous competitive advantage over those that are slow to adapt. The difficult part is changing business thinking. On demand business challenges long-held notions about organizations and hierarchy—but "silo" thinking and obsession with control are obstacles on the path to the future.

COMPLEXITY IN IT

One of the most difficult challenges facing IT organizations today is ensuring alignment with business objectives in terms of quality, flexibility, initial cost, and time to market. In computing, opportunity breeds complexity. Moreover, complexity begets systems that can be unreliable and difficult to manage. In most medium to large-sized IT organizations, there are now numerous applications and environments that weigh in at tens of millions of lines of code, and they require substantially skilled IT professionals to install, configure, tune, debug, upgrade, and generally maintain them. This means that the difficulty of managing today's computing systems goes well beyond the administration of individual software environments. There is a need to integrate several different environments into corporate-wide computing systems and make them work. This goes beyond company boundaries into the Internet and introduces new levels of complexity. Computing systems' complexity appears to be approaching the limits of human capability, yet the relentless march toward increased interconnectivity and integration rushes ahead unabated. New technologies, such as wireless, will increase the complexity even more.

We do not see a slowdown in the progression of Moore's Law. (For a more detailed discussion of Moore's Law, see Chapter 5.) Rather, it is the IT industry's exploitation of technological growth inherent in Moore's Law that leads us to the verge of a complexity crisis. Software companies now have massive computing power, which can produce ever more complex applications that run on even more complex IT infrastructures. Add to this mix network and communications technology and the complexity increases by several orders of magnitude. The domino effect applies here. Software packaged applications aren't providing much, if any, relief from the traditional organizational need to customize enterprise applications. They pose system and network management challenges that also aren't getting any simpler to handle. The result is more complexity. More complexity means more time and more resources to manage the complexity; so the costs begin to rise.

Many surveys have been conducted that ask CIOs and their staff the following basic question: *"What IT applications or technologies are becoming too complicated to manage?"*

The responses and results have been predicable.

1. Integrating the Web and standard legacy-based systems.
2. Implementing custom software packages.
3. Integrating new Java™-based software.
4. Constructing object-based and distributed architectures.
5. Data warehousing.
6. Implementing new e-business systems.

SIMPLIFYING THE IT INFRASTRUCTURE

Most CEOs would cringe at the idea that IT infrastructure—the way architectures and associated technology resources are organized—will determine the agility with which companies can carry out good strategy. Yet the difficulty and cost of modifying today's rigid IT architectures—dominated by big enterprise applications, such as Enterprise Resource Planning (ERP), and large application suites, such as Customer Relationship Management (CRM) and many others—can be so high that some companies would rather abandon new strategic initiatives than make a single change to the applications they already have in place.

Businesses need to reduce costs and sprawling networks as well as respond more quickly to changing business environments. In today's typical IT environment, there may be three to four tiers of computing, with caching and security servers on the front end, application servers as a middle layer, and transaction and data processing servers on the end. Add to this another layer of complexity with Internet servers, Web services, and portals, and it gets even worse.

By reducing the tiers of computing, customers may gain cost savings and create an environment where they can deploy new technologies, such as Linux and grid solutions, to create a dynamic operating environment capable of responding more flexibly to changing business or customer requirements.

Businesses reducing the tiers of computing are using a scale-out and scale-up approach. Scale-out systems, such as Blade servers, allow customers to add compute capacity by the processor; while scale-up systems—mainframe and mainframe-class servers—grow like building blocks. Buy when you need it. Install it, and use it.

Good news is on the horizon in the form of service-oriented architectures, which promise to reduce, if not remove, the current obstacles to less complexity.

AUTONOMIC COMPUTING: ONE ANSWER TO COMPLEXITY

Costs are also rising dramatically due to complexity. In the 1990's, approximately 80 percent of the cost of major computer systems revolved around hardware and software acquisitions, according to IBM studies. Now, the human expenses are roughly equal to equipment costs. If nothing changes, the human costs will double that of equipment in the next five to six years.

Adding to this complexity is the proliferation of multiple-vendor and technology environments, which require the components of a given solution to be integrated and customized into unique customer business processes. The increased need to distribute data, applications, and system resources across geographic/national and business boundaries further contributes to the complexity of the IT infrastructure. The additional complexity, which continues to grow exponentially, keeps the costs of managing (deploying, tuning, fixing, securing) the IT infrastructure very high.

In IBM's view, autonomic computing systems must follow the four principles described in Figure 2.2. They must be self-configuring (able to adapt to changes in the system), self-optimizing (able to improve performance), self-healing (able to recover from mistakes), and self-protecting (able to anticipate and cure intrusions). Systems with self-managing components reduce the cost of owning and operating computer systems.

COMPLEXITY—THE ENEMY OF CIOs

IT must start taking positive steps forward if it wants enable of growth, rather than hinder it. Business units are demanding a higher level of service from IT, and CIOs are taking a hard look at how they run their operations, spend their money, and plan for tomorrow. In the long run, CIOs can implement new systems that are expected to radically change IT operations and reduce staff and costs.

Here are some of the symptoms of complexity in IT:

1. Frequent and reoccurring software crashes of critical applications due to incompatibility of data, files, errors, or network protocols.

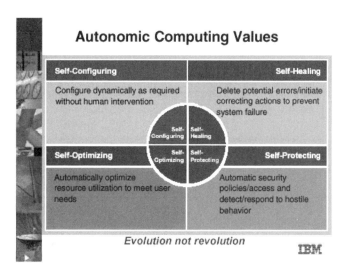

Figure 2.2   The core values of autonomic computing.

2. Longer timeframes for IT staff to solve the problems in item 1.

3. A significant increase in IT budgets, including hardware, software, human capital costs, training, and support.

4. Increase in the level of application outsourcing—if there is a problem, it is better to let some other vendor deal with it.

5. High turnover of critical IT staff due to frustration, long hours, and burnout.

6. Unexpected surprises in new technology, new languages, or applications leading to increased time in understanding and managing projects that use them.

7. Longer timeframes to satisfactorily test and install new applications or software packages.

8. Growth of expensive hardware and software in IT architectures—the "silent sales" syndrome.

9. Incompatibility between competing vendor software packages—i.e., file structures, databases, transmission protocols, and parameters—due to lack of standards.

10. Frequent but necessary software upgrades of packages, operating systems, and application development languages, resulting in yet another round of errors and incompatibility problems.

11. Incessant requests for new business systems to be developed and installed within what appears to be unreasonable timeframes.

IT COMPLEXITY TRANSFORMATION

To rid themselves of unnecessary complexity, corporations will need comprehensive self-assessment to create a plan for transforming their systems and making them simpler. Corporations can take immediate steps to untangle most of their unwanted IT complexity by focusing on the following six specific activities, which, taken together, will help them transform the way they use and manage IT, thus making IT organizations leaner and companies better prepared for the end of the downturn:

- Understand and target the root causes of complexity.
- Install self-managing systems, such as autonomic computing.
- Consider consolidation of hardware and software.
- Regenerate the company's IT architecture.
- Plan for outsourcing of certain applications.
- Develop a management culture in IT.

By reducing this kind of IT complexity, corporations position themselves to benefit as growth continues. They will then need to add systems, but they will be able to do so more quickly and at far less expense by pruning complexity now. Adding an application to a streamlined, integrated IT platform, for example, requires less systems development and integration work.

THE COST OF IT COMPLEXITY

Technology should obviously make it possible to streamline processes and reduce costs. Often, it does. But during the 1990s, companies added wave after wave of novel technologies, often starting new projects before completing earlier ones, with disappointing results. By not fully changing business processes to reap the value of the new systems, these companies made processes more complex—not more streamlined—and increased costs, particularly in IT.

Rapid mergers and globalization added to the complexity. Integrating and rationalizing systems after a merger can be a massive job that takes months, sometimes years, to complete. For example Bank One, the nation's fifth-largest bank, has been acquiring smaller banks over the last ten years and is continuously integrating new accounts into its systems. In the interim, companies may have to grapple with operating systems and business applications that don't mesh fully or even partially; trying to get data to flow between two recently merged companies is a straightforward aim, but may turn out to be frustratingly difficult. Meanwhile, as companies expanded into new markets around the globe, they added systems to support new supply chains, local human resources and legal requirements, new financial structures, and the flow of information in a variety of languages—all of which increased costs due to added complexity. As almost every computer user can confirm, the "hidden costs" of computing are huge. That is, after paying for the hardware and software, considerable time is required to address software installation, upgrades, maintenance, enhancements, configuration, tuning and optimization, problem detection and resolution, and security considerations.

A few companies have decided that IT cost-cutting provides a great opportunity to untangle their systems and projects. Rather than taking the short-term view—"Can we live without this piece of IT now?"—these companies are looking to the longer run, transforming their business activities and IT processes in ways that will strengthen their systems and, at the same time, eliminate the deeper causes of bloated IT spending. In a sense, the companies are finishing a job they didn't have time to complete during the bubble years.

IT costs soared in the 1990s as companies adopted systems and applications to support new channels and products, expansion into new markets, and tighter coordination with suppliers. The rapid pace of competition often meant that such companies implemented these systems quickly—in "Internet time"—without fully integrating them with existing systems (and retiring older ones) or making the business changes needed to exploit technology's potential for helping to automate and streamline business activities.

Indeed, companies *can* make short-term cuts and save while, at the same time, addressing the costly longer-term roots of IT complexity, but only if senior IT and business leaders commit themselves to keeping these goals in mind. Companies are reaping big savings by rethinking the way they manage multiple channels—for example, by closing a failed Web site or keeping the Internet channel and outsourcing a call center. The same treatment is being accorded to product portfolios supported by disparate and often uncoordinated IT systems: Banks and telecommunications companies, for example, are dropping some older offerings. Companies are also consolidating their database-management systems and other infrastructure technologies and redrawing their IT architectures—the blueprint for the IT structure supporting the business. They are giving themselves the ability to take advantage of new outsourcing arrangements that will ease overall complexity.

In summary, there are many advances that can be made to lessen existing IT complexity. Here are some suggestions:

1. To establish the level of complexity, seek and secure senior IT management authorization to review the entire corporation's IT infrastructure, resources, applications, processes, and operating procedures. Write a report with metrics and recommendations to define priority recommendations—see the next section on Corporate Complexity Assessment.

2. Establish what can be done in the short term:
   - **Server consolidation**—Determines what can be consolidated to reduce costs and lessen complexity.
   - **Outsourcing**—Review all applications to establish what, if any, applications can be outsourced.
   - **System Management**—Review new automated system management software to determine if automated updating, new software releases, patches, and updates are needed.

○ **Application Development**—Review all application development software, and consolidate where possible.

The impact of complexity on IT systems thinking is fundamental. Instead of basing our strategies and actions on *prediction*, with the development and implementation of a plan designed to take us from "here and now" to "there and then," we need to adopt a more creative approach. This implies more frequent monitoring and reassessment, with an awareness and capacity to change targets and goals, to make use of what is working and reduce what does not. This is an approach that recognizes the constant need to learn about what is happening and to try to make sense of it as fast as possible—before the complexity increases to unmanageable proportions.

CORPORATE COMPLEXITY ASSESSMENT

The first step in beginning to identify corporate complexity should be to perform an assessment. Results of the complexity assessment are used to define the most cost-effective, appropriate complexity implementation plan to meet corporate goals.

The complexity assessment is performed to measure the potential for practicing complexity in a corporation, to determine if the corporation is ready to embark on a complexity reduction program, and to define where to focus its efforts to gain the maximum benefit. The emphasis is on a business viewpoint, looking at the reasons why complexity has evolved, how a reduction policy and the introduction of simplicity can help, and the expected business value to be gained from complexity reduction or elimination. The result of the complexity assessment can be used as the basis for defining corporate complexity goals, complexity reduction adoption strategies, the domains in which to practice simplicity instead of complexity, and the complexity reduction program implementation plan.

GOALS

The complexity assessment is performed to help successfully introduce complexity reduction into a corporation. The purposes of the complexity assessment are as follows:

1. Evaluate a corporation's current complexity strategy and the implementation of that strategy in current software projects and various systems groups.
2. Use the results of the assessment to determine a corporation's complexity goals, elements of a complexity program to achieve those goals, and domains in which to focus complexity efforts.
3. Recommend actions to take to implement its complexity strategy.

Instituting the practice of complexity reduction across a corporation is a large, complex task in itself, especially if the ultimate goal is to practice complexity reduction practices above the project level—that is, across teams, across product lines, and across software groups/organizations. Success requires careful planning, cooperation, and good management practices. To ensure success, a corporation needs to determine how ready, willing, and able it is to practice a complexity-reduction-driven development approach and what actions it needs to take to prepare itself to accomplish its complexity objectives and goals.

The assessment will investigate both technical and management/organizational complexity issues. On the technical side, some important issues include:

- Identifying and defining core business objects and other kinds of components.
- Defining guidelines and standards for core business objects (once they exist) and for creating or re-engineering core business objects.
- Defining the organizational structure and classification scheme for the complexity library or libraries.

On the management/organizational side, issues include:

- Defining personnel support for core business objects/components.
- Establishing complexity training programs.
- Establishing the complexity measurement infrastructure (i.e., complexity metrics and measurements, corporate complexity policy, complexity incentives).

INFRASTRUCTURE ASSESSMENTS

Conducting an IT infrastructure management assessment would help corporate IT users and senior management to prepare their IT environments to incorporate emerging capabilities, such as automated provisioning, autonomic computing, and business systems monitoring.

Infrastructure management assessment services are key components of complexity management offerings. The services provide ongoing assessments of corporate IT systems with special focus on the following areas:

- **Systems Management:** Ongoing operational health checks using proven methods for monitoring system availability across multi-platform IT hardware, software, and network resources.
- **Asset Management:** Systematic, multi-vendor asset management through consolidated assessment and tracking of hardware and software assets to managing even complex monitoring and usage environments.
- **Resource Management:** Health checks on what resources are being used where and at what cost.
- **Problem Management:** An assessment of problem management determinations and how problems and issues are tracked, resolved, and documented.
- **Change Management:** Processes that help decrease risk of IT system downtime.
- **Service Management:** Interlocking of test, migration, and production schedules for smooth integration and transition of new technologies into an existing data center environment.

- **Security Management:** Assessment of security strategies, policies, and protocols for deploying security techniques.

By having clear assessment of the IT environment, the services help users define the technical and business requirements designed to enable improvements in server, storage, and network utilization; standardize their computing environment; and evaluate their security needs using automation software and processes.

Customers that manage their own data centers have a huge opportunity to reclaim money spent manually directing the hundreds or thousands of computer systems in their enterprise. By designing an IT framework based on industry standards and proven business processes, customers can substantially increase the efficiency and utilization of their existing IT resources.

Just as enterprise resource planning and Six Sigma made company manufacturing and supply chains more efficient and flexible, applying more discipline to a corporate data center can bring similar benefits to a company's overall IT operations.

SUMMARY AND CONCLUSIONS

Complexity is becoming a major issue for all IT departments, whether acknowledged or not. Many CIOs are still in denial. This is not industry hype; rather it is reality. Complexity is not just an academic theory, since it has emerged into the IT world. Complexity in IT increases costs and affects productivity. This is a new threat to progress and future success that must be addressed. There is no future in the status quo. To let IT infrastructures and architectures become increasingly complex with no action is unacceptable and irresponsible. If the eventual solution is to throw more skilled programmers and others at this problem, it is clear that chaos will be the order of the day. Reliability and performance of critical corporate applications will be called into question. Confidence in the IT department, already battered in the past, will be the next issue on senior management's checklist. Until IT vendors solve the problem of complexity, the same problems will be repeated and continue to plague the industry. There is no way that these complexities can be managed through skilled staff alone, even if they are available.

Corporations and forward-thinking CIOs should start with a complexity reduction management policy. This policy will set out an approach for dealing with complexity and present solutions, such as autonomous computing. The management, and ultimate reduction, of complexity and a move to simpler solutions will not be easily achieved. Consider the boxed quote from IBM's Alan Ganek.

In the IT industry, we are operating in one of the most difficult and complex business environments that any of us have participated in during our business careers, and it is vital that we address complexity NOW.

<table>
<tr><td>

THE AUTONOMIC GOAL IS ONE OF SIMPLICITY.

"The goal is to increase the amount of automation that businesses need to sustain. Because the more that you can get human error out of the loop, the more efficient your business will become—whether you are a financial institution, a shipping company, or an online retailer. The beauty of it is that all of these complexities are hidden from the user."

—Alan Ganek, the Vice President of Autonomic Computing for IBM Corporation's Software Group[3]

</td></tr>
</table>

RECOMMENDED READING

1. *Simplicity,* Edward De Bono. New York: Penguin Putnam Books, 1998.
2. *Simplicity, the New Competitive Advantage,* Bill Jensen. Cambridge, MA: Perseus Books, 2000.
3. *The Clock of the Long Now*, Stephen Brand. New York: Weidenfeld and Nicolson Press, 2000.
4. *Information, Entropy, and Progress: A New Evolutionary Paradigm*, R Ayers. American Institute of Physics, New York: Woodbury Press, 1999.
5. *The Alchemy of Growth: Kickstarting and Sustaining Growth in Your Company*, M A Baghai et al. London: Orion Business, 1999.

Note to readers: Regrettably, there are no IT books on this subject.

NOTES

1. See *http://www.fda.gov/cdrh/ocd/panamaradexp.html.*
2. Frederick P. Brooks, *The Mythical Man-Month: Essays on Software Engineering.* Boston: Addison-Wesley, 1995.
3. See *www.eetimes.com/issue/fp/OEG20020412S0056.*

CHAPTER 3

AUTONOMIC PRODUCTS AND APPLICATIONS

INTRODUCTION

In this chapter, we shall review some examples of autonomic products and their applications. This will illustrate the benefits and advantages of autonomic computing, which is in use today, not just in commercial enterprises, but in other industries, such as space exploration, where autonomic software has been under development for over five years.

IBM'S DB2 DATABASE MANAGEMENT SYSTEM

DB2 is not a single software product; rather it is a family of tools, utilities, and products supporting the database management system itself that can run on several operating platforms. DB2 has had a long and successful history going back 20 years in the global database industry. The current version of DB2 expands its autonomic computing foundation with key new capabilities that reduce complexity in deploying, managing, and configuring relational databases. Today, the DB2 family of products spans a wide variety of UNIX®, Linux, and Windows platforms and the IBM iSeries™ (OS/400® operating system) and zSeries™ (OS/390®, z/OS®, VM, VSE, and Linux) server lines. DB2 Everyplace™ supports handheld devices and embedded Linux environments, and provides data synchronization with larger systems. Common tools have been delivered for application development and database administration across the family. Innovations from all family members and the Informix database line feed the growth of the entire family.

DB2 technologies of today address emerging customer requirements in several new areas:

1. Autonomic computing requires servers, operating systems, and middleware including DB2, to diagnose and correct problems without human intervention. Database self-

    management and automation for the database administrator are areas of particular emphasis in the most recent edition of DB2.

2. Standards-based Web services have emerged as a new style of application processing with full support from DB2.

3. Grid computing, or the idea of large-scale computing resources used as a utility or service, such as a database service, takes advantage of the vast clustered scalability of DB2 to support large databases and large numbers of simultaneous users in an available manner. Standards-based Web services are another key component of grid computing supported by DB2.

4. The e-business on demand business model requires an operating environment built on open standards to allow quick and cost-effective innovation and reconfiguration. The infrastructure to support e-business on demand must be reliable, scalable, and secure. DB2 is an essential part of that infrastructure.

DB2 software plays an important role in this infrastructure—the e-business on demand operating environment. All elements of the portfolio (database servers, business intelligence software, enterprise content management software, data management tools, and information integration software) are developed with four key e-business on demand attributes in mind: They are integrated, open, virtualized, and autonomic.

There are a number of DB2 capabilities supporting these attributes.

1. **Integrated:** Built-in support for both Microsoft and Java™-based operating environments; integration into WebSphere®, Tivoli, Lotus, and Rational products and plans; cross-platform DB2 family capabilities; integration with Web services and message queuing technologies; heterogeneous data source support via DB2 Information Integrator; support for both structured and unstructured information.

2. **Open:** Deep commitment to and support for Linux and standards for Java, XML, Web services, grid computing, distributed database interoperability; and multivendor, multiplatform exploitation.

3. **Virtualized:** Federation and integration technologies in DB2 Universal Database and DB2 Information Integrator that provide a pragmatic alternative to data centralization; clustered scalability to support expansion of a virtualized information environment.

4. **Autonomic:** Self-tuning capabilities of DB2 Universal Database; rapid DB2 deployment via optimized configuration tooling; dynamic adjustment and tuning; simple and silent installation processes; integration with Tivoli® for system security and management.

DB2 TODAY

The current version of DB2 (v8.1) has several existing autonomic features that have been in use for sometime as illustrated in Figure 3.1.

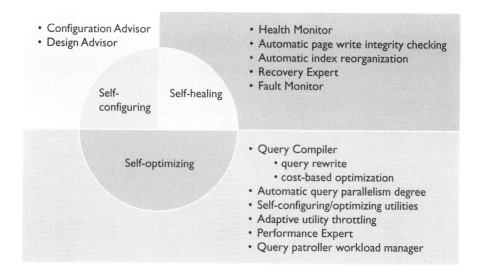

Figure 3.1   The autonomic features of DB2 version 8.1.

The full-function autonomic features are available to all DB2 clients. Autonomic capabilities examples listed from the above figure include the following:

- The Health Monitor: provides monitoring of key DB2 performance and reliability metrics and offers advice on resolving any problems that may occur. DB2 performs the following self-healing functions:

  ○ Monitors its own health right out of the box.
  ○ Notifies upon encountering unhealthy conditions: email, page, logs.
  ○ Advises on severity of condition, and suggests resolutions.
  ○ Initiates corrective action if required or requested.

- The Configuration Advisor allows even a novice or expert systems programmers to configure a system much more quickly—often doing in a few hours what previously would have taken an expert days to accomplish. For example, the Configuration Advisor automatically detects and senses system-related data about the required operating environment so that the configuration can be automatically updated when the hardware changes are detected.

  System information data is collected, such as:

  ○ Number of physical disks
  ○ Physical memory size (RAM)
  ○ CPU information

○ Number of online CPUs

○ Number of configured CPUs

○ OS features

○ OS type and release (OS2, Windows, NT, Unix, etc.)

Database information is also collected, such as:

○ Size of the database

○ Number of tables

○ Number of indexes

○ Number of tablespaces

Buffer pool information is collected as well, such as:

○ Name and size of each buffer pool

○ Number of buffer pools

FUTURE AUTONOMIC FUNCTIONALITY IN DB2 RELEASES

In the future releases of DB2—for example version 8.2, which is about to be released—there are more and richer autonomic features available.

Automatic Maintenance Policies

Here DB2 will create a policy for maintaining the database—when and where and what is to be achieved. This is accomplished by defining what needs to be completed—either offline or online.

- Policies are used to specify the settings for automatic maintenance:

  ○ Specified in XML documents.

  ○ Stored in tables in the database.

  ○ The Configure Automatic Maintenance wizard in Control Center & Health Center configures these policies.

- Common Policy:

  ○ Specifies maintenance windows for online and offline activities.

- Utility-specific policies:

  ○ Specifies settings relevant to the particular utility.

  ○ Each utility uses the common policy maintenance windows when automating maintenance activities.

Automatic Database Backup

This is an autonomic feature for backing up data automatically. Again, DB2 creates a policy that describes the requirements needed to back up the database(s).

- The policy defines the following:

  ○ Backup location.
  ○ Criteria for determining when a backup is required.
  ○ Maximum time between backups.
  ○ Maximum log space used between backups.

- Automatic backup runs online if in archive logging mode, offline if in circular logging mode.
- Health indicator alerts if manual backup is required.

Conclusions

DB2 is not just a relational database, as it adds value with these rich autonomic computing features that provide customers today with self-managing facilities. Expect more and increasingly sophisticated autonomic features in future releases, such as version 9.1.

The bottom line is DB2 is a leading example of autonomic computing in the database market.

AUTEVO FROM INTAMISSION

IntaMission is a British company that is working to develop an autonomic software suite of products called Autevo. Autevo is an integrated suite of infrastructure components that enable the development of distributed enterprise systems in an unusual way. The architecture underpinning the Autevo model views applications as being composed of sequenced flows of data objects through a virtual information space that is distributed, persistent, and transactional. This approach is useful in addressing a wide variety of business needs, and particularly encourages systems that are easy to change, robust to failure, and scalable. These are areas where traditional N-tier models often struggle to meet expectations.

Based upon cross-platform Java technology, Autevo is supported on all major contemporary platforms and handles heterogeneous environments with ease. It includes components that are fully compatible with the JINI and JavaSpace standards, which define a powerful, self-healing, service-oriented architecture for enterprise systems.

Autevo allows companies the freedom to change architectures and applications by decoupling the business from application-specific data models and processes. Removing the tight interdependencies between system components enables parts of the system to be changed with no downtime or knock-on impacts across the system.

Autevo is not a software application but a new way of thinking about middleware. Autevo allows incompatible and inconsistent applications to share common information. This allows a business to define and model its information and processes around the services required, rather than being rigidly bound and directed by the limitations of the systems in place.

Some specific areas this product addresses are:

- Building a common data model to deliver improved collaboration and service reliability, while simplifying the underlying infrastructure;
- Allowing service providers to consolidate and migrate complex systems in a way that reduces risk and drives down the cost of change;
- Monitoring services end-to-end across the domain from a single point, allowing the business to drive down support costs while boosting the quality of service; and
- Enabling grid computing through Autevo—processing power is spread across your entire network, maximizing the use of your existing hardware.

Autevo provides the framework for a self-healing and flexible system that is service-oriented from the ground up. Based on open industry standards, Autevo is specifically designed to enhance and enrich existing systems investments.

What's in Autevo?

The core infrastructure component is the Autevo Engine. This is a shared, persistent, and transactional "network memory" that can be concurrently accessed by many remote processes. It serves as a hub and data repository for collaboration and communication between services and their clients. It is accessed using a simple, consistent object-based interface that employs template matching (a.k.a. query-by-example) to locate desired data without requiring the use of a query language.

The other two key components are the Lookup Service, a distributed network of software agents that track and advertise available services to clients, and the Transaction Manager, which manages two-phase distributed transactions. Figure 3.2 describes the model architecture.

Internally, these Autevo components use the standard Java Remote Method Invocation (RMI) protocol to intercommunicate. Autevo allows the automatic transfer of both complex object data and behavior across the network without any manual schema and stub definition. Autevo also includes the Explorer and Profiler user tools, which assist system development, administration, and task monitoring.

Autevo embraces a number of technologies, including the JINI services framework and the JavaSpaces API, both from Sun Microsystems. Below are listed five key fundamental design and technology characteristics that together underpin the Autevo product:

- Dynamic registration and discovery allows services to automatically locate and connect to one another without any need for administrative intervention.

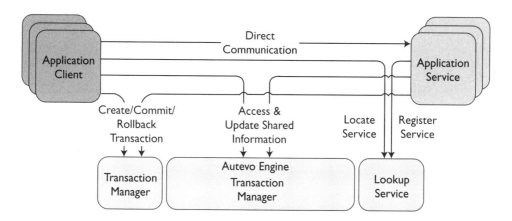

Figure 3.2 The basic architectural model of the Autevo Engine.

- Decoupled communication enables organizations to build systems of interconnecting services that collaborate and intercommunicate without need for prior knowledge of identity or location.
- Network mobile objects support service changes without any redevelopment work and provide natural load balancing through the use of the Autevo Engine.
- Built-in evolution enables information structures to change without service interruption.
- Automatic resource reclamation simplifies development and freeing unused network resources.

Autevo Applications

The Autevo Engine excels at supporting high volume Publish-Subscribe messaging, especially guaranteed messaging scenarios where durable and transactional messages are required. Publishers write the message into the Engine with topic and other routing criteria attached. Subscribe can either register to passively receive notification of relevant incoming messages or actively query the engine. A variety of protocols can be employed to sequence or prioritize delivery order and to detect and recover from delivery failures. Autevo can improve flexibility and information exchange in J2EE systems. For example, the Autevo Engine can allow Enterprise Java Beans (EJBs) and Servlets distributed on multiple application servers to share and synchronize state objects, without the overhead of writing to a database. The Engine's network-accessible memory can meet the frequent need for an efficient shared object cache. Such approaches can provide a compelling alternative to clustering when architecting coordinated multimachine J2EE systems.

Many powerful application models can be constructed that employ the Engine for load balancing and task control. Load balancing and job farming across a network of machines always require some mechanism for matching tasks to available resources and collecting results or responses.

One or many task dispatchers can write request objects into the Engine's memory, making it visible to all resource machines. Worker processes take requests from the engine, perform them, and write back a response when finished. The scalability, persistence, and transactional integrity of the Engine's store ensure that such systems continue operating despite the partial failure of any individual participant.

Autevo Summary

The Autevo Engine and related products and software comprise a different viewpoint from the IBM autonomic computing model. This viewpoint is interesting, but needs case studies and implementation experience to validate its methodology. This software could have significant potential if marketed in the United States.

AUTONOMIC SPACE SYSTEMS

Space is the last great frontier that awaits us. However, due to the size and nature of space and the distances involved, there are some basic fundamental problems that must be solved. The successful exploration of space will require a large number of cheap, agile, and smart spacecraft that can undertake ambitious missions to the far corners of the universe.

Spacecraft will be very different from the vehicles that we have developed over the last 30 years. The new age of space exploration will require spacecraft to be independent, autonomous, and smart. They must be capable of self managing and solving problems without human intervention. In the past, vast numbers of staff were needed to carry out all the necessary functions to design, launch, track, manage, and retrieve a spacecraft, and then interpret the data or results.

This approach is no longer viable or acceptable due to a number of factors, such as:

- Space is massive and requires travelling huge distances.
- Missions have been very expensive.
- Large-scale automation is necessary for deep space exploration. Automation implies sophisticated software.
- Humans cannot endure multiyear space flights, hence unmanned missions are required.

To engage in this approach, organizations such as NASA have been developing numerous autonomic based technologies to address many of these issues. NASA's New Millennium Project (NMP) is one such example. It is the first example of autonomous based software that will, in combination with other Artificial Intelligence software, completely control a space exploration mission. The NMP will accelerate the infusion of technologies into the space and Earth science missions of the 21st century. The program plans a series of technologies—anticipating a rate of two flights per year—which will demonstrate technologies for deep space and Earth-orbiting missions that will work successfully. In tandem with developing and validating new technologies, NMP is also undertaking new management approaches, particularly in the area of partnering between government and industry. A novel application of the concept of integrated product development teams (IPDTs) is being pursued: one in which cross-organizational teams, made up of members from government, industry, and academia, create road maps for development of high pay-off technologies, such as agent technology, that NMP intends to validate through flights. The IPDT approach is expected to reduce costs and improve product. These are examples of the management challenges that must be addressed today to more efficiently undertake space exploration and Earth observation in the 21st century and beyond.

How Do the Costs Compare?

To give some perspective on how much taxpayer money is being spent to accomplish these extraordinary goals in space exploration—and ultimately to enhance mankind's understanding of the universe we live in—consider this comparison. The budget for the movie Titanic was over $200 million, which was more than the budget for the Deep Space One (DS1) mission from 1998 to 2001 ($139.5 million). DS1 flew by an asteroid and returned information on the kind of celestial body that might once have slammed into Earth million of years ago. DS1 also flew by a comet and took pictures and measurements of its tail, gathering information that might give scientists clues on the origins of the solar system—all for less than the cost of a single Hollywood movie. NASA created the most advanced spacecraft artificial intelligence software yet developed for launch aboard DS1.

The Deep Space One Mission

The robotic Deep Space One (DS1) spacecraft carried no crew and with a total mass of 945 pounds, was much smaller than conventional craft—see Figure 3.3—but its autonomic computer intelligence program, known as the Remote Agent, shared the same basic goal of operating and controlling a spacecraft with minimal human assistance.

The autonomic computer software on board DS1 represents a big step forward in spacecraft autonomy. It is designed to allow spacecraft to make a wider variety of decisions for themselves than they were able to in the past. DS1's Remote Agent software is capable of planning and executing many activities onboard the spacecraft, with only general direction being given from ground controllers on Earth. In contrast to remote control, this software acts as an autonomous "remote agent" of controllers because they rely on it to achieve particular mission goals. Ground controllers do not tell the agent exactly what to do at each instant of time, as they do with conventional spacecraft. The software logically reasons about the state of the spacecraft, and the Remote Agent considers all of the consequences of its actions. The Remote Agent was

Figure 3.3 The Deep Space One craft looks familiar to normal spacecraft—but it is completely self sufficient, self-managing, and autonomous.

developed in a collaborative effort between NASA, Ames, and the Jet Propulsion Laboratory (JPL), Pasadena, CA.

Autonomous Models

The Remote Agent should enable future spacecraft software to be more easily designed. The first version of Remote Agent was the most difficult to create and test. Now, NASA should be able to copy it for the next mission, making improvements rather than redeveloping the software from scratch. It will be continuously improved with knowledge gained from each mission.

This is made possible by model-driven software. Models of the spacecraft's components and environment are given to the Remote Agent, which figures out the necessary detailed operating procedures on its own. Only the models need to be updated for each new spacecraft.

Given NASA's continuing efforts to develop many smaller, less expensive science spacecraft, there is a need to perform each mission with less than a dozen ground controllers instead of the hundreds of people previously needed to run a major planetary science mission. The large distances inherent in planetary exploration result in communications that can be painfully slow during normal operations and totally unacceptable during emergencies. Even signals from the nearby planet Mars take 11 minutes to be received. And sometimes your communication pathway is blocked when a planet is between the spacecraft and Earth.

Three parts of Remote Agent work together to demonstrate that it can autonomously operate a spacecraft: High Level Planning and Scheduling, Model-based Fault Protection Explorer, and Smart Executive. See Figure 3.4.

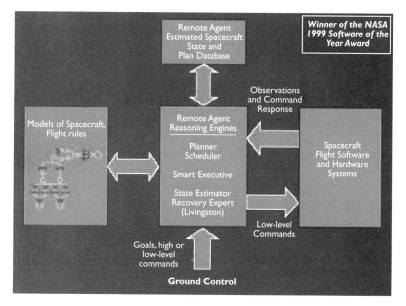

Figure 3.4   The autonomic architecture diagram of the DS Remote Agent technology.

Some estimates show a 60 percent reduction in mission costs using the Remote Agent. The software would replace a large section of the human spacecraft control team back on Earth.

The High Level Planning and Scheduling part of Remote Agent will constantly look ahead to the schedule for several weeks of mission activities. The Planner is mostly concerned with scheduling spacecraft activities and distributing resources such as electrical power. The Planner allows a small spacecraft control team on Earth to command the spacecraft more effectively by sending goals instead of detailed instructions to DS1.

The fault protection portion of the Remote Agent, known as "Livingstone" (named after the missionary and African explorer of the 19th century), functions as the mission's virtual chief engineer. If something should go wrong with the spacecraft, Livingstone would use the computer model of how the spacecraft should be behaving to diagnose failures and suggest recoveries.

The third part of the Remote Agent software, Smart Executive, acts as the "executive officer" of the mission, issuing general commands to fly DS1. The Executive has to be able to execute the plans that are produced by the Planner and Livingstone. If the Planner had to worry about every single detail, it would be hard pressed to produce a plan. So, the Executive takes care of the details.

The Executive also can receive a plan or single commands directly from ground controllers. However, if the ground plan won't work, the Executive can say, "Sorry, Ground, I can't do that." This can actually be a big help to ground controllers, who currently expend enormous effort double-checking every command and still don't always get it right. In a sense, they can test different scenarios in real time.

In the event that the Remote Agent won't cooperate under some unusual circumstance, NASA is developing a surgery mode, where ground control can really get into Remote Agent and take corrective action. Remote Agent may someday lead to software that would be incorporated into a space robot that would be as intelligent as HAL 9000 in the movie *2001:A Space Odyssey*.

The New Millennium Program has accelerated technology development in autonomous based spacecraft automation by at least ten years. The Remote Agent will open up new exploration opportunities, allowing us to really begin the in situ era of space science. Future systems also should be able to learn about their environment and act in partnership with scientists to find and analyze new discoveries. The key issue for the program in the next few years will be to continue to make it work successfully.

Looking ahead even further, NASA plans to build a fleet of these smart spacecraft, called constellations or armadas, and let them explore different places, share their findings, and even divide amongst themselves the work of achieving complex scientific goals. Systems like the Remote Agent will be crucial to supporting components of this vision.

Implications for Future Missions

If DS1 shows that electric propulsion works as well as expected, there will be many new missions that will take advantage of it. Ion propulsion is not of value for missions that require high acceleration, and it often will not be worthwhile for missions that can be done quickly using conventional propulsion systems (such as missions to the moon). But for a wide variety of missions with high energy requirements (such as missions to asteroids and comets, Mercury and the inner solar system, and some to the outer solar system), the low but steady acceleration of ion propulsion wins out over the less efficient bursts from chemical alternatives.

The real benefit of spacecraft autonomy is to enable a new kind of space exploration where the spacecraft will face much higher degrees of uncertainty. Such missions include exploring the oceans of Europa and the terrain and atmosphere of Venus. The Remote Agent software will also allow a faster response by the spacecraft to in-flight situations when ground controller intervention is not possible due to communication delay. For instance, autonomy capability is needed to maneuver a spacecraft in a hazardous environment, such as landing on an active comet where there are dangerous flying rocks. Furthermore, mission development and operations costs will also be reduced.

The magnitude of the benefits is difficult to quantify however and cannot be fully realized through flying the Remote Agent on one or two experimental flights. The full benefits of this software can only be realized over time and by maturing the technology through use on many future missions.

After DS1, NASA intends to work on even more autonomous spacecraft that could reconfigure themselves. If some part of such a spacecraft performed differently during the mission than expected, the craft would be able to detect this and change software models and algorithms to self-adapt. Deep Space 1 exceeded all its goals in successfully testing autonomic technology for self-managing space missions.

For more information visit The New Millennium Project at *http://nmp.jpl.nasa.gov/*.

SUMMARY AND CONCLUSIONS

These few examples illustrate the potential, scale of autonomic computing. The adoption and development of this type of technology has numerous benefits for corporations and commercial software in general. Today's modern society is totally dependent on the Internet and other information systems. But our current information systems need to be more reliable and better managed before society can put their trusts in such systems. With widespread automation through autonomic computing much of the complexity is removed, the systems begin to manage themselves—so it must be considered a desirable and achievable goal to implement autonomic computing.

INDUSTRY DEMAND

4

THE IT INDUSTRY—
AN ENGINE
OF GROWTH
AND OPPORTUNITY

INTRODUCTION

In this chapter, we will review the growth, significance, and future of the software industry that has been created over the past 50 years.

The now global software industry feeds into the wider range of activities that constitute global economic growth. In order to understand and to be able to situate these activities, it is necessary to briefly explore the characteristics of this industry. By understanding the various stages of dynamic software growth and components, a more dynamic analysis becomes feasible when considering the industry in context.

A SNAPSHOT INTRODUCTION

For more than 50 years, the IT industry has been a catalyst for global growth and opportunity. The dynamic effects on our society, including commerce and all types of industries, have been astonishing. The global market for all IT products surpassed $1 trillion in 2002 and is projections to reach $1.4 trillion by 2005[1] despite economic uncertainty. In addition, the IT industry has generated millions of highly skilled workers worldwide who, in turn, are paid above-average salaries and are able to contribute to better standards of living and stable societies. In addition, millions of jobs have been created in related industries, such as services, support, and training. In the United States, for example, nearly 11 million people are employed in IT. Add to that nearly 14,000 IT companies that employ 50 or more employees.[2] The United States is the world leader in IT, representing over 35 percent of global IT spending, or over $350 billion.[3]

The IT industry can be classified as a "transformation technology." This is because it affects economic and social systems dramatically and is frequently compared to earlier transformative technologies, such as electricity, the telephone, and the automobile. Analysis of enterprise growth and productivity over the last 50 years has shown accelerated development in almost every industry employing IT products and services. From its earliest beginnings after World War II, where a small group of companies targeted large enterprises with big, expensive mainframes, to today's standard, where millions of cheap and powerful desktop computers and sophisticated software are universal, IT has continued to grow. Add to this scenario the superglue called the Internet, which ties hundreds of millions of these computers and their associated networks and corporations together, allowing information, transactions, and ultimately revenues to flow across global borders 24 hours a day.

One measure of IT growth is to analyze per capita spending by country. Figure 4.1 illustrates this trend. Note that despite its very high population, the United States is in the top three.

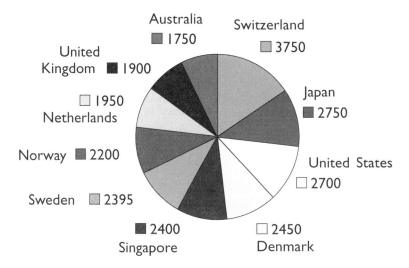

Figure 4.1   Per capital spending by country.

IT also presents significant opportunities for developing countries. In the past 20 years, countries such as India and China have created IT industries and can now compete in the global market-place. They do so with IT products that have quality, service, and support that rival, and in some cases exceed, many Western-based enterprises. Many IT companies are well established in delivering services in North America and Europe, with world-class capabilities. This trend is expected to expand and continue. Many organizations familiar with the economic struggles of these nations believe that IT and the Internet will provide a more level playing field and enable those countries, to use economic jargon, to "leapfrog" many stages of their development. IT will catapult them into societies that rival our Western culture, with its associated benefits and advantages. It also means that these countries will share the economic pie; where in the past they have been excluded. Again, this is an excellent example of how IT is a transformation technology.

India's IT industry illustrates the benefits that developing nations can realize from the commercial software model. Between 1994–1995 and 2000–2001, gross earnings from India's software industry grew from $835 million to $8.2 billion, while the value of software exports grew from $485 million to $6.2 billion.[4] India had over 16,000 IT firms in 2001 (double the number of firms just six years earlier), which employed over 561,000 workers. Overall, IT spending in India grew an average of 20.6 percent annually from 1995 to 2001 and is expected to increase to 26 percent annually from 2001 to 2005.

IT INDUSTRY SEGMENT FUNDAMENTALS

While for many the IT industry is well understood for the purposes of this book, we shall roughly describe its topology. The IT industry has evolved into an exceptionally diverse series of companies, firms, and corporations, which can be simply classified into the industry's three basic segments—hardware, software, and communications.

Hardware

Hardware can be divided into three subsections.

- Hardware—Always the most visible elements of the IT industry. When many people see a box they think it's a computer. Hardware can be broken down further into subcategories of IT systems, such as mainframes, servers, workstations, and their related components, such as microprocessors and storage devices.
- Peripherals—In this subcategory are classified printers, scanners, and other external devices, which provide overall functionality for IT systems.
- Data Communications—The hardware that allows IT systems to communicate with each other, such as classify modems, routers, switches and network hubs in this subcategory.

Hardware enterprises engaged in manufacturing are often faced with the known challenges of designing and assembling equipment. However, there are key differences because most hardware firms are engaged in highly specialized design and development and are required to bring their products to the marketplace in ever faster cycle times. In addition, hardware firms employ a higher percentage of skilled, qualified engineers and designers than non-IT manufacturers.

The line between hardware and software is becoming increasingly blurred as hardware firms now construct and develop software embedded in their products to make them more efficient or to enable a given functionality. The term "middleware" is used to describe such products.

Global IT spending on hardware exceeded $410 billion in 2002 and is projected to average 4.3 percent growth to over $459 billion by 2005.[5]

Software

Software is seen by many as the driving force behind the entire IT industry. It creates new opportunities in other industry segments such as hardware. Subcategories are as follows:

- Corporate—The software needed to manage corporations will include custom-designed applications as well as off-the-shelf software packages, whose sales have exploded in recent years.
- Consumer—This subcategory covers software such as word processors, email programs, spreadsheets, and many other types used by the individual consumer.
- Utilities and Languages—This category defines required software development tools for managing data, the necessary operating systems and languages with which we have become familiar, such as COBOL, and more recently Java, C++, and others, to generate and manage corporate software.

It is software that is the medium for doing all the new things in computing that hardware makes possible—whether simple numeric calculations or increasingly sophisticated functions like symbolic processing, graphics, simulations, and artificial intelligence. As the IT hardware industry has experienced rapid growth in the corporate, consumer, and general markets, so too has the software industry. Analysis of software growth has shown several cycles in software acceptance over the last 50 years—from the monolithic days of COBOL and FORTRAN in the 1950 and '60s to acceptance of IBM's PL/1 (Programming Language 1). Then in the early 1980s came the emergence of Fourth Generation Languages (4GLs) and CASE (Computer Aided Software Engineering), where corporate applications could be generated from diagrams and specifications. With the acceptance of the personal computer, there came client/server applications, and subsequently the Internet came bolting out of the academic world to unite hardware and software.

With so many great software development tools and standard yet rigorous methods of software generation, a software industry of enormous diversity and scalability has emerged. One person and a PC can create fabulously successful software with the potential for worldwide sales. Linus Torvalds, the creator of Linux, is a case in point. At the other end of the spectrum, vast programmer farms churning out highly specialized code for corporate software exist in abundance. IBM, Microsoft, Sun, and Texas Instruments are examples.

Innovation is a key aspect of the software industry. While quantifying innovation is notoriously difficult, two useful proxies for measuring innovation are investments in research and development (R&D) and the impact of new products on users. By either measure, the commercial software industry is highly innovative. For instance, in 1998, the U.S. software and computer services industries invested an estimated $14.3 billion in R&D, which exceeded the level of R&D spending by the U.S. motor vehicles, pharmaceuticals, and aerospace industries combined. Furthermore, innovations in software have enabled businesses across the economy to become more productive. As a recent study by the U.S. Department of Commerce concluded, innovative new software programs have enabled firms "to create extraordinary efficiencies and improve decision making within their own operations and supply networks."

Software vendors have made enormous strides on standards and sharing of data—once a severe obstacle to growth. The result of these innovative efforts is that literally hundreds of thousands of off-the-shelf hardware and software products on the market today can communicate and exchange data. Further evidence of these efforts can be seen in the IT systems of large enterprises, which often include a range of hardware, software, and platform products from several different vendors. Sharing data between the disparate elements of these systems typically would have been difficult or impossible only seven or eight years ago. Now, industry efforts to promote open standards—including support for the Internet as a common communications layer—have helped to create an environment today in which data can be shared among most elements of these IT systems with much greater ease.

Communications

Communications was once considered an unrelated stand-alone industry, but data and networks have become more integrated, leading to what is now a vital part of the IT industry. The communications segment of the IT industry now provides a mix of both hardware and software, integrated into products along similar lines as software. Subcategories include:

- Corporate—Offerings for the management of high volume and high bandwidth networks that transport data at very high speeds to customers and consumers alike.
- Consumer—Individuals are now are able to log on to high speed networks and the Internet from anywhere they choose.
- Utilities—Products that monitor and control networks, routers, security, traffic, and other essential elements of telecommunications.

Indeed, the merger of IT and telecommunications, now regarded as an integral part of IT, is almost complete. Since the early 1990s, as the Internet emerged as the primary engine of growth for IT innovation, the telecommunications industry has begun to benefit substantially. The PC revolution has transformed the IT industry, giving users access to data anywhere in the world. Starting with a minority share, Internet traffic now exceeds international voice traffic by volume and is expected to constitute more than half of all telecommunications by the end of 2004.[6]

For much of the last 50 years, most countries have had to rely on a single telecommunications provider. AT&T in the United States and British Telecom in the United Kingdom are two examples. Telecommunications deregulation started in the early 1980s and became widespread during that time, with 1982 seeing both the breakup of AT&T into the seven "Baby Bells" and the introduction of a second carrier in the UK. Deregulation of labor and product markets also became common in the 1980s, and these processes of deregulation have been adopted in varying degrees in developing countries during the 1990s.

Because of their monopoly and the regulatory framework, the large single carriers were insulated from any significant competition and had little incentive to lower prices or strive for network improvements and innovation. Thankfully for consumers and corporate entities alike, this framework of single provider regimes has been dismantled and all customers now have many choices. Governments can best achieve the growth of affordable high bandwidth telecommunications services at lower costs to the customer by eliminating those practices that impede innovation and competition. Consumers will benefit the most if competing providers are free to offer a wide range of services.

THE SOFTWARE GENERATIONS

First Generation

During the 1950s, programming a computer required changing the wires and adjusting a set of dials and switches. Next came punched paper tape (which looked like ticker tape from the telegraph), followed by the punched card. With these tapes and cards, the machine was told what to do, and when and how to do it.

To have a flawless program, a programmer needed to have a very detailed knowledge of the computer. A small mistake would cause the computer to crash—which it did frequently. Today we call this the First Generation Languages.

Second Generation

Because the first generation "languages" were regarded as very difficult to use, researchers set out to create something else, faster and easier to understand. The result was the birth of the Second Generation Languages in the mid 1950s. This generation made use of symbols called assemblers and machine code languages.

An assembler is a program that translates symbolic instructions to processor instructions. A programmer did not work with ones and zeros when using an assembly language. These symbols are called mnemonics because of the mnemonic character these symbols had (STO = store; LDA = load a register). Each mnemonic stands for one single machine instruction.

But an assembler still works on a very low level with the machine. For each processor a different assembler was written.

Third Generation

At the end of the 1950s, the pursuit of "natural language" interpreters and compilers was begun. But it took some time before the new languages were accepted by enterprises. The oldest Third Generation Language (3GL) is likely the scientific language FORTRAN (Formula Translation) which was developed around 1953 by IBM. Standardization of FORTRAN started 10 years later, and a recommendation was finally published by the International Standardization Organization (ISO) in 1968.

COBOL (Common Business Oriented Language) was developed around 1959 for the commercial world. With 3GLs, there was no longer a need to work in symbolics. Instead a programmer could use a programming language that more closely resembled natural language. In the 1970s, well-known so called "high level" languages like BASIC, Pascal, ALGOL, FORTRAN, PL/I, and C were developed.

Fourth Generation

In the early 1980s, came development of the fourth generation. A 4GL is a language or system that the end user or programmer can use to build an application. Therefore, knowledge of a programming language not needed!

The primary feature is that you do not indicate HOW a computer must perform a task but WHAT it must do. In other words, the assignments can be given on a higher functional level. This became known as procedural language.

A few instructions in a 4GL will do the same as hundreds of instructions in a lower generation language, such as COBOL. Applications in 4GLs performed tasks like screening requests for data, changing data, and reporting. In most of these cases, the 4GL was linked to a specific Database Management System (DBMS).

The main advantage of this kind of language is that users can develop and debug an application in a much shorter time than would be possible with older generation programming languages. Also, a customer can be involved earlier in the project and can actively take part in the development of a system, by means of simulation runs, long before the application is actually finished.

Today, the disadvantage of a 4GL lays more in the technological capacities of hardware. Since programs written in a 4GL are large, they need more disk space and demand a larger part of the memory capacity than 3GLs. But hardware of technologically higher standard is made more available every day so, in the long run, restrictions will disappear.

There were problems with the code generated that impaired performance and required substantial investment in hardware. In the 1990s, expectations for 4GLs were too high. In most cases, the 4GL environment was misused and became shelfware. In a few cases, the use of such programs increased end-user productivity.

Figure 4.2 illustrates a timeline of computer software generations.

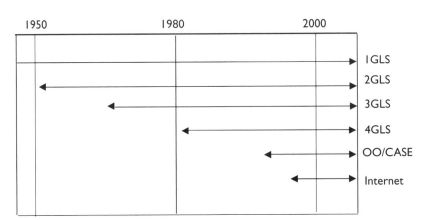

Figure 4.2   The development of the generations has stopped at the fourth level, although the Japanese attempted to deliver the fifth generation.

THE FIFTH GENERATION—ALMOST

In the early 1980s the "Fifth Generation" was an attempt by the Japanese to deliver a system of artificial intelligence—computers that think. This was Japan's challenge to the world to build sophisticated, intelligent machines in a ten-year project. This development—in contrast to machines that merely respond to preprogrammed instructions—would not merely have been another quantitative improvement in computing technology, with all the economic implications. It was an attempt at a new qualitative leap for human civilization and the world economy. Japan learned many things from the major industrialized countries at the dawn of the computer age, and today's Japanese computer technology was fostered on this knowledge.

It had been predicted that such an intelligent computer would be able to communicate in natural spoken language with its user, store vast knowledge databases, and search rapidly through these databases, making intelligent inferences, drawing logical conclusions and processing images and sees objects in the way that humans do.

While many new subtechnologies were developed, the overall goal was never realized. Many of the Japanese scientists and engineers involved in the Fifth Generation project were actually skeptical about the direction of the project and not very hopeful about spectacular results. Their doubts were well-founded.

By 1992, the project was seriously behind schedule and had only produced a few deliverables. It has since been suggested that research into other technologies, such as neural networks, may present more promising approaches to artificial intelligence. These results were considered an immense and embarrassing anticlimax.

THE INTERNET—FROM WHENCE IT CAME

Never before has there been a medium that has had such a profound, dramatic, and rapid effect on our society and culture, and the way we conduct business, in such a short time. Not since the invention of electricity, flight, the wheel, and perhaps gunpowder has there been a technology that has been accepted so quickly. The Internet has sprung almost from nowhere and burst upon society in a few short years. It has been in existence since the early 1970s, but only as a military and academic tool. Probably over 90 percent of users have come to the Internet since 1992, when the World Wide Web (WWW or Web), a key Internet technology became available. But the Internet is much more than just the Web. It has abundant resources in newsgroups and email. The factors that have brought about this boom deserve some further analysis:

1. The pursuit of the global economy—Corporations large and small, small businesses, and individuals are now required to seek new markets for goods and services—in areas that they would not have considered 10, or even five, years ago. The Internet is a means for achieving this objective by allowing anyone in any part of the world that has a computer and telephone to communicate with anyone else in the world and conduct business.

2. The powerful personal computer—The PC has evolved in power, capacity, and speed, and the cost has dropped considerably since it was first introduced. The Internet would only be available as a corporate and academic tool if the PC had not been invented—access and growth would have been severely limited. Imagine trying to access the Internet via an old-style device or green screen for any length of time.

3. Falling communication costs—Cheap, fast communication is a very important part of the equation. Expect to see costs continue to drop and access speeds continue to rise. The newer, faster, and improved Internet services or the Next Generation Internet project that is proposed will be needed sooner, rather than later. Internet access speed is key to future success. We want to access information much faster—by a factor of at least 100.

4. User demand—When users demand a service, if the market is large enough, corporations and entrepreneurs supply it. Users want faster and cheaper access to information. They demand to see and experience other cultures; the pursuit of education and knowledge are also driving forces to Internet growth.

5. Simpler software—The increased development and widespread availability of good, high-quality software that everyone can use—and can use quickly to find information—is also driving IT growth.

6. Support and services—This final, but nonetheless important, category provides much needed support and services to the IT industry in the form of training, call centers, IT consulting, and outsourcing services, to give just as a few examples. This sector of the IT industry has experienced robust growth in recent years due to the ever-increasing

sophistication and complexity of applications and the associated infrastructure required to operate them.

Twenty years ago, most corporations did not have any formal IT support or services. The Help Desk did not exist. If users had problems, they would simply call up the IT person they knew who could fix the problem. The entire IT services framework has developed in this time. It is perhaps the youngest sector of the overall IT industry. As the complexity of IT applications has grown, the services sector has grown with it, albeit at a slower pace than in previous years. The current and future market opportunities for IT consulting, systems integration, IS outsourcing, and IT training services continue to vary by vertical market.

Given the voracious worldwide appetite for all things IT, enterprises must graduate from ad hoc assembly of skills and resources to strategic attraction, development, and retention of people who can drive IT services excellence within their enterprise. Those enterprises that are serious about keeping their edge in innovation and learning will focus subsequently in investment funds for IT human capital management. Enterprises that underestimate the need for human capital management will be quickly be surpassed in the market for talent.

Three of the biggest growth areas over the next few years will be in outsourcing, administrative outsourcing, and development and integration, all of which are IT services.

SLOWER ECONOMY—SMALLER IT BUDGETS

Since the beginning of the new millennium, and despite the impressive growth we have discussed so far, world economic growth and spending have slowed significantly. For the foreseeable future, the majority of CIOs are not getting any increases in their budgets, which means they have to make the most of what they already have and be cautious about further spending. Any request to the Board to sign off new projects will come under close scrutiny for essential value to the business.

In the wake of the slowing economy, a "bare bones budget" approach to technology spending has taken over and created new buying patterns, with the focus on selecting the most affordable option that can deliver the quickest return on investment. This is taking the form of smaller, highly measurable projects and, increasingly, an interest in automating many IT functions, in an effort to reduce staff, boost efficiency, and save money. IT technology must keep a business up and running while also giving the corporation the competitive edge. This is the process most sought after by senior management. This is where autonomic computing can have significant impact of the future IT budgets.

Certain key steps can be taken to maximize IT budgets to the fullest. To ensure this, the budget-conscious CIO should:

1. **Maximize the existing software and hardware.**

   Hardware costs traditionally form the largest part of precious IT budgets, and typically, individual servers are poorly used. A recent survey of large companies by Morgan Stanley found that 67 percent of servers are utilized at less than 60 percent of capacity—this is a shocking waste of IT dollars and can be a source of future income. Grid computing, for example, is just one way to allocate that wasted money and, in turn, create a greater workload output.

2. **Reduce the complexity and consolidate.**

   By reducing complexity throughout the IT infrastructure, consolidating everything from files to databases to servers and data centers, enormous savings can be achieved. In addition, most companies struggle with a disconnected mix of mainframe, client/server, and Web applications, and this complexity is further compounded by any merger and acquisition activity, which can occur at any time—usually at an unexpected time, from an IT perspective.

3. **Spend wisely.**

   Today, businesses of all sizes should concentrate on investing their IT budgets in technology that maximizes their existing infrastructure. This allows them to focus on their core business, while taking a longer-term strategic view to ensure that they have the necessary technology in place to emerge from the current economic downturn ahead of the competition. Those who spend wisely today will be well placed to be the winners tomorrow.

4. **Evaluate potential new automated technologies.**

   CIOs would be wise to keep a business eye on new technologies that offer greater self-management and increased automation. As all IT human capital costs soar, there will be a direction from senior management to reduce staff or focus existing staff on creating more business value. It is inevitable.

The most crucial step in this process of assessing the value of an IT infrastructure to the overall business is to understand the business requirements and to map technology investment to them.

SOFTWARE PREDICTIONS

Although the market is difficult at present, there are several areas where new products and interests are emerging. These include the following:

- Web services have the potential to revolutionize the corporate software business by moving applications to a services-based architecture.
- Consolidation and mergers among software vendors both large and small will surely continue.
- Business intelligence, security, portals, content management, grid computing and self-managing systems are critical growth areas.

- New U.S. laws, such as Basel II and Sarbanes-Oxley, are fuelling interest in records management systems and applications.
- Open source software continues to gain ground both in the consumer and corporate world.
- Open standards-based software will gain ground in the next few years as the benefits become real in the corporate world.
- Wireless technologies to support mobile workers and devices are beginning to attract serious interest.
- Linux continues to make an impact on the corporate world as an alternative to other operating systems and thanks to investment by large vendors such as IBM.

Microsoft remains the largest vendor with 2002 business software revenues of $25.9 billion. IBM was second with $13.1 billion of software sales, followed by Oracle and SAP with sales of $6.9 billion and $6.8 billion, respectively. No other vendor achieved software sales of greater than $3 billion in 2002. Three mature world markets—the United States, Western Europe, and Japan—accounted for about 90 percent of global software sales, but more rapid growth was expected to come from emerging markets in Asia—especially China—and Latin America.

The global information technology services market is forecast to reach $707 billion by 2007 and in the process record a compound annual growth rate of 5.7 percent. The primary growth drivers will be governments, manufacturing, communications, and financial services. Industry observers, such as Gartner Group, further predict that the highest percentage in growth will occur in the Asia Pacific region, followed by Eastern Europe, the Middle East and Africa, Japan, Latin America, North America, and Western Europe.

However, this forecast has to be seen in the context of the generally uncertain economic outlook. In a climate of lower investment, the major players, who are able to provide complete *one-stop solutions,* are cornering a larger share of the market. Customers are primarily interested in a rapid return on investment. Longer sales cycles are expected as corporate customers use the software they have for longer periods of time.

PREDICTIONS FOR 2004 AND BEYOND

On the good news front, industry sources are predicting a recovery for software markets in 2004 and beyond. In general, and not only for software, there will be a release in pent-up demand (frustrated need) stronger than the constraint that is the allocated budget. IT managers will still have to fight for increases in budgets—but many of them will win.

The unrelenting pressure from business units for agility in a fast changing world will continue to grow.[7] When a business wants to modify its processes, products, or services, it cannot afford to wait for long IT development cycles. It must be possible to change the way application systems work by simply altering the components that are already in use, rather than buying or coding new components or whole systems from scratch.

Wireless and mobile should take another step toward maturity in 2004. The base technologies are now being offered at reasonable prices, and businesses are realizing that continuous supply chains must include a continuous information chain.

The demand for innovation and software vendor and venture capital investment in innovation will continue to increase despite low business confidence in the value of IT, which will continue to restrict new license sales for all software markets.

Models for IT organizations are changing substantially. In a global, speed-based, information-driven, fluctuating economy, a multiplicity of competing and complementary imperatives arises. In the past, the drivers for these varied initiatives included decentralized organizational constructs, in which achieving enterprise-level synergies was subordinate to the expectation that the business units succeed or fail independently, as well as the nature of an infrastructure as a collection of shared resources. Currently, organizational models and work processes are highly collaborative and fluid, which will usher in the on demand world.

As Figure 4.3 illustrates, the path to on demand organizational flexibility is driven by numerous factors.

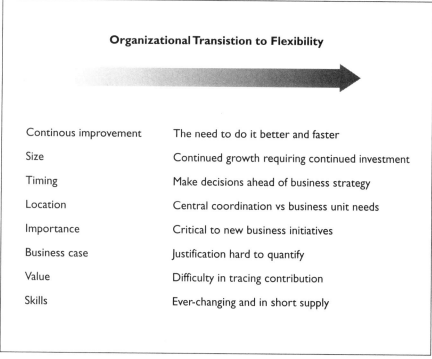

Organizational Transistion to Flexibility

Continous improvement	The need to do it better and faster
Size	Continued growth requiring continued investment
Timing	Make decisions ahead of business strategy
Location	Central coordination vs business unit needs
Importance	Critical to new business initiatives
Business case	Justification hard to quantify
Value	Difficulty in tracing contribution
Skills	Ever-changing and in short supply

Figure 4.3 Flexibility factors.

IBM AND ON DEMAND

IBM is the largest IT vendor with the broadest portfolio of offerings. Its breadth has resulted in financial stability during tough economic times. In late 2002, IBM's new CEO, Sam Palmisano, described IBM's new corporate strategy, pulling together most of the established elements of IBM's portfolio—plus new elements, such as business consulting—toward a single vision called "on demand."[8]

According to IBM, an on demand business is a dynamic business that is flexible from its business processes to its software infrastructure to its hardware infrastructure. On demand is not just about efficiency and cost cutting, it is also about increasing the value of IT to the business. It is about a paradigm shift for IT, as well as growth for IT vendors that can provide on demand services and solutions. IBM's new strategy shifts the focus of its business divisions. The challenge for IBM will be executing such a broad, integrated strategy across all of its service, software, and hardware organizations. The evolution toward the on demand environment will:

- Reduce capital and labor costs through more efficient use of resources and more automation.
- Shift the IT cost structure from fixed to variable, so costs can expand and contract with business demand.
- Increase agility by enabling the IT infrastructure to dynamically change and repurpose itself in response to changing business needs and priorities.
- Improve service levels through greater underlying IT service and component intelligence to predictively manage service levels in an automated way, as well as providing faster response when failures do occur.

SUMMARY AND CONCLUSIONS

The intensifying process of economic integration and political interdependence that we know as globalization is clearly tearing down barriers and building new networks among nations, peoples, and cultures, at an astonishing and historically unprecedented rate. It has been fueled by an explosion of IT technology that enables information, ideas, money, people, products, and services to move within and across national borders at increasingly greater speeds and volumes.

It is important to point out that globalization need not benefit only the advanced nations. Indeed, in developing countries, too, it brings the promise, but not the guarantee of a better future. More people have been lifted out of poverty during the last few decades than at any time in history. Life expectancy in developing countries is up. Infant mortality is down. And, according to the United Nations Human Development Index, which measures a decent standard of living, a good education, and a long and healthy life, the gap between rich and poor countries actually has declined since 1970. However, much remains still to be done.

With half the world's people struggling to survive on less than $2 a day, nearly 1 billion people are living in chronic hunger. Almost a billion of the world's adults cannot read. Half the children in the poorest countries still are not in school. So, while many of us walk on the cutting edge of the new global economy, alarming numbers of people still live on the bare razor's edge of survival. The IT industry and its technology are a vital part of this enabling process. We should not lose our sense of responsibility to those who desperately need it.

The key conclusion is that today's IT industry is by no means considered to be mature. Those who say that the IT industry is now so large that it can only grow at the rate of the overall economy are mistaken. First, the history of other technologies and media, such as electricity, telephony, and television, suggests that the true capability of any new technology does not become fully evident until societal usage becomes pervasive. The IT industry is still a long way from that, even in the U.S., let alone most of the rest of the world. Other than perhaps email, very few Internet applications are even close to achieving their full potential. The finish line in the IT industry race will never be fully reached.

Secondly, and probably more importantly, the IT industry should not be viewed as just another economic sector, such as retail or health care. Instead, IT should be viewed as an ever more important part of just about *every* industry. From this perspective, for the foreseeable future, growth is, at least theoretically, virtually unbounded as more and more business processes become inseparable from their underlying technology, and many new forms of business value-added have an essential technology component.

Internet growth will continue to fuel the IT industry worldwide. About 10 million U.S. adults hooked up to the Internet for the first time in 2002, boosting the overall number to 168.6 million, or 79 percent of the population.[9]

It took less than five years for the Internet to reach over 50 million users. When we compare that growth to other technologies it startles the imagination:

- Cable Television took 10 years to reach 50 million.
- Regular Television took 13 years to reach 50 million.
- Telephone took 48 years to reach 50 million.

Worldwide, the number of people with home access to the Internet hit over 600 million by the end of 2002. This figure was up 17 million from the previous year. As countries in the Far East, such as China, continue to grow, so does their Internet population. US surfers accounted for 29 percent of users, with Europe accounting for 23 percent.

Growth in user numbers the UK, Italy, and Germany outpaced that in the US in 2002 on a percentage basis, with spectacular growth in countries such as Spain and Brazil. The Internet will continue to expand in all countries with some maturity leveling expected in larger countries. Almost 62 percent of Web surfers ages 14 and up—94.9 million people in the United States— will purchase goods and services online in 2005, up from nearly 60 percent, or 81.2 million users in 2002.

But can this expansion continue along the lines we have discussed here? Is the rate of expansion part of the future problem? Will complexity of the technology tear down what has been successful so far? This is the key challenge for Autonomic Computing to address.

NOTES

1. United Nations 2002 Conference on Trade and Development IT Report, Trends and Executive Summary, p. 3.
2. "Where Can I Start?" Published by the Information Technology Association of America (April 2002), p. 2.
3. Ibid.
4. United Nations 2002 Conference on Trade and Development IT Report, Trends and Executive Summary, p. 6.
5. Ibid.
6. ITU Telecom Conference 1999. Paper by Yoshio Utsumi, *The Spirit of TELECOM: Past, present and future*, p. 5.
7. Speech on November 12, 2003, IBM Chairman and Chief Executive Officer Sam Palmisano—one of several of his speeches on this subject.
8. Speech on December 10, 2002, IBM Chairman and Chief Executive Officer Sam Palmisano
9. Data taken from Neilson ratings. See *www.nielsen-netratings.com/*.

CHAPTER 5

FAST AND FASTER

INTRODUCTION

Speed is the one word that typifies the description of our way of life, our society, and future. We lead a hectic, frantic lifestyle at home or work. Everything around us seems to be moving fast or faster. We are required to move at the same pace as others. If we do not, then we are worried about the consequences. The technology of computers, networks, mobile phones, pagers, and the Internet feeds on this lifestyle. Technology has a rapid heartbeat, and yet this is the choice we have made for ourselves. Some of us thrive on it; others do not. Our ability to live, work, and play at this pace can give us a sense of power—a buzz, or feeling of exhilaration. This feeling is similar to what our ancestors felt in the heat of battle.

No one can deny the acceleration in the pace of business life that has happened in the last 50 years—since the evolution of the computer and its associated technology. It is an "instant" society that we live in: instant coffee, instant results, instant replays—ironically shown in slow motion for emphasis—instant gratification. In Japan, some restaurants actually charge by the minute. Patrons are required to eat fast or literally pay the consequences. Our addiction to speed has led us to behave in various ways we may not have otherwise. We are influenced by the actions of the society around us. Consider the following illustrations of these events. Make a note of how many times you have acted in this fashion.

- We travel fast in our cars on highways or freeways. We change lanes frequently, trying to get ahead of the person driving in front.
- When entering an elevator, we push the "close door" button—even if someone has entered ahead of us and pushed the button already. As the elevator stops at different floors, there is always the temptation to press the close door button again to ensure that we reach our destination in the shortest time possible.

- When using a microwave oven, we tend to frantically push the same button twice as the guide to cooking—for example, pressing "2,2" or "3,3" in rapid succession. Our intent is to get the meal cooked as soon as possible.
- When standing in line at a location, such as a bank or fast food outlet, that has multiple lines, we will switch lines to what we perceive as the fastest moving line to get served as quickly as possible.
- We choose health care providers, such as doctors or dentists, by how quickly we can get in to see them and how quickly we can receive the treatment.
- Escalators are designed to transport people from one point to another. Individuals who are apparently in a hurry, and who are not content to allow themselves to be transported at the normal escalator speed, set off to their destination by climbing two or more steps at a time.

Does any of this sound familiar? Psychologists have termed this behavior, "Hurry Up Syndrome." But with the fast life comes anxiety and ill heath. "Burnout" is a phrase that did not exist thirty years ago. If we cannot act in the same fashion as everyone else or achieve what is expected of us, then we are prone to rapid heartbeats and a rise in blood pressure. Sociologists in several Western countries have come to the conclusion that increasing wealth and education have contrived to create tensions about time and how to spend it. Alvin Toffler caught the essence of speed before the Internet with his landmark book *Future Shock*, first published in 1970. Then, in 1980, he published *The Third Wave*, about society based around information technology. The Third Wave Information Society is more than just technology and economics. It is not just "digital" and "networked." Painful social, cultural, institutional, moral, and political dislocations often accompany our transition from a brute force to a brain force economy.

Adding to this lifestyle is the daily reminder to keep up the pace of life. Companies extol products and services by advertising that "speed is good." A small selection of those companies is reproduced in Table 5.1 to emphasize this point.

It appears that even the great American egg is a victim of this fast lifestyle. Speed is important in the digital economy. Take the example of Mr. Jeff Bezos, the CEO of online bookstore Amazon, who is known, for running through the office. He says he is just hyperactive, but there is no denying a fundamental truth of his approach: if you're going to succeed in today's business world, you have to move fast. One wonders how many other managers run through the offices at Amazon and how many accidents happen?

LIFE AT INTERNET SPEED

Welcome to the world of Internet speed. If one thing increasingly defines the modern workplace and workers' lives, it's that fast is no longer fast enough. The crush of new technology descending on the workplace—designed to provide quantum leaps in productivity and improve communication—is leaving many feeling alienated, disoriented, and burned out. People are bombarded with information, data, and deadlines. And many individuals aren't sure how to cope. Corpora-

Table 5.1   A Selection of Slogans for a Fast Lifestyle

Name of Company	Slogan
American Egg Board	"Think eggs—think fast"
Anacin	"Fast, fast relief"
Citibank	"The Citi never sleeps"
Coca-Cola	"Three Million a Day" (in 1917) "Six Million a Day" (in 1925)
Federal Express	"When it absolutely, positively has to be there overnight"
GEICO	"Fifteen minutes could save you 15 percent or more on car insurance"
Kentucky Fried Chicken	"There's fast food, and then there's KFC"
Lendingtree.com	"Up to 4 offers in hours"
Panasonic	"Slightly ahead of its time"
Rolls-Royce	"At 60 miles an hour the loudest noise in the new Rolls-Royce comes from the electric clock"
Western Union	"The fastest way to send money"

tions are not much better. As competition escalates and pressure builds, many corporations believe they must respond with increasing speed to stay in the game. Customers, employees, and managers continue to develop expectations about doing business with organizations through the Internet—at Internet speed. For some it is an absolute necessity. Unfortunately, the technology often moves faster than the ability of people, and particularly corporate cultures, to adapt. While it is tempting to blame this problem solely on the technology, the issue is as much about work habits, time management, corporate culture, and human resources practices. Unless people take control of the technology and learn to manage it, they're likely to find themselves managed *by* it. But at many companies, there are simply too few rules. Human Resources and senior management must take the initiative in solving these problems.

The dynamic digital workplace wasn't supposed to be like this. In the 1980s, pundits envisioned a society replete with laborsaving technology and an increasingly short work week. It was to be the "golden age of leisure." Yet the road to leisure has encountered more than a few potholes along the way. In Jeremy Rifkin's excellent book and bestseller, *The End of Work* (G.P. Putnam's Sons, 1995), readers glimpse a future where there isn't enough work to go around and large numbers of people are unemployed or underemployed—all as a result of technology. It's not uncommon for most mid-level and senior managers and professionals to find themselves constantly tethered to their jobs. They make calls on their cell phones as they commute. They incessantly check their pagers and voice mail at business meetings, in their kitchens, at the grocery stores, and at restaurants. Our restaurants would all be a lot quieter if cell phones were banned, These "professionals" take their work home and plug into the Internet in the evening, checking and responding to email before going to bed at a late hour—only to rise again at an early hour and start where they left off.

Vacations now suffer because of the need to constantly check email and voice mail, and respond to demands. It may be easier to take an hour each day to respond to emails, rather than face a backlog of over 1,000 emails on return from a week's vacation. For some managers, there could be even more at stake. They cannot be out of the loop while away. They want to know the decisions being made that might affect them. It's unrealistic to ignore a crucial project or a spate of email messages asking for additional information. Many a family vacation has been cut short by the need to "get back to the office."

Some companies are attempting to gain control of technology and exorcise the demons of speed. This includes training in time-management, and work-life programs to help people better manage their lives. Some corporations even provide business-life coaching and one-on-one counseling.

No amount of training can eliminate all the pressures that come with Internet speed. Human resources can, however, define rules and guidelines for communication and interaction. People must have realistic expectations. They have to learn that it is okay not to respond to an email message within two minutes, and that it is occasionally all right to turn the email off when they're busy with an important project or at a meeting. Organizations also have to establish methods and processes that help employees conduct their personal lives, so they can go on vacation without constantly being on call. The secret is to make the technology work in the best interests of individuals, and ultimately the corporations. In the end, there's no one way to succeed. However, companies that devise a well-planned strategy for integrating and adopting technology are far more likely to boost productivity and success. Working smarter with advanced technologies will help provide better quality of life for all concerned with it.

NO PATIENCE?

Technology has made so many things faster—microwaves, ATMs, jet aircraft, processed foods, satellites, email. Technology has made us the fast society—two-minute noodles, one-hour photo processing, 24-hour loan approvals. At this rate, can we be far from a home study course called "Teach Yourself Brain Surgery in 12 Days"? Since so many things take so little time, when something or someone slows us down, we lose our patience, quickly.

Most people today live in cities and towns, not on farms. Very few people are involved in raising animals or growing crops—activities that inherently require patience. It's easy to imagine a city worker impatient with a train being five minutes late. It's hard to imagine a farmer being impatient because his calves aren't becoming cows fast enough or because his summer crop isn't ready to harvest in springtime.

Another reason patience is becoming rarer in our society is because of the way we link achievement and success with personal worth. For us, to fail at an activity means to fail as a person. But that hasn't always been the case. In other times and other places, failure in an activity meant the opportunity to learn something new, to try again, and to experiment or try another approach, an opportunity to grow and mature. Most of the great scientists of the past—such as Newton, Galileo, Copernicus, and Einstein—are great examples of this. Their contributions didn't come in one flash of inspiration, but over decades of patient work with as many failures as successes. Our society says, "Succeed and succeed now!" There is no time to be patient and persistent. In truth, we need these qualities to ultimately be successful.

MOORE'S LAW

The IT industry has its own measure of speed. For more than three decades, it has been an unshakable principle of the computer industry that every 18 months, the number of transistors that will fit on a silicon chip doubles.

The phenomenon known as Moore's Law, named for the semiconductor pioneer who first observed it, has been the basic force underlying the computer revolution and the rise of the Internet. Moore made his prediction in 1965 for an article he was writing for a magazine.[1] Later, he had to revise his initial prediction of 24 months for each doubling of chip capacity. And while it is not an actual physical law, his observation has taken on an almost mystical quality as the clearest expression of the power of human science and engineering. In fact, many industry executives have come to see it as a self-fulfilling prophecy. As transistors have been scaled ever smaller, computing performance has risen exponentially, while the cost of that power has been driven down. And it has been assumed in the industry that the rate of progress would hold for at least another 10 to 15 years despite recent debates to the contrary.

Table 5.2 lists the trend is the number of transistors on a chip over time.

Table 5.2   Processor Evolution and the Number of Transistors on a Chip
Source: Intel Corporation

Processor Type	Year of Introduction	Transistors
4004	1971	2,250
8008	1972	2,500
8080	1974	5,000
8086	1978	29,000
286	1982	120,000

Table 5.2   Processor Evolution and the Number of Transistors on a Chip
Source: Intel Corporation (Continued)

Processor Type	Year of Introduction	Transistors
386™ processor	1985	275,000
486™ DX processor	1989	1,180,000
Pentium® processor	1993	3,100,000
Pentium II processor	1997	7,500,000
Pentium III processor	1999	24,000,000
Pentium 4 processor	2000	42,000,000

Figure 5.1 illustrates the point.

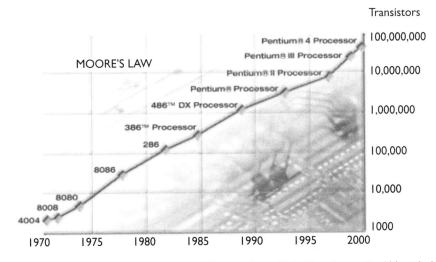

Figure 5.1   The graphical representation of Moore's Law. Note that the vertical Y scale is logarithmic—that is, 10 times the previous scale.

To be sure, such dire warnings have been made periodically in the past—an article in *Scientific American* in 1987 said Moore's Law was unlikely to be maintained through the 1990s—and each time semiconductor designers have shown remarkable ingenuity in surmounting seemingly impossible barriers. This means those computer speeds will continue to increase. If Moore's Law had operated in the automobile industry, it would be possible to purchase a Jaguar S-Type for less than $5 and have it run on gasoline for over 200 miles to the gallon. While this is perhaps a crude analogy and calculation, the conclusion is inescapable. It's all about high speed and low cost.

SPEED IN BUSINESS

To stay competitive and to continue to produce profits, corporations are shortening most processes, products, and services—everything in sight. They have shortened product life cycles and aim to introduce products quicker than their competitors. Manufacturers are striving to lower costs and increase market share by implementing just-in-time inventory control. Faster product development is essential, for speed kills the competition. In the automobile industry, new cars took used to take years to get to the marketplace—now they take months. When a customer orders a new car, instead of weeks, it is delivered in days. In the semiconductor industry, chips are produced and manufactured, then delivered in days.

Other corporate examples of legendary speed in business include:

- In the late 1990s, Citibank completely recreated its procedures for approving home mortgage loans, moving from being an also-ran to a market leader. The company reasoned that consumers would want to do business with a lending institution that gave them fast turnaround of a loan application. Citibank's new mortgage approval procedure went from a lengthy turnaround time of 45 days to just under 15 days.
- Federal Express started out by promising overnight delivery of a letter or package by noon the next day. Later, came the promise overnight delivery by 10:30 a.m., Priority Delivery. After FedEx had captured significant market share with fast, dependable service, it developed real-time computerized tracking of any package in the FedEx system and gave customers a choice of two classes of delivery: Priority Overnight and Standard Overnight. FedEx has consistently developed new products that enable it to achieve and maintain a prominent position in the marketplace.
- In 1993, Marriott opened up the Courtyard hotels, its version of a moderately priced hotel chain. When it went after this niche opportunity, Marriott did a good job of identifying customer needs and wants. It empowered a cross-functional team to develop the new product, which first appeared as a prototype hotel in Gaithersburg, Maryland. After a successful test marketing of the new hotels in Atlanta, Courtyard has become an important addition to the Marriott product line, with more than 200 units around the country.

Countless other examples exist; including Black & Decker, IBM, Hewlett-Packard, Honda, and Motorola, to illustrate how real companies must act quickly to meet the needs of the demanding customer. The message is clear to all senior business managers—act fast and adapt or die. "Business as Usual" is a phrase that many companies will never use. It deserves to be tossed on the scrap heap of history due to the rapid pace of technology. Business will NEVER be usual again. The new motto is "Business Unusual." There is one fundamental enabling factor in all this fast product development and implementation—the computer. Without adaptable, flexible computer systems that manage and produce these products, speed is not possible. New terms in our vocabulary have evolved which describe the speed at which we work—"Internet speed" is one example and "Warp speed" is another.

It is now estimated that the knowledge we have for any given technology doubles every 12 to 18 months. Moore's Law should now relate to technology in general rather than just transistors on a chip.

The effect on the economy with this approach is dramatic and anti-inflationary. Alan Greenspan, longstanding chairman of the U.S. Federal Reserve, made the observation that inflation in the United States would have increased one percent more if it had not been for the widespread use of IT technology.[2]

Just a few days prior to Mr. Greenspan's comments, the U.S. Department of Commerce issued a report noting that although the information technology industry accounts for only about 8 percent of America's gross domestic product, it generated more than one-third of the nation's economic growth from 1995 to 1998.

Meanwhile, the technology industry showed dramatic increases in productivity: an average of 10.4 percent annually from 1990 to 1997, compared with less than one percent outside the technology sector.[3]

SUMMARY AND CONCLUSIONS

The process of innovation is neverending. Indeed, many argue that the pace of innovation will continue to quicken in the years ahead, as companies exploit the still largely untapped potential for e-commerce, especially in the business-to-business/consumer arena, where most observers expect the fastest growth.

It appears to be only a matter of time before the Internet becomes the prime venue for the trillions of dollars of business-to-business commerce conducted every year. The ranks of online retailers seemed to be decimated after the dot-com bubble burst, yet e-commerce has grown steadily. E-tail sales in the U.S. totaled about $31 billion during the first nine months of 2002, an increase of 34 percent, compared with just a 4 percent rise in retail sales overall.[4] The essential contribution of information technology is the expansion of knowledge and its obverse, the reduction of uncertainty in all these areas.

Indeed, it is the widespread acceptance of information technology throughout the economy that makes the current period unique. The remarkable combination of technologies that we label IT has allowed us to move beyond efficiency gains in routine manual tasks to achieve new levels of productivity in routine information-processing tasks that previously depended upon other facets of human input—computing, sorting and retrieving information, and acting on pieces of information. As a result, information technologies have begun to alter fundamentally how we do business and create economic value, often in ways that were not readily foreseeable even just a decade ago. This has happened at relentless speed.

The demand for new computer applications will no doubt continue to spur demand for those with the creativity and the higher-level conceptual skills to increasingly harness technology to produce greater client value. Economists say the most important driver of long-term economic growth is productivity—the output workers produce per hour. Increasing productivity enables companies to pay higher wages without raising prices, thus improving our standard of living. The importance of technological innovation in sustaining productivity growth is widely recognized and accepted today.

There are certain basic factors that propel information technology. The three laws that guide this technology are well known. The first is Moore's Law, which we have already identified and discussed. The second law is the law of networks popularized by Metcalfe. John Chambers, the chief of CISCO, pointed out that when computers were being extensively installed in enterprises in the 1970s, a debate arose in the United States about the productivity paradox of the computers. Are the computers giving increase in productivity commensurate with the investment involved in installing them? This doubt was removed once the era of network was born. Starting with the local area network to the wide area network and now the era of Internet, which is growing so rapidly that it is setting new records in its reach and pace of development, the doubt about IT and productivity is now resolved. Metcalfe pointed out that when the computers were made to talk to each other and network, productivity increased because the power of the network is equal to the square of the number of computers connected in a network.

In was back in 1989 that the eminent economist Lestor Thurow wrote his book *Head to Head* trying to estimate the shape of global trade in the decade beyond 2000. He predicted a situation evolving where in the future, global competition will be not an exercise in live-and-let-live but instead a fierce head-to-head competition. There will be winners and losers. This is because all of the major global players will be focusing on the same seven technologies: microelectronics, computer software, civil aviation, biotechnology, new materials, telecommunication, and robotics. Quite a few of these technologies have a bearing on information technology. In other words, information technology becomes the common denominator of the key technologies deciding global competition in the early 21st century.

These years of extraordinary innovation are enhancing the standard of living for a large majority of citizens of all countries. We should be thankful for that and persevere in policies that enlarge the scope for competition and innovation and thereby foster greater opportunities for everyone.

NOTES

1. G.E. Moore, "Cramming More Components onto Integrated Circuits," *Electronics*, 38:8 (April 19, 1965), available at *http://www.intel.com/research/silicon/moorespaper.pdf.*

2. *The Revolution in Information Technology.* Remarks by Chairman Alan Greenspan before the Boston College Conference on the New Economy. Boston, Massachusetts, March 6, 2000.

3. Commerce Department Study, *The Emerging Digital Economy II.* U.S. Government Publication.

4. Data from the U.S. Census Bureau report. See *http://www.census.gov/mrts/www/current.html.*

CHAPTER 6

HUMAN CAPITAL

INTRODUCTION

I n the last 50 years of the 20th century, the nation has witnessed momentous changes in the size, composition, and characteristics of the U.S. labor force. The same social, demographic, and economic forces that influenced the growth and composition of the labor force during the past 50 years will continue to influence the workforce in the decades ahead. Chief among those influences has been information technology, which has brought so much automation, along with communications networks, speed, and the ability to produce goods and services for the global marketplace.

Another part of the growth of the labor force in the past 50 years has been the so-called Baby Boom generation. This Baby Boom swelled the ranks of the labor force during the past three decades, and their exit will have a profound impact on the labor force during the next two decades. Boomers will remain a force of change even in their retirement. A large portion of the current IT workforce can be categorized as Boomers, who grew up with the emerging computer technology during this time. They have embraced all aspects of computer technology.

The productivity enhancements of IT have been significant for the labor force. The impact has been felt in increased standards of living and the creation of a society that is the envy of most countries in the world.

U.S. POPULATION GROWTH AND EMPLOYMENT TRENDS

The U.S. population is expected to increase by 24 million between the years 2000–2010, a slightly faster rate of growth than between 1990–2000 but slower than from 1980–1990. Continued growth is good news for the IT industry, as it will mean more consumers of goods and services, spurring demand for workers in a wide range of occupations and industries driven by computer systems. The effects of population growth on various occupations will differ. The differences are partially accounted for by the age distribution of the future population.

Population is the single most important factor in determining the size and composition of the labor force, which is comprised of people who are either working or looking for work. The civilian labor force is projected to increase by 17 million, or 12 percent, to 158 million between 2000–2010.

Total employment is expected to increase from 146 million in 2000 to 168 million in 2010, a rate of 15.2 percent. The 22 million jobs that will be added by 2010 will not be evenly distributed across major industrial and occupational groups. Changes in consumer demand, technology, and many other factors will contribute to the continually changing employment structure in the U.S. economy.

Analysis of trends indicates that services and communications will be two sectors where the biggest expansion will occur, leading to many new jobs in both areas.

- **Services:** This is the largest and fastest growing major industry group. It is expected to add 13.7 million new jobs by 2010, accounting for three out of every five new jobs created in the U.S. economy. Over two-thirds of this projected job growth is concentrated in three sectors of the service industry: business, health, and social services. Business services—including personnel supply services, and computer and IT processing services—will add 5.1 million jobs. However, employment in computer and data processing services—which provide prepackaged and specialized software, data, and computer systems design and management, and computer-related consulting services—is projected to grow by 86 percent between 2000 and 2010, ranking as the fastest growing industry in the economy. Health services—including home health care services, hospitals, and offices of health practitioners—will add 2.8 million new jobs, as demand for health care increases due to an aging population and longer life expectancies.
- **Communications:** Employment in the communications sector is expected to increase by 16.9 percent, adding 277,000 jobs by 2010. Half of these new jobs—139,000—will be in the telephone communications industry; however, cable and other pay television will be the fastest growing segment of the sector over the next decade, with employment expanding by 50.6 percent. Increased demand for residential and business wireless services, cable service, and high-speed Internet connections will fuel the growth in communications industries.

Figure 6.1 graphically illustrates the projected changes in employment trends. Services, which are mainly comprised of IT, will be the fastest growing industry in the United States.

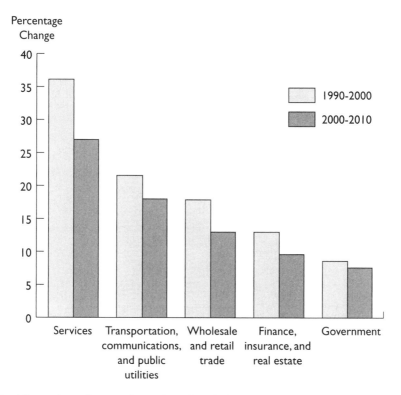

Figure 6.1 The projected comparison of services industries and percentage changes in wages/salaries. Note that the projected rate from 2000–2010 is not as great as the period from 1990–2000 in all sectors. *Source:* U.S. Department of Labor—Bureau of Labor Statistics[1]

OCCUPATION GROWTH

The question to ask now is what types of occupations will grow in the next ten years? Professional and related occupations will grow the fastest and add more new jobs than any other major occupational group. From 2000–2010, a 26 percent increase in the number of professional and related jobs is projected, a gain of 6.9 million. Professional and related workers perform a wide variety of duties, and are employed throughout private industry and government. Nearly three-quarters of the job growth will come from three groups of professional occupations—computer occupations, health care practitioners and technical occupations, and education, training, and library occupations—which will add 5.2 million jobs combined.

We can break this down further and say what specific occupations will grow the fastest over the next ten years. Figure 6.2 lists the main growth by occupation type. Note that out of the top 10 fastest-growing occupations, eight are IT-specific categories.

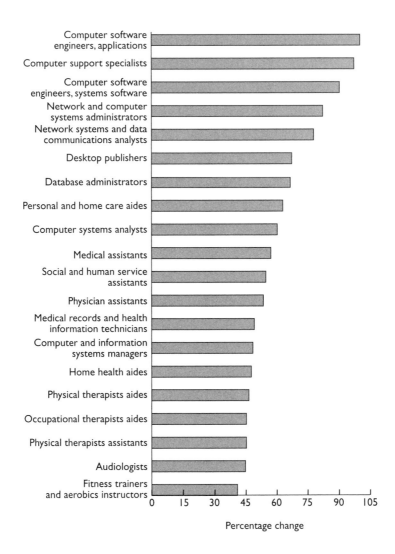

Percentage change

Figure 6.2 The fastest growing occupations for the period 2000–2010. *Source:* U.S. Department of Labor—Bureau of Labor Statistics

They are listed here, along with the percent growth expected over the next 10 years:

  1. Computer Software Engineers, Applications, 101 percent
  2. Computer Support Specialists, 98 percent
  3. Computer Software Engineers, System Software, 91 percent
  4. Network and Computer Systems Administrators, 86 percent
  5. Network Systems and Data Communications Analysts, 80 percent

6. Desktop Publishers, 71 percent

7. Database Administrators, 70 percent

8. Computer Systems Analysts, 62 percent

There is no question that these very large numbers of people will be needed, but asks the question, "If there are chronic shortages of IT staff now how will the industry recruit these new people?" There is no clear answer to this question.

THE DYNAMICS OF THE IT LABOR MARKET

After the recession years of the early 1990s, the IT market picked up rapidly as new systems were required and the Internet started to have its impact. The market for IT staff reached a fever pitch by the middle of 1996. Corporations could not recruit or retain IT staff fast enough. Outrageous deals in salaries, bonuses, stock options, and other compensation were made to attract the right staff. As a result of this, job-hopping became rampant. By 1998, another problem was looming that would last for several years—the year 2000 or Y2K bug. The year 2000—thanks to the open question of whether legacy computer systems would be able to handle the rollover in century—posed one of the most significant challenges ever faced by the IT industry, which had an enormous impact on business applications, package solutions, and systems software. The year 2000, however, posed a significant business opportunity for external service provider (ESP) vendors. Suddenly, those with older skills, such as COBOL programmers, could command the same compensation packages as cutting-edge Internet and e-commerce specialists. Addressing the Y2K bug was the largest project ever undertaken by most corporate IT organizations. Enormous numbers of IT staff, both internal and external, were drafted to solve the problem. And solve the problem they did. Now, Y2K is a distant memory.

Next came the Internet and e-commerce stampede. Almost all corporations rushed to put up Web sites, intranets, and extranets in the hope of rapid transition to globalization. The stampede lead some corporations to the edge of the cliff and then over. "Dot.gone" and "Dot.bomb" became new phrases in the English language. Now that the dust from the Internet stampede has settled, and consolidation has produced a stable of fine companies and products, the long-talked-about Internet prophecy is starting to be realized. But as globalization and the growth of e-business continue to raise the levels of IT diversity most companies must manage, the need for some sort of unifying framework is more important than ever. And much harder to achieve.

ORIGINS OF IT STAFF SHORTAGES

The next question to ask is, "How did the IT industry get into this situation?" More importantly if this question can be answered, what strategies need to be put in place to prevent it happening again? The answer to the first question is complex and seated in many factors, none of which are individually responsible for the problem.

1. **Growth of the economy**—With the rapid growth of Western-based economies in the last five years, there has been an explosion in the need for new corporate computer systems. The Internet has been an engine of growth requiring new IT skills that have not been readily available. The demand for Internet systems was very strong for several years, 1999–2001 particularly. Corporations were scrambling to install Web-based systems to keep up with competitors.

2. **IT dependency**—Senior corporate management now acknowledge, albeit reluctantly, that there is a strong dependence on IT departments for success. No corporation—large, medium, or small—can effectively compete in the global marketplace without substantial modern computer systems.

3. **The education gap**—Universities and educational establishments have been slow to recognize that there is a gap in the need for qualified IT staff. IT curriculums based on modern technology were not readily available when needed. Most universities were slow to adopt the Internet as a medium for education and delivery of distance learning. A notable exception to this observation is the University of Phoenix, which was an early innovative leader in online learning. Because trained IT staff was not readily available, corporations looked to other nations, such as India, to fill the gap. However, there is another side to this issue. Many corporations do not promote IT awareness, do not contribute time, resources, staff, or equipment to schools and college communities. They do not help academic institutions strengthen their curriculums and do not create learning environments appropriate to new graduates. Subsequently, they have paid the price of IT shortages. Education must be a partnership to be successful.

4. **IT retention practices**—CIOs and other senior IT managers have paid too little attention to good retention practices, which has resulted in a flight of IT staff. Clearly, the need to address IT salaries and benefits, and the IT environment is now recognized outside the IS organization.

5. **Rapid changes in IT technology**—The technology of the IT industry is very cyclical. Languages, systems, and methodologies become fashionable very quickly, only to be replaced with the next silver bullet after a few years or less. We briefly touched on this subject in Chapter 1. Over the last twenty years there have been a number of technology cycles. From Fourth Generation Languages (4GLs) in the early 1980s to the Computer Aided Software Engineering (CASE) products of the later part of that decade, technology has continued to change. In the early 1990s client/server technology was very much in vogue, with large database technology such as IBM's DB2, and Oracle. After that came the Internet from the middle of 1995 onward, with object-oriented and Java-related languages, C++, and Web-based systems. Each cycle requires staff to be fully trained, and frequently corporations are scrambling to find staff to fit the technology. It is a continuous game of trying to catch the hare.

6. **Complexity**—As the number of installed custom-designed applications, software systems, and packages has grown in many corporations, the need for all-embracing archi-

tectures and communications networks to support them has also grown. This means that large numbers of highly skilled systems programmers, architects, and database specialists are needed to make sure the systems are running smoothly. As we noted in Chapter 2, most installations are required to maintain systems that have tens of millions of lines of code. This is a significant undertaking, and it provides the stability that must be present for critical applications to run without problems.

It is important to note that no one of the above issues is the culprit for the IT staff shortages. But collectively, they represent the scenario that has led us to this point.

HIGH-TECH VISAS AND LEGISLATION

Attempts have been made in the past by the U.S. Government and many high-tech firms to address the IT shortage. Many companies have recruited in countries such as India and China for skilled workers using the H-1B visa method. This permits workers to legally work in the United States for periods up to six years. However, a large number of high tech firms suggested that the number of H-1B visa holders were not sufficient and needed to be increased because of the IT staff shortage. After some lengthy debate, in October 2000 President Bill Clinton signed into law the bill S. 2045, the "American Competitiveness in the Twenty-First Century Act," and H.R. 5362, an Act to increase the fees charged to employers who petition to employ H-1B nonimmigrant workers. The law increases the number of H-1B visas available to bring in highly skilled foreign temporary workers and doubles the fee charged to employers using the program, thus providing critical funding for training U.S. workers and students in return. The Acts recognize the importance of allowing additional skilled workers into the United States to work in the short-run, while supporting longer-term efforts to prepare American workers for the jobs of the new economy.

At the core of President Clinton's IT strategy was the belief that fiscal discipline and freeing up capital for private sector investment must be accompanied by a commitment to invest in human capital. The growing demand for workers with high-tech skills is a dramatic illustration of the need to "put people first" and increase the investments in education and training. Many companies are reporting that their number one constraint on growth is the inability to hire workers with the necessary skills. In today's knowledge-based economy, what you earn depends on what you learn. Jobs in the information technology sector, for example, can pay 85 percent more than the private sector average.

The quota of issued H-1B visas increased to 195,000 for each of fiscal years 2001, 2002, and 2003. (It then drops back down to 65,000 in fiscal 2004.) However, other provisions of the legislation should result in a noticeable number of H-1Bs not being counted toward the cap who had been counted in past years, resulting in an even greater effective increase in numbers for high-tech firms.

This legislation was further enhanced in November 2002 when President George W. Bush signed into law the "21st Century Department of Justice Appropriations Authorization Act," Public Law 107-273. This law corrected and fine-tuned S. 2045 by adding extensions to applications to allow foreign workers to extend their H-1B visa. The H-1B worker is entitled to continuing extensions, in one-year increments until and unless the labor certification is denied.

This legislation was a big step forward in the battle against IT shortages, despite some vigorous opposition from domestic organizations in the United States. Since its introduction, this legislation has been somewhat successful. CIOs and other IT management have welcomed the government initiative and lobbied hard for its success. It is encouraging that the United States government will respond to calls from the IT industry to correct imbalances in IT staff shortages. However, once a concern has been raised, the time taken for the legislation to be formed, written, debated and enacted is not insignificant. Government legislation is not known to be rapid or provide swift solutions. It has not been the complete answer to the IT shortages that have been experienced; other solutions are still needed.

COSTS OF THE IT RECRUITMENT CRISIS

The continuing crisis of recruiting IT staff is not new. In the past, there have been numerous studies showing that the lack of skilled IT staff has had significant and negative impact on the U.S. economy. For example, in 1999, the Computing Technology Industry Association, a non-profit organization, released a report that indicates the IT service and support personnel shortage costs to the U.S. economy in spending on salaries and training a total of *$105.5 billion annually.* The association's study, "Crisis in IT Service and Support," analyzed data from the government as well as participating companies.The study also found that about 10 percent of IT service and support jobs, or 268,740 positions at that time, remained unfilled, costing U.S. companies $4.5 billion a year in lost worker productivity due to unresolved technical issues.[2]

CURRENT IT UNEMPLOYMENT

This author has problems with the future projections and figures issued by the Bureau of Labor discussed earlier in this chapter. At present, we have widespread unemployment in the IT industry. Unemployment in the IT profession reached 6 percent in 2003, and the media is reporting "unprecedented" levels of unemployment for a career path that, until recently, was a sure path to a well-paying job. IT unemployment rates were as low as 1.2 percent in 1997, but rose sharply to 4.3 percent in 2002—see Figure 6.3.

The growth in unemployment over the past five years in the IT industry can be traced to multiple shocks to spending and employment trends, including many of the following events:

- The end of Y2K projects in 1999.
- The bursting of the Internet and telecom "bubbles" in 2000.
- Dramatic reductions in corporate IT spending.

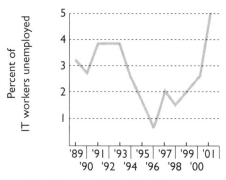

Data: Bureau of Labor Statistics

Figure 6.3   A graph showing IT jobless rates in the United States from 1989–2001. *Source:* U.S. Department of Labor—Bureau of Labor Statistics

- The U.S. economy in recession.
- The 9/11 terrorist attacks.
- The subsequent war in Afghanistan and Iraq.
- Big swings in the world stock markets, creating uncertainty.
- Constant moves to outsource major applications and networks overseas.
- Investor and business uncertainty as the WorldCom, Enron, and Tyco frauds, the mutual fund controversy, and other business scandals of the late 1990s and early 2000s unfolded.
- Continued market caution after the liberation of Iraq and the uncertainty of the reconstruction outcome to democracy.
- Accelerating global IT competition.

In addition, a half million jobs, or 10 percent of the U.S. IT professionals currently working in IT services firms, will be displaced in the next 18 months as their jobs move overseas, according to Gartner, Inc., the Stamford, Conn.-based research firm. This would bring total IT job losses to one million, when added to the 500,000 IT professionals estimated by the Bureau of Labor Statistics to have lost their jobs in the United States since 2001.

So the question of how will autonomic computing impact these figures arises. Will this technology make unemployment worse than it already is? In the future, automation improvements and the development of autonomic applications may harm some IT career paths. So perhaps the career advice should be is to avoid the technical aspects of the profession and focus more on IT management. It is not clear how IBM and other autonomic vendors are addressing this unemployment issue.

IT SKILLS DEVELOPMENT

If new technologies, such as autonomic computing, are to succeed, it will be necessary to create a skills development program. One of the surest ways to align strategies and workforce competencies with corporation vision is to create a road map from vision to execution. A skills management process starts in the future and works its way back to the present. An IT skills management process, for example, links the corporation's vision to a technology forecast. The technology forecasts to the required skills, the required skills to the IT skills inventory, the skills inventory to the IT staff's competence levels, and the competence levels to gaps and to the time frame during which those gaps need to be filled. Leadership, team building, marketing, business savvy, project management, manufacturing know-how, functional expertise, and institutional knowledge all are part of the skills picture.

As shown in Figure 6.4, skills management serves as an order for managing the workforce. It lays out a road map for skills development, work role definition, career tracks, resource management, staffing allocation, workload balancing, and learning. With a road map, all members of the workforce can fit their strengths, weaknesses, and alternatives into the corporation's plans.

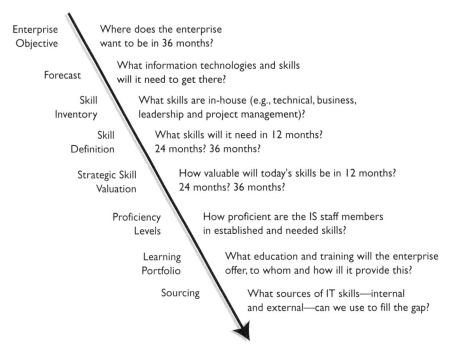

Figure 6.4 Skills management—a road map for the workforce. *Source:* Gartner Group

Skills management is becoming a lifeline in a turbulent IT labor market. Midsize and large corporations, businesses in the private and public sectors, aggressive and conservative companies—all are looking at skills management with renewed interest. Many corporations now recognize that the combined lack of corporation planning, imagination, and foresight are as much to blame for today's labor crunch as is the shortage of relevant IT skills. In that climate, skills management can be a powerful tool for bringing discipline, rationale, and cross-pollination to an underused process. Even more enticing, many IT professionals, under the mantle of career "entrepreneurism," will throw in their lot with corporations that have clearly committed to and funded skills management programs. Having a road map with which to guide career development is more meaningful than wandering until serendipity strikes.

Before moving on, it is beneficial to make sure that everybody is speaking the same language. In the Gartner[3] Group's definition of perspective, skills management is *a robust and systematic approach to forecasting, identifying, cataloguing, evaluating, and analyzing the workforce skills, competencies and gaps that corporations face.* Although many programs and initiatives adopt the label *skills management*, most of them focus on skills inventory and fall short in analysis and forecasting. A well-designed skills management process injects a stronger dose of discipline, coordination, and planning into workforce planning, strategic planning, professional training and development programs, resource allocation maneuvering, and risk analysis and assessment.

Corporations can reap several lessons from skills management. Skills management works if it does the following:

- Defines skills for roles
- Forces forward thinking
- Forces some documentation of what makes an IT professional especially proficient
- Strengthens the overall organization
- Leads to focused training, risk assessment, sourcing strategy, and resource allocation via gap identification
- Attracts high-level endorsement from senior management

Skills management does not work when it:

- Does not define work roles
- Lacks plans or incentive for refreshment
- Communicates its purpose poorly
- Provides differing language and terminology
- Force-fits skills and work roles to policies, rather than driving new frameworks

KEYS TO A SUCCESSFUL SKILLS MANAGEMENT ENDEAVOR

Three areas must be worked out for a skills management initiative to be successful:

1. Employees have to adopt the program as their own, rather than as a management dictate. The employees must assume control of their own professional development.
2. Supervisors have to surrender some control over employee development.
3. Executives must ensure that employees use metrics as a tool for professional development, not as a weapon in cutthroat competition.

As enterprises turn to technology such as autonomic computing to reach the next level of corporate performance, IT organizations should identify the skills they need to meet corporate objectives. Through a program of skills identification, IT organizations can see the holes in their coverage, set priorities for projects, define what training is required, and determine which skills may need third-party coverage. A commitment to funding for training is essential.

SKILLS MANAGEMENT FOR AUTONOMIC COMPUTING

Although the purpose of autonomic computing is to implement self-managing systems while at the same time hiding the complexity, its purpose is not to exclude IT people entirely. The stated aim here is to reduce the need for IT staff to work on the mundane, but necessary, tasks of supporting, configuring, and maintaining the systems themselves. These are necessary tasks that can be automated.

It will not be possible in the next 20 years for IT people to be eliminated entirely from managing autonomic or any other technology. Therefore those staff chosen to be responsible for the management of autonomic computing systems must acquire the necessary skills to be successful. Corporations must not neglect the very important task of developing a skills management program for autonomic computing systems. For the skills will be fundamentally different from what most IT staff have learned in the past.

The following is a list of considerations that must be reviewed when developing a skills management program for autonomic computing.

- Develop and implement a total autonomic computing culture.
- Acquire the ability to accept and trust decisions presented by autonomic computing systems.
- As IT infrastructure becomes more autonomic, learn how executing a business policy will become the focus of IT management.
- Accept that the management of the business and of IT will no longer be separate, possibly conflicting, activities.
- Understand and accept that the self-configuring and self-optimizing technologies drive efficiency in running and deploying new processes and capabilities.

- Learn how the actualization of self-configuring systems speeds the deployment of new applications required to support emerging business requirements.
- Understand that workforce productivity is enhanced when the focus is on management of business processes and policies, without the need to translate these needs into actions that separately manage supporting technology.
- Realize that autonomic systems that self-manage free up IT resources to move from mundane system management tasks to working with users to solve business problems.
- Understand and accept that the aim is to deliver system-wide autonomic environments for maximum operational efficiency.

Only a few years ago, when large organizations first began covering the area of skills management, it was a process reserved for the most progressive corporations. By methodically and meticulously forecasting, classifying, analyzing, and taking inventory of skills, progressive corporations could identify the urgency and volume of skills gaps, create focused training programs, and add some rational thinking to their sourcing strategies. Skills management continues to satisfy those needs, even fostering a niche market of consultants and software developers that are eager to bring order to IT Human Resource management. This is particularly important with autonomic computing.

SUMMARY AND CONCLUSIONS

The shortage of IT staff is not projected to be solved any time soon; according to figures presented here, the shortage will continue to at least 2010. This is despite widespread layoffs and sector unemployment. Almost daily reports suggest that the modern 'knowledge economies' will struggle and become less competitive if the shortage cannot be overcome. The problem is worldwide. One report noted that a Spanish company had gone as far as signing up students before they begin their final year of studies and that Spain had 22,000 computing and telecom posts vacant. In Germany, there is a shortfall of 75,000 jobs in high-tech workers (Center for Immigration Studies, 2000). Other countries, such as Australia, the United Kingdom, and Ireland, have reported similar problems. As we have seen, the effects and the costs to the U.S. economy can be significant and serious.

It is time to challenge all high-tech companies to redouble their efforts to find long-term solutions to the rapidly continuing demand for workers with technical skills. A strategic global initiative is needed to address and present rapid effective solutions. This will require doing more to improve college education systems—a collaboration of universities and high tech companies. Collaboration between countries and the sharing of knowledge and solutions, upgrading the skills of our existing workforce, and recruiting from under-represented groups, such as older workers, minorities, women, persons with disabilities, and residents of rural areas and other emerging countries must also be attempted. Many IT companies have important initiatives in these areas, but we clearly need to be doing more.

Historically, IT organizations have typically met all that was expected of them with staff members who had the necessary skills. However, because of the scarcity of skills and the vast complexity of computing compared to legacy mainframe systems, IT organizations must change their approach. They will have to create a blend of internal and external resources by finding motivated IT professionals able to work in a collaborative environment and possessing the necessary critical skills.

In addition, we must look beyond these identified solutions and use the software tools that we have to provide more automation. If we can design and implement software products and services that can address the functions and processes that IT staff perform, this will help in the solution.

One of autonomic computing's main objectives is to reduce the need for and dependency on IT staff. If we can use this software to relieve skilled workers of monotonous tasks, it will allow them to concentrate more on the business objectives.

Autonomic computing will provide the following:

- Software installation and regular configuration.
- Required and periodic upgrades.
- System monitoring to ensure optimum performance.
- Automatic data and file management, such as backups and checkpoints.
- Self-healing software that will automatically recover from system failures, errors, and runtime faults.
- Embedded security features that can detect and prevent data, files, and systems from being infected or stolen.
- Software that can manage resources and apply them where needed to maximum effect.

As an industry primarily concerned with providing effective software automation, IT should look inward upon itself and adopt higher levels of automation wherever possible.

NOTES

1. U.S. Department of Labor–Bureau of Labor Statistics, *www.bls.gov.*
2. Computer Technology Industry Association, Worldwide Corporate Headquarters 1815 S. Meyers Road, Suite 300 Oakbrook Terrace, IL 60181-5228.
3. Gartner Report. *IT Staff Retention and Recruitment: Addressing a Critical Problem for the IS Organization*, Industry Trends & Directions (ITD), September 28, 2002.

CHAPTER 7

THE NEW AGENDA— E-BUSINESS ON DEMAND

INTRODUCTION

IBM has come to the realization that business is entering a new era, an era where customers, suppliers, manufacturers, and every department in the corporation will need tighter integration, and greater information and application requirements to react to the new marketplace. At the other extreme, corporations must deal with limited or reduced spending, and greater review and control over internal budgets. Senior management and shareholders demand lower costs and greater efficiency each year. Speed and time to market are the driving factors. Customers once needed products in a few days or weeks. Now customers frequently require delivery in hours. Whoever delivers the best quality in the shortest possible time scale at the best price will win the business. There are no exceptions. This is the environment we discussed in the first section of this book. If corporations do not act accordingly, we will see a repeat of the dot.com bust where business failed to adjust to changing customers needs.

To achieve this new business objective will require a transformation for almost all corporations. It will need the e-business on demand approach. As corporations need to respond to their customers' changing requirements, they will need the speed and flexibility of e-business on demand solutions. This new business model requires a corresponding on-demand technology environment that matches and is closely aligned with the business. If the business is moving fast, the systems and solutions must match in partnership.

IBM defines e-business on demand as

> An enterprise whose business processes is integrated from end-to-end across the company and with key partners, suppliers and customers—can respond with speed to any demand, market opportunity or external threat.

E-business on demand will not happen quickly, and many companies will need to rethink their strategies to move to this new business model. E-business on demand will be different from just e-business. IBM has identified four steps necessary for an e-business to be classified as on-demand.

1. **Responsive**—Companies must have the technology and operating environment to be responsive to a new dynamic business model–to react quickly to unpredictable or unplanned changes in orders, supply, or demand, market changes, client needs, partner changes, supplier demand, or unexpected moves by competitors or new product entry. Companies must change in *hours*—not days, weeks or months.

2. **Variable**—The new companies must have a flexible and variable structure to be able to respond quickly. This means creating new cost structures and business models that are driven by speed. This can increase corporate productivity, drive down costs, and managing risk levels.

3. **Focused**—If corporations concentrate on core competencies that differentiate them from their competitors, they will increase market share. Tight integration with a set of like-minded strategic partners who think and act the same way will drive new sales and greater profit.

4. **Resilient**—The new model corporations will need to be able to operate globally, 24/365 in all markets. However, when changes are made, they need to be implemented without any difficulties or delays. Robust procedures are necessary, to meet the unexpected changes that will drive the marketplace or to respond to threats, such as denial of service, floods, fire, or unusual spikes in orders.

Corporations that concentrate on these essential core steps, shown in Figure 7.1, will need to manage the company as a whole—total holistic management. This means corporations that are geographically dispersed in different time zones. This is more than just operational efficiency; it is about opening up new value and profit.

Corporations that enact and install e-business on demand operations will be able to react to new business opportunities in many new ways.

- A nationwide television news service can react to an overload of its Web site when a new or exciting story breaks. This means that millions of Internet users can quickly access the latest news events as they happen in real time. Organizations such as CNN would have benefited from an e-business on demand environment during the terrorist attacks on September 11, 2001, when the Internet traffic at their Web site was doubling every few minutes.

- Shifts in global stock markets could be analyzed in real time to provide banks and brokers the means to uncover new stock opportunities and recommend them to clients immediately by cell phone, email, pager, or other chosen method. Also, as an audit con-

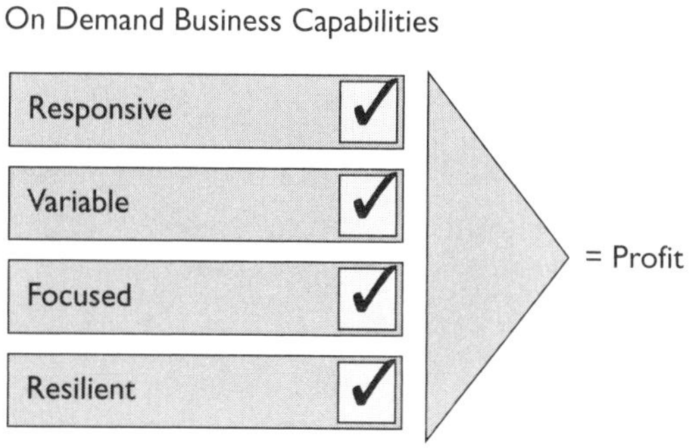

On Demand Business Capabilities

Responsive ✓

Variable ✓

Focused ✓

Resilient ✓

= Profit

Figure 7.1   The four categories that make up e-business on demand capabilities—and, in turn, lead to profit.

trol mechanism, banks can monitor stock trades to ensure that they meet federal guidelines, thus preventing or uncovering fraud.

- In all types of manufacturing industries—large, medium, or small—from office staples to aircraft to automobiles to customized Chinese lanterns, inventory management could be driven by e-business on demand. This means holding inventory parts for minutes rather than weeks or months. The corresponding cost savings will be enormous.

- Supermarkets and megastores can order new products as the demand increases. If a product becomes popular overnight and thousands are needed, e-business on demand can provide the necessary order fulfillment. Thus, shoppers will not be disappointed nor will they see store signs saying, *"On order—more expected next Tuesday—please check back then."* When demand fluctuates and a store is vastly overstocked on an item, excess inventory can be quickly delivered to stores that need it.

E-BUSINESS ON DEMAND CHALLENGES

One immediate concern raised by senior corporate management is that a total transformation model such as e-business on demand will be prohibitively expensive to introduce. This may be solved a number of ways. For example, e-business on demand outsourcing will no doubt evolve to assist corporations and companies to move to the new business model quickly. It will be possible to outsource a single application, one business unit, or the entire corporation. The e-business on demand outsource organizations will use the e-business on demand model themselves. It makes sense to adopt a model such as e-business on demand. The e-business on demand mantra should be: "Adapt and adopt or don't and die." But very few companies can draw the slate clean and start over. Therefore, they are compelled to begin this new adventure by utilizing their existing infrastructure. E-business on demand allows for this.

Another concern might be business risk. With such a dynamic and changing business model, there is a higher risk of business failure or disruption. In the world, where information flows readily and at constant streams 24/365, the accuracy and integrity of the data must be paramount. Similarly, privacy and security concerns are equally important, and the e-business on demand model can enhance already established, operational procedures.

E-BUSINESS ON DEMAND OPERATING ENVIRONMENT

A new e-business on demand operational environment is needed. To gain all the advantages of e-business on demand will require customers to move away from the complicated, difficult to manage, and extremely costly IT infrastructures of today to the new dynamic e-business on demand model.

The e-business on demand-operating environment has four essential attributes.

1. **It must be integrated.**

   Corporations have been more successful and more profitable by creating internal and external integration. This allows access to large amounts of valuable data, files, systems, and reports, sharing custom applications where applicable and needed. Integrating outside suppliers, partners, and customers allows for a holistic but very tight integration. After doing so, you will have an integrated universe where everyone with an interest stands to benefit. You can network in real time, keeping on top of events as they happen, achieving accuracy and integrity while managing risk at the beginning of a fully operational e-business on demand model.

2. **It must be based on open standards.**

   Open standards are one of the most significant movements in the IT industry in the last 50 years. Open standards make IT work at its best. The opening of standards continues with the adoption of Java, XML, Linux, and others. These standards are critical to making e-business on demand work successfully. When multiple partners, suppliers, and customers come together, they will have a mix of systems and applications. E-business on demand will allow them to share and integrate data and systems, working in the same environment. Open standards will make e-business on demand work.

3. **It is must be virtualized.**

   Customers will always use the solution that fits best with their own objectives and benefits them most. E-business on demand is a utility computing approach. It can be served up when needed, whether internally or across secure Internet connections. Other technologies, such as grid computing, can allow for the introduction of huge computing resources—not one computer, but thousands creating one very large *virtual* computer. It is expected that the grid solution will be adopted by large corporations and become known as "intragrids." So when that huge spike in orders or traffic on the Web site is detected, computing resources can be made available immediately to solve this problem. Computing will become a utility that will be traded, bought, and sold as needed like other commodities, such as pigs, soya beans, rubber, spices, timber, coffee, and palm oil. Like traditional utilities, such as telephone and electricity, Web services will be metered, and customers will pay for their use of what will be called by the new term eUtility. The terms of use (called service level agreements or SLAs) of eUtilities will include functionality, availability, performance, resources, and reliability. These terms of use may vary from customer to customer, and they may change over time. The big payback for corporations will be when they can purchase only the computing commodities they want at future prices, for delivery only when needed. Again, the savings will be gigantic. E-business on demand will create a new breed of IT vendor and related services to go with it. A corporation using e-business on demand will have lots of choices as to what to do and who to buy from.

4. It must be Autonomic.

In the e-business on demand world, there is no place for managing complexity. That will be the domain of software and systems. With the large numbers of open systems and the tight integration required, the virtual world will need the automation provided by autonomic computing. Balancing workloads, managing automated service level agreements (SLAs), reallocating adequate system resources, and so on cannot and should not be done manually by IT staff. Eventually autonomic computing will manage e-business on demand itself with minimal human intervention. E-business on demand cannot properly function without autonomic computing.

For a summary, review Figure 7.2.

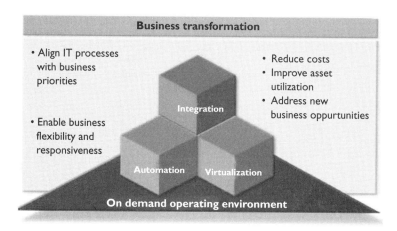

Figure 7.2   The e-business on demand operating environment will grow from the building blocks of integration, automation, and virtualization.

THE EMERGENCE OF THE E-BUSINESS ON DEMAND ENTERPRISE

Since the earliest days of business, it has been possible to boil the process down to a few fundamental elements:

- Identifying or creating a market for an offering.
- Creating the offering.
- Supplying it to the customer.
- Getting paid for it, and managing the customer relationship.
- Repeating the process.

These fundamental business principles haven't changed in hundreds of years—not even recently with the false dawn of the dot-com era and the so called "new economy"—and those companies that remain focused on them will survive through all market conditions.

Over the past decade, however, the changing economic perspective has had a profound effect on how companies do business and how they compete. Among the factors are the following:

- The Internet and related network technologies have ushered in new business models.
- Certain industries, such as financial services, telecommunications, transportation and utilities, have deregulated worldwide, throwing open the doors to new competition and consolidation.
- Globalization and other initiatives, such as the Euro and NAFTA, have impacted how we do business with the rest of the world.

It is the advent of those new business models that has brought us to the cusp of a major shift in business design and management thinking: the emergence of the e-business on demand enterprise.

The promise of e-business on demand is that companies or institutions can respond dynamically to whatever business challenges arise. They can provide products and services "on demand," in real time. They can adapt their cost structures and business processes to reduce risk and drive business performance. They can optimize their IT infrastructures and resources to cut costs and boost productivity. And they can be flexible—prepared for whatever challenges may arise.

A BRIEF HISTORY OF E-BUSINESS ON DEMAND

By the mid-1990s, IBM recognized that advances in network technology were going to fundamentally change the way companies could manage their core business processes. Companies quickly realized that the Internet's value was not in fancy Web pages, but in exploiting the technology to make business processes more efficient—what IBM calls e-business. Companies have since invested heavily in process reengineering, applying network technologies to traditionally labor- and paper-intensive processes to make them faster, cheaper, and more direct. While this has been beneficial, we need to do more. We need e-business on demand.

Business Transformation Begins

Today, companies are recognizing another benefit of e-business: The real value in applying network technology to business processes is not in merely automating them in isolation, but in gaining a greater understanding of how the processes relate to one another.

With that insight, companies can reconfigure their existing IT assets to streamline their operations. They can start managing their processes horizontally to improve performance throughout the enterprise instead of in organizational silos. They can find and exploit the hidden value in their operations by building flexible, integrated business process systems that can anticipate, accommodate, and quickly adapt to new conditions to improve performance and productivity. A manufacturing company, for example, might develop a touchless process, from the time an order is received until the product hits the loading dock. A financial services company could offer straight-through processing. These companies would become e-business on demand enterprises.

Optimizing an IT infrastructure and creating an integrated business process model are challenging tasks, in themselves. Managers are being held accountable for the performance of their particular lines of business. So they have chosen business processes and IT infrastructures designed to boost the performance of their isolated units. The result? Single enterprises operate multiple business processes on disconnected applications, middleware, servers, and operating systems—an ad hoc collection sometimes too complex to fathom, and another example of complexity gone mad.

But now companies are starting to overcome that complexity. Many of IBM's customers are asking for help in integrating their existing IT assets. They are tapping into IBM's knowledge to look at their business processes in concert and revise their business models. Always with an eye on return on investment, they are partnering with IBM on many levels, from complete outsourcing and application management to hosting and utility computing services.

Taking a step-by-step approach to improving the IT infrastructure and processes they already have, these companies are building businesses that are almost intuitive in their responsiveness to changes in demand, supply, pricing, labor, capital markets, and customer needs. With the savings that accrue from restructuring their existing IT assets, they are often self-funding their e-business on demand journeys; bottom-line benefits derived from streamlining operations can be reapplied to new initiatives.

Integrating the Retail Supply Chain

For example, IBM is working with some of the world's largest retailers and manufacturers on pilot versions of integrated business process networks. The networks, which use open standards to ensure communication across systems, enable those companies to automatically respond to the tiniest variables throughout their supply chains. Products are tagged with radio frequency sensors, and there are tag readers in the factory, on the truck, at the distribution center, in the store, and at the checkout. So at any time, every participant in the network can view the location of every product in the supply chain. They can respond to variables like customer demand, parts delays, traffic accidents, floods, fires, or even strikes.

The same technology can enable the customer to check out by simply walking the shopping cart through a tag reader. The reader detects all of the products in the shopping cart and bills the customer's credit or debit card. The retailer, in turn, gains information on the buying habits of individuals or groups, which can be used to predict and respond to demand runs.

In total, this pilot has integrated the core business processes—supply chain, customer care, and payment systems—in a real-time network that enables all participants to respond to demand and other variables automatically. It's a pilot that demonstrates the potential power—not to mention return on investment—of this business model.

Making Insurance an E-Business on Demand Service

Another emerging technology is serving as the catalyst for business process integration in the insurance industry. Telematics technology, which has become commonplace in cars for navigation systems, automatic credit card payments at tollbooths, and even remote engine diagnostics, may become a common way to determine insurance rates.

A leading insurance company is working with IBM to build a voluntary auto insurance program with telematics as a key enabler. A chip will measure the exact usage of a car—where and when it is driven and where it is parked. In doing so, the company can gain an exact risk profile for the customer, and drivers can pay for variable policies that reflect their precise risk profiles. Insurance premiums can even be paid on a daily basis as risk is incurred, with the chip debiting payment in the same way it would for tollbooth fees. The insurance company is using new technologies to integrate customer care and payment system business processes. It can offer a service that will enable greater business efficiency in understanding and profiting from risk variables, while providing demand-based flexibility for its consumers.

Transforming the Pharmaceutical Industry

In the pharmaceutical industry, IBM predicts that advances in medical technology over the next 10 years will usher in an era of customized drug treatments. IBM is at the forefront of this technology movement with its Blue Gene program.

Advances in genomic research, drug discovery, and manufacturing capabilities will enable a treatment-on-demand scenario; whereby doctors, according to patients' unique requirements, prescribe increasingly customized drug programs. This vision will require integrating genetic-data computing systems, data systems that manage patient data in real time, and possibly, dynamic payment systems.

As the pharmaceutical industry comes under increasing cost pressure to reduce product development times and research investments, this type of treatment system may become an economic necessity rather than just a vision.

Flexibility and Adaptability Are Key

Companies are looking to become more flexible and adaptive in response to the tremendously competitive international economic environment. They need to be able to respond immediately to variables in their marketplaces. But they also need to focus on their own core competencies, to maximize efficiency, exploit opportunity, and minimize risk.

This approach can only be accomplished by optimizing IT infrastructures and integrating business processes in a way that enables the enterprise to respond automatically to internal and external variables. Utility computing—which eliminates up-front infrastructure investments and limits long-term costs—is another key; customers pay only for the IT capacity they use, enabling them to meet peak demand without having to maintain such a high level of readiness.

In each of the examples above, emerging technology is the catalyst for business process integration and, ultimately, business transformation. Some companies are taking it a step further by outsourcing their new, integrated business processes. One of the world's largest energy companies, for example, has built a comprehensive analytics tool that provides an enterprise-wide view of business process performance. The company then outsourced the management of that analytics process, and the financial management responsibility for all of its business units and processes, to IBM.

This type of transformation requires a keen business insight, married to a deep understanding of the kinds of technology that will make these systems possible. IBM is a technology leader in grid, autonomic, research, and utility computing—all the technology and infrastructure elements necessary to dynamically link core business processes. IBM has experience in industries ranging from financial services to health care. To further support change within its clients' organizations, IBM made a change within our own. IBM recently established a formal research group that will work with IBM consulting teams to help customers realize the true value of business process integration. Through this team, IBM will be able to provide customers access to the world's most advanced research labs and the world's largest patent portfolio. If the prospect of becoming an e-business on demand business sounds good, take the first step: Consider how you might benefit from optimizing your IT assets or improving your business processes.

E-BUSINESS ON DEMAND, A CASE STUDY—TEINOS

Established in 1999, Teinos is an Italian health care company that develops solutions for managing, transmitting, and archiving patient data and diagnostic imaging. Its primary offering is P@ris, a Web-based platform for radiological examination management that includes reservations, medical reporting, and archiving.

Background

After developing an innovative Web-based radiology service management system, Teinos turned to IBM for e-business on demand services to reduce the infrastructure cost of deploying its solution. Teinos sought to generate new market opportunities with a Web-based radiology service, P@ris. The service would enable smaller health care providers to leverage the expensive radiological equipment generally available only at larger health care organizations.

Diagnostic imaging is critical for quality patient care, but radiological equipment is expensive for health care providers to support. Teinos' radiological service management system addressed health care providers' unique business challenges, but to make the system economically feasible, the company needed to deliver its solution through a flexible IT infrastructure. Teinos needed to pay only for the IT capacity it used, just as its customers would pay only for the radiological services they used. The solution was obvious: e-business on demand. Teinos could have developed the infrastructure necessary to support P@ris itself, but this effort would have entailed tremendous start-up and ongoing costs. Instead, it decided to focus on core competencies and partner with IBM for its infrastructure needs. IBM's e-business on demand services, which are built on open standards, allowed Teinos to deploy a world-class infrastructure on an as-needed basis. The arrangement represents the first European partnership for deploying e-business on demand in the health care industry. IBM stores all of Teinos' radiological data at its Internet data centers, which ensure maximum security and access speed. Service levels are consistently high, and all aspects of the P@ris system are seamlessly synchronized.

The Results

Using P@ris, patients at small hospitals undergo radiological tests at large hospitals, and their doctors access the results—including reports and diagnostic images—through a secure Internet connection. The client hospitals are charged on a per-use basis, limiting their costs, while the larger hospitals defray the expense of operating the equipment. In addition, the patients' doctors are able to quickly and securely share test results with other physicians—a key element of the diagnostic workflow. For Teinos' customers, P@ris reduces staff time by enabling faster authorization and scheduling of radiological treatment. It allows physicians and health care providers to collaborate more efficiently, with rapid access to patient information and radiology results. And it ensures patient confidentiality with high security standards.

For Teinos, the key to P@ris' success has been IBM e-business on demand. Teinos was able to rapidly roll out and expand its offering because it did not need to build either the initial infrastructure or the capacity to meet peak demand. The company continues to benefit from reduced complexity and increased agility, while meeting its customers' needs and expectations.

THE NEW REALITY: E-BUSINESS ON DEMAND IS HERE TO STAY

Unstoppable drivers are creating a new e-business on demand environment where competition is intense, change is continuous, financial pressures are unrelenting, and threats are unpredictable, as shown in Figure 7.3 below. For corporations rooted in traditional mindsets, this new market reality promises increased pricing pressure, as customers demand more for less. Lost market share, as more nimble competitors respond rapidly to changing customer needs. Stranded assets, due to market requirements that have evolved beyond the fixed investment infrastructure; sudden risks, from unexpected business, geopolitical and natural disaster shocks; and lower levels of profitability. But, for a new breed of businesses prepared for the inevitable market realities, this supercharged environment serves as an incubator for a brand new phase of accelerated value creation. Due to increasingly transparent markets, competitive intensity is growing in severity as existing players and new entrants scramble to provide value to customers.

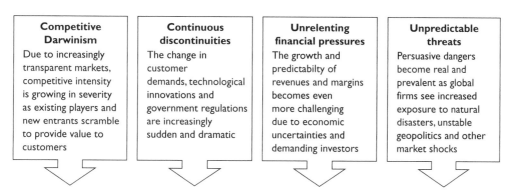

Figure 7.3 The emerging and unforgiving business world. Combating these factors requires an e-business on demand approach with autonomic computing.

The changes in customer demands, technological innovations, and government regulations are increasingly sudden and dramatic. The growth and predictability of revenues and margins becomes even more challenging due to economic uncertainties and demanding investors. Pervasive dangers become real and prevalent as global corporations see increased exposure to natural disasters, unstable geopolitics, and other market shocks.

WHAT THE NEW AGENDA REQUIRES

E-business on demand businesses address competitive Darwinism by focusing on differentiating capabilities. They become far more responsive, allowing them to successfully navigate continuous discontinuities and spend less time and money building inflexible business models based upon inevitably wrong predictions. While these corporations can't escape unrelenting financial pressures, they migrate more of their cost structure to variable models, which can adapt quickly to changes in demand, moving away from committed investments. In addition, they develop resilient operations that can withstand a multitude of unpredictable threats. Successful organizations master these four dimensions—becoming focused, responsive, variable, and resilient—and, in doing so, they make e-business on demand their new agenda, accelerating the creation of value for their customers and other stakeholders. Figure 7.4 below explains.

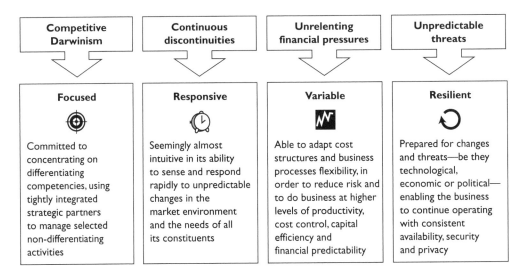

Figure 7.4 The responses to the four unrelenting business pressures—an e-business on demand operating environment.

Charles Schwab—Enabling Information E-Business on Demand

> **A WORLD CLASS INVESTMENTS COMPANY TWEAKS ITS SYSTEMS TO ALLOW E-BUSINESS ON DEMAND RESPONSES TO CUSTOMER INQUIRIES.**

Charles Schwab, a well-known and respected financial services company and long-time IBM customer, wanted to investigate autonomic and grid technology and what it might mean for its business. It defined an e-business on demand challenge for IBM to solve: How can Charles Schwab's employees provide immediate, real-time help to customers within an IT infrastructure that currently necessitates customer callbacks?

Why become an e-business on demand?

When customers phone Schwab with questions, they frequently can't get immediate answers, because the application that employees use is too slow in responding: Instead, customers have to wait for a return call. Speeding up the application would increase customer satisfaction. This means more business.

How and where did they start?

IBM and Charles Schwab's Advanced Technology Group took an existing application that ran on non-IBM systems and grid-enabled it with the Globus Toolkit running Red Hat Linux on IBM eServer xSeries 330 machines.

What benefits did they achieve?

This solution reduced the processing time on the application from more than four minutes to 15 seconds: a 94 percent improvement. Since this particular application scaled extremely well in an autonomic/grid environment, proving the potential for autonomic/grid-based services in a financial services environment, Schwab hopes to implement the solution sometime soon. The two companies are now looking at ways to expand the grid activities to other financial services organizations.

Finnair—Air Carrier Turns to IBM for E-Business on Demand Transformation

> **AIRLINE SEEKS TO SURVIVE INDUSTRY CONSOLIDATION, AND DOMINANCE BY BIG AIR CARRIERS.**

Finnair, one of the world's oldest operating airlines, wants to be the travel industry's digital champion, estimating that more than half of its passengers will soon be using the Internet for airline services, from making ticket reservations to clearing check-in. To meet this anticipated customer demand, Finnair came to IBM not only to transform its service chain and IT systems, but to create an innovation center for incubating new solutions for the airline industry, such as wireless check-in, e-ticketing via the Internet, and wireless ticket sales.

Why become e-business on demand?

Finnair had been using IBM products for years. But when it chose to explore a real business transformation, Finnair chose IBM for its broader business value: its depth in research and technology, and long airline industry IT experiences.

How and where did they start?

IBM is working with Finnair to move to a digital service chain so that every customer contact is becoming more personalized, available as a record, and integrated with related records. This requires integrating its internal business processes, so the effect of variables in one process can be seen across the enterprise as a whole, and the use of integrating middleware, in order for Finnair's different computer systems to work together. By using open standards, Finnair can interact with any company, supplier, and partner.

What benefits did they achieve?

Moving to the e-business on demand utility model will allow Finnair to scale up or scale down according to demand and to pay only for the computing capacity it uses.

Additional benefits Finnair will enjoy from this approach include flexibility to respond dynamically to any kind of variable across its systems or in the marketplace. Improving its competitiveness; moving its cost structure from fixed to variable; reducing IT-related expenses and releasing capital for its core airline business; and reinvesting a significant portion of resulting cost-savings in business transformation will help Finnair realize its vision of being the digital travel industry champion.

Metro Group: The Future of Retail Is E-Business on Demand

> **PROVIDING RETAIL CUSTOMERS THEIR PRODUCT CHOICE AT THE RIGHT TIME AND PLACE, IN AN EVER-INCREASING E-BUSINESS ON DEMAND WORLD.**

Metro Group, a major retail corporation in partnership with IBM, has opened a futuristic supermarket in Germany to test new retail technologies with customers. These technologies bring the promise of increased efficiency and customer responsiveness, key differentiators in the tough retail market.

Why become e-business on demand?

A major problem for retailers is keeping track of their stock and being able to provide their customers the right product in the right color or size at the right time in the right place. "Shrinkage"—the disappearance of articles by theft, damage, or loss—costs retailers billions every year. Metro Group chose IBM for its radio frequency identification (RFID) technology, which means products can be tracked at any point in the supply chain, eliminating significant inefficiency and shrinkage while better satisfying customer demand.

How and where did they start?

IBM's business consultants began by redesigning the supermarket's supply chain process, integrating a system that now includes "Smart Shelves" that have the ability to communicate— warning the stock rooms when the razor rack is nearly empty, for example, or triggering promotional advertising on a nearby screen as a customer picks up a shampoo bottle.

The RFID gives a complete picture of where each item is in the store, unlike bar codes, which only track by groups of identical items. RFID tags in the shopping carts tell store management how many carts are in the store. If there's an increase, additional checkouts are opened to accommodate the extra volume, bringing an end to delays at the checkout.

What benefits did they achieve?

1. Reduction in stock carrying costs through better inventory management.
2. Fewer sales losses caused by empty shelves.
3. Reduced theft, because tags raise alarm at exits unless products are scanned at a checkout.
4. More effective staff, because Personal Digital Assistants (PDAs) provide real-time information on stock.
5. Increased sales through targeted in-store promotion.
6. Access to information on customer buying habits, data that can be used to predict demand and automatically fed back through the inventory management systems to better tailor stock to customer needs.

SUMMARY AND CONCLUSIONS

As more and more corporations enter the global marketplace, the need to manage internal IT complexity, infrastructure, and increased service delivery will become paramount. Geographical borders are becoming increasingly irrelevant. Senior management are fully aware that they will lose customers to their competitors if they do not supply supreme quality service, yet without the dependent IT technology to implement that service, there is no way of providing it. The retention of customers is something that corporations ignore at their peril. Every department, not just IT, must work towards retaining customers. Customers constantly change their habits. They know they have the power. They can shop for the best prices, discounts, and contracts and are constantly looking for the best deal. They are very unforgiving and will tell the world when you disappoint them.

Most corporations began their e-business journey at a time when the economy was booming in the middle half of the 1990s. Business was booming, profits were good, and the outlook was positive. Many things have changed since them and the circumstances are much different. As discussed in Chapter 4, after the shakeout of the Internet stampede, we now have a greater understanding on how the marketplace changes rapidly and the need to adjust quickly. Adapt or die!

Today, few CIOs would disagree with the need for more sophisticated and less complex business-oriented delivery models. As e-business evolves in many different ways, a unifying structure for IT is needed. This structure should have the following components:

- Proactive, sophisticated tools—The IT department must embrace the application of more intelligence and automation to the problems of managing the complexity and infrastructures that they have developed. There is a growing realization that this is inevitable. IT vendors are coming to the same conclusion, so new products and services will begin to appear.
- Fewer resources—To reduce costs and solve problems, it is desirable to let automation handle operational and technology problems, thus freeing staff to concentrate on the business itself.
- Flexibility of standards—There is still a pressing need to integrate the many different vendors, products, and protocols, so they can work more easily together. This may be the root of the complexity problem. There is no "one size fits all" model. Software vendors must work together to solve this problem. National and international standards must be agreed to and implemented.
- Wider markets—Products and solutions must be aimed at a wider market. Global corporations are not the only markets that have complexity, infrastructure, and service delivery problems. Small- to medium-sized businesses suffer the same pressures as their larger competitors. The problems are universal, and it is not only the large corporations that will benefit from the new e-business models. IT vendors must address this.
- Ease of implementation—The new business models must have better and more successful implementation methodologies. Much-needed repeatable processes will enhance and make implementation easier and safer. If a product is not easy to implement, it will be an agent of increasing the complexity. Graduated levels of implementation are desirable.
- Protection and security—If products can provide automation as well as the same levels of protection and security, they are necessary. The same great threats, such as more sophisticated viruses, denial of service, and information theft, will still exist, even in the e-business on demand world.

Is this the brave new world? No—it is the logical progression of the marketplace. E-business on demand is a bold initiative and it's a new agenda. IBM's move into on-demand computing is a natural evolution of current initiatives rather than the introduction of a more disruptive technology or theme. It's the next generation of the Internet e-business initiative that began in the middle of the 1990s that we referred to earlier.

The underpinnings of eUtility computing have been most clearly articulated in the marketplace by IBM. IBM is offering products and architecture. Web services standards provide interoperability among applications, and initiatives such as Grid Computing will allow distributed comput-ing resources to be shared and managed as a single, virtual computer. Higher bandwidth provides a conduit for all kinds of data and messages to be passed.

Early adopter companies are already experimenting with elements of e-business on demand and eUtility computing, selectively outsourcing a portion of business processes and computing applications. Several vendors already offer utility-based pricing for server and storage capacity. Web services and grid protocols are gaining credibility, even at a time when technology spend-ing is mostly confined to the essentials. Autonomic computing plays a key role in dealing with the complexities and costs of managing complex, distributed networks in the e-business on demand world.

PART **3**

AUTONOMIC COMPUTING— MORE DETAIL

- AC Architectures
- Autonomic Computing and Open Standards
- Autonomic Implementation Considerations
- Grid Computing—An Enabling Technology
- Autonomic Development Tools
- Independent Software Vendors
- Other Vendors
- The Tivoli Management Suite—Autonomic Features

CHAPTER 8

AC ARCHITECTURES

INTRODUCTION

So far, we have discussed the overall picture of autonomic computing and its component parts. In this chapter, we will define how autonomic computing systems might be built, and the architectures needed for implementation and success. While at this time the detailed autonomic architecture are still evolving and under development, we can still review the necessary elements and describe a framework of the most important aspects of the architecture.

Specifically, an IT architecture defines the components, or building blocks, that make up the overall information system. It provides an environment from which products can be procured and systems developed that will work together to implement the overall systems for today's corporations. It thus enables the management of IT investment in a way that meets the needs of the corporation.

An effective IT architecture is critical to business survival and success, and is the indispensable means to achieving competitive advantage through IT. Today's CIOs are aware that the effective management and exploitation of information through IT is the key to business success. An IT architecture addresses this need, by providing a strategic context for the evolution of the IT system in response to the constantly changing needs of the business environment. It is the very foundation on which the systems and applications are built.

CONTROL LOOPS

In an autonomic computing architecture, the basic management element is a control loop, depicted in Figure 8.1. This acts as manager of the resource through monitoring, analysis, and actions taken on a set of predefined system policies. These control loops, or managers, can communicate and eventually will negotiate with each other and other types of resources within and outside of the autonomic computing architecture.

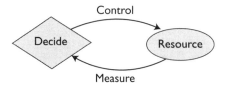

Figure 8.1   An example of a basic autonomic control loop.

This collects information from the system and makes decisions based on that data and then issues instructions to make adjustments to the system. An intelligent control loop can provide functionality of autonomous computing, such as the following:

- Requesting additional processing cycles when needed.
- Installing software and upgrades.
- Restarting a system after a failure.
- Initiating backups after daily processing.
- Shutting down systems after detection of an intrusion.

These are many of the self-managing functions that we have been discussing so far. They will be available in embedded software or system tools. An alternative approach is to install control loops in runtime environments for faster responses and actions. When fully operational, control loops will hide complexity from end-users and IT professionals.

A more detailed picture of the structure and components of the autonomous control loop is shown in Figure 8.2.

In Figure 8.2, we see the control loop is divided into two basic subelements:

> 1. **The Managed Element**—This can be any component in the autonomous system, such as a server, a database, or a file, or it can be numerous related larger elements, such as a cluster of servers, a complete software application, or even a business unit. This means that managed elements are highly scalable. The sensors and effectors control the managed element.
> 2. **The Autonomic Manager**—This manages the collection, filtering, and reports of the data collected from the element from the sensors. It also analyzes, models if necessary, and learns about the element, gaining knowledge. With this knowledge, it can predict future situations. The planning part provides the structure the mechanism needs for the actions it takes to achieve the desired goals and objectives of the autonomous system. The planning part also uses the predefined policies that establish the goals and objec-

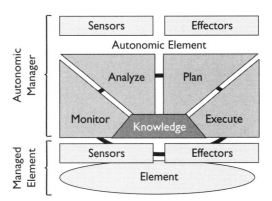

Figure 8.2 A diagram of an intelligent control loop, which facilitates the self-management functions of the autonomous system architecture.

tives. These policies are described in the system. The execute part of the autonomic manager provides control of the commands being accomplished. It will establish whether the commands completed their required actions.

The sensors provide the mechanisms to collect data on the state of the element. To trigger the sensors will require a "get" instruction—for example, "get the information of the customer database"—or for the element to change in a material fashion, such as volume or time. An example of the last trigger would be "get the transaction information when the database completes the daily update."

The effectors are the mechanisms that change the state of an element. In other words, they act or alter the configuration of the element from the data provided from the sensors. The effectors are a set of software commands, or application programming interfaces (APIs), that alter the element's configuration.

AUTONOMIC COMPONENT DESCRIPTION

The data from the four autonomic components are available as shared knowledge. This shared knowledge comprises many types of data, such as metrics, commands, system events, logs, performance data, and policies. It can be described as follows:

1. The sensors and effectors collect the information from an element, such as a file, database, or a similar system segment.
2. The data from the sensors and effectors is analyzed during the analysis phase to determine if the policy is being adhered to, or if corrective action is needed, an example of self-managing.

3. A policy is defined as a set of behavioral constraints or preferences that influence the autonomic manager.

4. The plan component is responsible for interpreting and translating the polices for the managed element.

5. The results, metrics, and commands are stored as knowledge.

This is the basic structure of the control loop. It relies on the technique of feedback control optimization. Control loops will be required to work with many different types of computing technologies and different software that exist in the IT world today. As the technology of control loops develops, more intelligence can be built in. There may be thousands of control loops in big, complex IT systems, and they will be required to work together. This is referred to as autonomic manager collaboration.

AUTONOMIC MANAGER COLLABORATION

If the IT systems of the future are to achieve the goals we have set for autonomous computing, the control loops and their autonomic managers must be able to collaborate, communicate, and negotiate. For example, a Web-based application must access data from a shared database through a Web server, store new data entered by site users, verify the accuracy of that data, and so on.

To illustrate the collaboration needed within autonomic managers consider the following example. We have an IT system consisting of a customer order entry application, which accepts online customer orders for products and updates databases that reside on several different servers. As orders are accepted through the order entry application, accepted orders are communicated with the supplier system to order the delivery of the necessary parts to the factory so that the orders can be constructed and delivered to the customer. The supplier data resides on different servers in a different geographical location. The main database is the customer database.

If we apply an autonomic architecture to this example, as shown in Figure 8.3, we can illustrate how autonomic managers will communicate with one other.

The autonomic managers in this example are:

- The Customer Database is the managed element and manages the file and interaction with the other managers.
- The Database Resource will be the collection point for the transfer of data to and from other autonomic managers.
- Database Management collects information from the customer order application and sends it on to the Database Resource and ultimately the Customer Database resource.
- The Vendor Relationship sends and receives data from the other autonomic managers when requested from the online application.
- Server Management controls access to and from the hardware server.

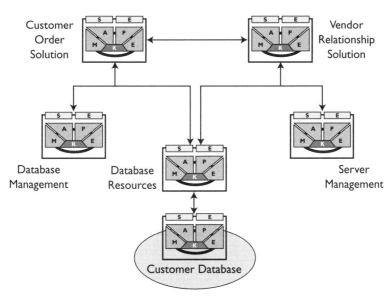

Figure 8.3 In this example, the customer database is managed by six autonomic managers. Note the collaboration and communication required.

This is a simple example, but it does illustrate how autonomic managers are required to work together, communicate, and negotiate the self-management of an element.

AUTONOMIC MANAGER DEVELOPMENT

In order for autonomic managers and their associated elements to work together in an autonomic architecture, there must be a set of tools that provide the basic structure. There are presently seven core capabilities available to developers:

1. Policy Determination
2. Solution Knowledge
3. Common System Administration
4. Problem Determination
5. Autonomic Monitoring
6. Complex Analysis
7. Transaction Measurement

Now let us review each of core capabilities in some detail.

Policy Determination

Achieving the objectives of an autonomic architecture requires an understanding of the specific policies under which it will operate. The policies will determine the decisions that autonomic managers will make. A policy defines the criteria. As shown in Figure 8.4 below, the policies are key parts of the decision-making process.

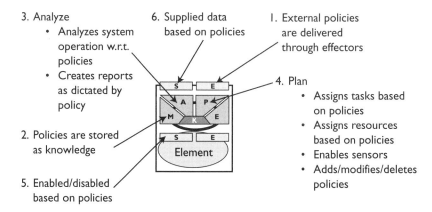

Figure 8.4 An example of a policy-based autonomic manager and its stored components. By defining policies in a uniform way, they can be shared across the individual components of an autonomic manager to enable entire systems to be managed as defined by a set of common policies.

We must be careful to be certain of the term "policy." In IT, it can mean different outcomes to different forms of interpretation. Some examples follow in Table 8.1.

Table 8.1   Examples of Policy

Policy	Example
Service Level Agreements	The customer report must be printed and delivered to the customer department by 9:00 a.m. each day
Security Policy	Identify sign-on by retina scans—report any variances. Set code level RED if variance detected above 1%
Business Process Policy	For all customers who have orders worth greater than $50,000 each day—apply discount of 5% for all orders over this limit

The secret to clarity and simplicity is commonality. The specification for autonomic policy definition includes the following common approach:

- A format and schema for specifying user requirements and criteria.
- A distribution mechanism for sharing policies among autonomic managers.
- Specification of configuration parameters for managed elements (files, databases, servers, etc.).

Solution Knowledge

This is one of the most important areas and one of the most difficult to manage externally. The IT industry has thousands of different software tools that provide installation, configuration, and maintenance functions for all types of solutions, platforms, and operating systems. The many different types of formats, parameters, return codes, and other data contribute greatly to the IT complexity that we now face. Add to these scenarios different protocols from the Internet with Web services and their associated software, and the problem is even larger.

To address this problem will require a standard approach provided by solution knowledge software. This software captures the configuration and installation requirements in a consistent manner. This data can be used in other areas of autonomic computing, such as optimization and self-healing.

Solution knowledge contains many types of data from multiple points such as operating systems, application languages such as Enterprise Java Beans, HTML pages, system utilities, and database tables and performance data.

The solution knowledge standards define a set of constructs for providing installable units and design patterns that make standards possible. An installable unit will consist of a descriptor that describes the content and the actual artifact that is to be installed. An artifact can be software that is to be installed. The descriptor and the artifact comprise the package, similar to a Java archive file. The target environment is called the hosting environment, where the artifact is to be installed.

There are three categories of installable units:

1. The smallest installable unit—This unit contains one artifact.
2. A container installable unit—This unit contains several artifacts for a container.
3. Solution module installable unit—This unit contains multiple types of container units in a block.

There are other tools available in the solution knowledge component that will aid the definition of configuration and maintenance processes:

- An installed database of units—This is a database that stores configuration details about installed units and their hosting environments.
- Deploy Logic—This is the software functionality that distributes the installable unit.
- An installer unit database—This is a library of installable units.
- An installer—This required software functionality allows the artifacts to be installed in the designated hosting environments.
- A dependency checker—This software checks whether the dependency of an artifact meets the requirements of the designated hosting environment.

With these tools available, developers can prepare and plan the installing, configuration, and maintenance of the many products that are available and in use at IT installations.

Common System Administration

A common console technology represents the look and feel for a particular application. These standards ensure that screens will be similar to one another in looks and will be indistinguishable from one another, in terms of control characteristics, naming conventions, etc. Basic intent for these standards is to ensure that the user finds navigating through the screens easy and not complex.

The goal of the autonomic common console is to provide that single approach that provides all the administrative functionality to manage servers, storage, and related software, be it individual systems or products. These administrative functions cover a wide range from initial setup to monitoring in real time, configuration, and control.

This common console functionality is a standard that has been defined by IBM for IBM products. It will evolve and be made available to independent software vendors (ISVs) to integrate this into their products, thus establishing the necessary standards.

A common console approach consists of a framework and a set of specific components. For example, administrative activities are executed in the autonomic architecture as portlets. The success of the common console approach will be determined by how other ISVs and manufacturers adopt and embrace the approach. Standards and agreement will take time to evolve.

Problem Determination

The different components of autonomic systems base their actions on what they detect, observe, or analyze in the managed element. Examples of these actions are optimizing, healing, and protecting. Problem determination is an important function for achieving these objectives. Therefore, there is a basic core need to provide problem determination in the autonomic manager. If there is a problem detected, the autonomic manager must take action.

The data to make the determination of the problem is available in multiple types—for example, legacy systems data, such as logs, traces, and memory dumps. The diversity is enormous. Solving this problem will require a standardized approach in the autonomic architecture. To filter and process the multiple types of legacy data, the architecture will provide plug-in adapter/agent infrastructure that will translate to the autonomic standard format. The data needs to be processed in a common way such as collecting all the required data and normalizing it in terms of format and content. This requires a set of base data that must be collected or created when the problem occurs. It provides the starting point for the problem determination.

Autonomic Monitoring

Autonomic monitoring is the process of providing the autonomic managers with the capability of gathering and filtering data from the sensors. With this data, autonomic managers can perform a range of analyses and actions to be taken within the architecture.

This can be achieved with the following functionality:

1. Built-in sensor filtering functions.
2. A common approach to capturing the data from the managed element sensors. This will involve the use of industry standards, such as Windows Management Instrumentation, JMX industry standards, CIM, and SNMP.
3. A set of predefined resource models that enable the combination of different pieces of sensor data to describe the state of the resource. Resource models describe the business-relevant "logical objects" from the perspective of the common problems associated with the objects. Software is available to create new models.
4. A methodology to integrate policy knowledge.
5. Methods to plug in specific types of analysis engines that provide root cause analysis and automate the instructions to start corrective action.

The reference model component of the autonomic monitoring function will provide a number of integrated best practices data that will facilitate management, such as:

- A log of the performance data related to each business object.
- Proactively managing the application through a set of predefined problem signatures.
- Continuously interpreting the quality of the business object against a set baseline and reports the variances.

Complex Analysis

All autonomic managers need the capability of performing complex analysis of data and initiating actions based on that data from the sensors. In addition, the managers can draw on the stored knowledge data. There will be large amounts of data to be processed and shared among the many autonomic managers in the architecture. The data will vary according to type; while some data will remain static and unchanged, other types will be dynamic. An autonomic manager's ability to quickly detect and analyze this data is crucial for the successful operation of the architecture. Common data analysis tasks will include data classification—such as static or dynamic—the clustering of data to illustrate complex states within the autonomic manager, and analysis to detect previous situations, predicted workloads, throughput, and so on. This will lead to problem determination and solution, followed by optimization and resource leveling.

The technology behind complex analysis is a rule-based language that supports reasoning through declarative, and some procedural, rules based on the collected and stored knowledge data. The underlying rule engines uses scripting as well as forward-based and backward-based inferencing using "if-then" type rules, predicates, and fuzzy logic. Application classes can be imported directly into the rulesets so that data can be accessed using the sensors and control actions taken using the effectors. The rules language has been designed to simulate the Java programming language, as many corporations now use that software and are familiar with it. XML is also used for ruleset representation. These two well-used languages allow portability in exchange for productivity improvement. When more complex analysis is needed, other technology components can be called on, such as JavaBeans, to access data from legacy flat files and relational databases to filter and transform the data into templates for use within the autonomic manager. Other technologies include the use of machine learning beans, software agents, neural networks, decision trees, and Bayesian classifiers to perform statistical analysis using numerous generic algorithms.

As a core autonomic technology, complex analysis is a vital component of the autonomic manager.

Transaction Measurement

Autonomic managers will need to know the flow of transactions across an autonomous architecture. This is important in the management of resources. Appropriate resources need to be in the right place at the right time. By monitoring these measurements, autonomic managers can change the resources to ensure optimal system performance. When transactions increase suddenly, restrictions in processing will occur. Transaction queues will build up and resources directed to that problem with instructions to solve it.

The problem of transaction management and measurement is expanded when there is a cluster or mix of servers. Because of existing complexity restraints in the IT infrastructure, it may be difficult to exactly identify where the problem originates. The problem gets even bigger when there are hundreds or thousands of servers involved spread over geographical areas. Today, it is extremely difficult for system administrators to manage this type of problem with conventional tools and techniques. Sheer hard work and step-by-step tracing is necessary. Furthermore, the average utilization of most installed distributed systems is very poor. Many e-business applications are incapable of handling large and sudden increases in transaction volumes—"server crash" is a frequent phrase used in the media to identify this problem.

The problem can be addressed by implementing an end-to-end transaction measurement infrastructure together with a distributed workload capability. The goal behind this approach is a policy defined—similar to the approach defined earlier. Defined goals can be implemented, for example:

> When all input transaction levels exceed 5,000 per second, initiate eUtility level 1 setup for extra processing cycles.

In an autonomic architecture, the key issue is to understand the transaction workflow and map the service requirements classes to that topology. When an understanding of the transaction environment is achieved, the autonomic managers can commit sufficient resources—at high priority when necessary—to the workload and manage changes over time to ensure optimum performance.

ARCHITECTURES—AS IS AND TO BE

We can make a comparison of autonomic computing architectures that will emerge and compare them to the existing IT architectures that we are familiar with today. For this comparison, we will categorize today's architectures using "As Is." For future autonomic architectures, we will use "To Be."

We start with the basic elements of architectures, and Table 8.2 shows the results:

Table 8.2   Comparison of AC to Existing Architectures

As Is	To Be
Configuration	Self-Configuration
Problem Solving	Self-Healing
Optimization	Self-Optimization
Security	Self-Protection

Configuration—As Is

Today, detailed planning, discussion, and preparation are required to configure and install any major software package or application. A detailed work plan will be constructed and agreed on, and resources tasked with checklists. Work may start sometime before the required installation—perhaps several weeks or months before, if the configuration is large and complex. Several types of configuration/installation may be required—for example, a new release of the software or perhaps service packs with patches and fixes that need to be applied.

Detailed testing is required before the installation can be released. Results need to be reviewed and signed off on. Cross-impacts with other software packages will need to be tested and reviewed to ensure compatibility and normal operations. System performance is another factor in the equation that will need to be monitored and reviewed to ensure that the new configuration runs at the previous levels.

Self-Configuration—To Be

An autonomic computing architecture will configure and reconfigure itself automatically under varying system conditions. These conditions may be unpredictable and unexpected. The control will come under the SLA that will be defined in precise detail. The self-configuration of the autonomic computing architecture will assess the risks involved. It may also contract for outside services—in an on-demand environment, if needed.

Problem Solving—As Is

Solving system problems and errors is an intense and time-consuming process that involves tracing events, logs, and software to obtain the root cause of the problem. It is a highly complex process that requires intense analytical ability. It is a high tech detective game. There may be substantial pressure on IT people to solve a system problem quickly so that systems can be returned to operational status. When the problem is detected or identified, a fix has to be put in place and tested. Again this takes more time and effort.

Self-Healing—To Be

An autonomic computing architecture will be able to recover from events that cause system failures or operational malfunctions. To achieve this, it will be required to understand the problems and their solutions or fixes. It will learn when new problems are detected and solved. A systematic process can achieve this.

1. Identify the problem.
2. Determine if there are alternative compatible solutions.
3. Provide services as needed and on demand.
4. Install optimal substitutes.

In the future, more sophisticated autonomic computing architectures will anticipate failures and respond accordingly, just as the human autonomic nervous system reacts when faced with a threat.

Optimization—As Is

Software tools exist today to monitor systems and maintain optimal performance. These tools are sophisticated, with embedded algorithms and mathematical programming solutions, such as linear or integer programming, as well as modeling tools. To use these tools, requires substantial programming background and training. The average Java or COBOL programmer does not have it.

Self-Optimizing—To Be

Autonomic computing architectures will automatically optimize all elements in the system. It will review each element according to a schedule and frequency, and if any variation is detected, a solution will be implemented. Depending on the type of tuning needed, the element will be assigned a solution or additional resources—for example, if a Web site's traffic suddenly doubles to excessive loads. The self-optimizing feature will trigger an action to boost the service. The system may check for prices and availability of purchasing and initializing extra services (memory and storage) to continue operations. This will be previously defined in the defined in the SLA.

Security—As Is

Resilient technology is crucial to building secure computing environments, but technology alone cannot completely answer all threats as they evolve. Well-designed products, established and effective processes, and knowledgeable, well-trained operational teams are all required to build and operate an environment that provides high levels of security and functionality. IT customers expect systems that are resilient to attack and that protect the confidentiality, integrity, and availability of the system's data at all times. Customers also are able to control data about themselves, and those using such data faithfully adhere to fair information principles.

Self-Protecting—To Be

For businesses to remain competitive, efficient and secure networked computing is more important than ever. Autonomic computing architectures will protect against defined and known threats, viruses, worms, and internal threats as well. Self-protection will detect the threat and recover from faults that might cause some parts of it to malfunction. It will extend those advantages to the system and any connected partners, customers, and suppliers.

Table 8.3 summarizes the aspects of self-management.

Table 8.3   A Summary of Current Management versus the Autonomic Self-Management of the Future

Concept	Current Computing	Autonomic Computing
Self-configuration	Corporate data centers have multiple vendors and platforms. Installing, configuring, and integrating systems is time-consuming and error prone	Automated configuration of components and systems follows high-level policies. Rest of system adjusts automatically and seamlessly
Self-optimization	Systems have hundreds of manually set nonlinear tuning parameters, and their number increases with each release	Components and systems continually seek opportunities to improve their own performance and efficiency

Table 8.3   A Summary of Current Management versus the Autonomic Self-Management of the Future (Continued)

Concept	Current Computing	Autonomic Computing
Self-healing	Problem determination in large, complex systems can take a team of programmers weeks	System automatically detects, diagnoses, and repairs localized software and hardware problems
Self-protections	Detection of and recovery from attacks and cascading failures is manual	System automatically defends against malicious attacks or cascading failures. It uses early warning to anticipate and prevent systemwide failures

SUMMARY AND CONCLUSIONS

An autonomic architecture is an enormous subject and cannot possibly be dealt with in one small chapter. As a starting point, we have presented in this chapter some high-level descriptions of the required architecture components. As with all new technology, the autonomic journey has only begun and will evolve and develop in the future.

As we have identified, the basis of the autonomic architecture is the control loop, supplemented by decision-making components that monitor, analyze, plan, and execute using common knowledge and data collected.

The value of autonomic computing will be seen in the combination of efficient process changes, skill evolution, and adoption of new technologies, new architectures, and open industry standards.

The important topic of open standards is discussed in the next chapter.

9

AUTONOMIC COMPUTING AND OPEN STANDARDS

INTRODUCTION

We briefly discussed the value and definition of open standards in Chapter 7. There we indicated how important open standards are to the IT community, corporations, and software vendors and suppliers. This is an approach where everyone can benefit. It benefits new technologies by allowing for flexibility and choice.

Standards evolve, develop, and are managed by standards organizations, bodies that manage the agreement on, development of, education in, and future research for standards between all interested parties. Today, according to the National Institute of Standards and Technology (NIST), a U.S. government body, there are close to 800,000 global standards on just about every conceivable product, service, object, or endeavor, from shoes to aircraft to mammograms. Cable TV, doorway heights, computer chips, and other innumerable products and services rely in some way on technology and standards.

The standards that apply to the IT industry have been both problem and solution. After 50 years of IT evolution, we are finally coming to the conclusion that it is in everyone's best interest to have standards for better communication and compatibility within and between vendors, suppliers, and users. It has taken us 50 years to reach this point, and we still have some way to go before open standards are universally accepted and implemented. Despite the unqualified benefits of open standards, many software vendors and corporations are reluctant to embrace the new approach.

Open standards address long-term, strategic business/industry issues, not simply the short term, tactical (technical) objectives of a single segment (or company) within the industry. Successful open standards expand the opportunities for the entire industry while providing users with long-term stability for technology. Standards also provide a sound foundation on which users can base their strategic business decisions.

A BRIEF HISTORY OF OPEN STANDARDS

In the 1980s, computing technology started to become more stratified with much more distinct horizontal structures. Vendors had very proprietary architectures, and it was extremely difficult to interface data and communications with other computer systems. This led to greater degrees of modularization and interoperability, and the development of a marketplace for peripherals. The net effect was an increase in the rate of innovation, greater value for customers, and a certain degree of loss of account control by hardware vendors. The software side of the equation also saw horizontal stratification. Operating systems started to become much more generic and independent of hardware platforms. The middleware layer evolved, allowing for greater cost-effectiveness and greater innovation at the client layer, since application vendors were freed from having to worry about the inner workings.

These developments started to force standardization, which became vital in the effort to exploit networking technology and the growing use of the Internet. The potential for computers to communicate with each other and for great stores of information to be virtualized was predicated on simple and standardized communications.

Therefore, while it may have been possible for a business to be an IBM, HP, or DEC shop in the past, it had become impossible for any one company to control the interfaces that ran the world's networks. During the 1990s, a number of major companies made strategic decisions to embrace this evolution toward open standards. These decisions were based on simple pragmatism: If we are going to live forevermore in a networked world, then that networked world must run on open standards. This development has been good news for customers of IT and the IT industry in general. The skill and resources of these industry players have been critical in the development of robust, functional, and highly practical interfaces, which are critical enablers of e-business.

The battle for "openness" is still being waged. For the most part, businesses are beginning to embrace open standards as a means of ensuring degrees of flexibility and vendor independence. Many vendors have also embraced open standards, because their role in the ecosystem as either provider of horizontal infrastructure or networking capability necessitates it. It is also their desire to participate in markets dominated by other players who use their market position to promote their proprietary interfaces. Some vendors have been successful in exploiting what economists call the "network effect"—the tendency toward adoption of a common platform owing to the intersecting interests and interdependencies of ecosystem participants, including consumers. In turn, these companies have been able to exert control over programming interfaces and document formats to protect their market positions.

A CASE FOR OPEN STANDARDS—DEPARTMENT OF HOMELAND SECURITY

The Department of Homeland Security (DHS), whose logo is shown in Figure 9.1 has called for the use of open standards and IT interoperability in the fight against terrorism and the development of a successful homeland security strategy and future information systems.

The sharing of location-based information—such as data on people, assets, and facilities—across departments and among agencies and jurisdictions is vital for rapid response and accurate reaction to crisis situations. For instance, many government agencies need to have immediate access to critical information. The agencies need to know where the emergency is occurring, what kind of structures are involved, what buildings or open spaces can be used for staging emergency responses, and how best to move emergency responders to the site quickly and safely. Yet, this information undoubtedly resides with different agencies and departments and in various data and vendor formats. Based on this, the DHS has called for the development of information integration architectures that will allow for easy sharing of homeland security information with state, local, and private organizations. The adoption of open standards will provide this information.

Figure 9.1 The logo of the Department of Homeland Security, where 22 government agencies have a critical need to share information with the people who need it, including intelligence and law enforcement, state and local partners, foreign governments, and the private sector. Broader use of open standards in information systems will facilitate this.

TYPES OF STANDARDS—PROPRIETARY VERSUS OPEN

We can analyze two types of basic standards:

- Proprietary, or de facto ("from the fact"), standards have evolved from a product line or specific vendor, such as the IBM PC, UNIX or Microsoft's Windows. These standards develop when such a product or vendor is widely accepted by a broad base of customers or users. It may become a dominant technology and if produced from a single company it is designated as "proprietary" or exclusive. The dangers should be apparent—a single supplier or vendor has total control over the functionality and usefulness of the product.

- Open, or de jure ("by law"), standards are developed and adopted by some authorized standardization body. Such organizations may be created by treaty among national governments or voluntary nontreaty organizations. General examples, such as the International Standards Organization (ISO) and the National Institute of Standards and Technology (NIST), were referred to earlier in this chapter. De jure standards develop because there is no underlying technology, dominant, or proprietary technology needed to implementation. For example, XML—short for eXtensible Markup Language—a specification developed by the World Wide Web Consortium (W3), is an example of an open standard.

Open standard technologies, including Linux and Java technologies, give choice. Developers can choose the fastest and most capable hardware systems to execute their applications and services. Users can start the development on small, relatively inexpensive workstations, such as Linux boxes running Java then scale up to larger servers from IBM, Sun, HP, or numerous other vendors as required later on. As a business, they can choose the most cost-effective hardware, software and service vendors to meet the needs. The entire industry of UNIX vendors, Java-based middle tier and application server companies, and database providers is at their disposal.

Put simply, open standards give users extreme agility and flexibility as they develop solutions and grow their businesses.

Table 9.1 compares the attributes of proprietary and open standards.

Table 9.1   A Comparison of the Attributes of Proprietary and Open Standards

Characteristics	Proprietary Model	Open Model
Reliability	Closed process—high degree of variability	Visible process—more likely to yield reliable results faster
Interoperabilty	At the disgression of a single vendor	Assured by definition
Risk	One vendor as control point—if vendor loses interest in the project for any reason, user rarely has recourse or resources to self-maintain	Depends on the community developing the project—if it has value to users, those users know that in the worst case, they can support the resulting product themselves
Power (who has it?)	Vendor	User
Speed of updates	Many enter market based on vendor requirements	Enters market depending on member needs
Quality	Depends on single source	Best of breed
Cost	May be less expensive initially, loss of choice may raise expected future costs	May reduce cost

WEB SERVICES INTEROPERABILITY STANDARDS ORGANIZATION

Introduction

One approach IBM has made in open standards is to invest in, then develop and manage the appropriate standard organization. A case in point is the Web Services Interoperability Organization.

In February 2002, IBM and Microsoft, together with over 50 more industry leaders, formed the new Web Services Interoperability Organization (WS-I), committed to promoting interoperability among Web services based on common, industry-accepted definitions and related XML standards support. Other WS-I founders include Accenture, BEA Systems, Fujitsu, Hewlett-Packard, Intel, Oracle, and SAP AG. It is open to all organizations committed to promoting interoperability among Web services based on industry-accepted definitions and open standards support.

WS-I brings the work of multiple standards development organizations together for the purpose of providing clarity and conformance around Web services. WS-I working groups will be chartered to produce specific sets of deliverables, such as testing tools and sample Web services. These deliverables will be targeted toward providing resources to assist Web services developers.

WS-I is an open industry organization chartered to promote Web services interoperability across platforms, operating systems, and programming languages. The organization works across industries and standards organizations to respond to customer needs by providing guidance, best practices, and resources for developing Web services solutions.

There is a strong, complementary relationship between WS-I and other organizations committed to the growth of Web services, including its relationship to the W3C, the Internet Engineering Task Force (IETF), and others in autonomic computing.

To create interoperable Web services, and to verify that their results are compliant with both industry standards and WS-I recommended guidelines will include alliance.

Key deliverables are:

1. Profiles, which identify version-specific sets of Web services specifications that interoperate to support specific types of solutions.
2. Sample implementations exposing interoperability issues.
3. Implementation guidelines with implementation scenarios, sample solutions, and test cases illustrating compliance verification.
4. A tool to monitor and log interactions with a Web service.
5. An analyzer conformance testing tool, which processes sniffer logs to verify that the Web service implementation is error-free.

WS-I is open to any organization supporting the goal of interoperable Web services.

WS-I will aggregate collections of key Web services standards into meaningful groups that are easier for customers to work with. It will also promote the evolutionary adoption of key standards and evolve the scope and definition of profiles as required by market needs and the maturity of underlying standards. Web services and their market must grow and evolve together. Web-services profiles will help that happen. The open standard Web Services Framework document published by IBM and Microsoft[1] will serve as the foundation for the new road map, an evolving document that will identify functional areas and capabilities to be addressed by future Web services specifications. This road map will guide implementers and customers so that their work can remain compatible with the specifications as they are developed.

A WS-I Profile

A profile is a named group of Web services specifications at specific version levels, along with conventions about how they work together. WS-I will develop a core collection of profiles that support interoperability for general-purpose Web services functionality. Profiles make it easier to discuss Web services interoperability at a level of granularity that makes sense for developers, users, and executives making investment decisions about Web services and Web services products. WS-I focuses on compatibility at both the individual specification and profile level. To be a useful concept and avoid confusion, the number of profiles should remain relatively small. At the same time, too few profiles would force some Web services products to add unneeded features simply to conform to some profile and assert interoperability. It will be an ongoing task of WS-I to design and update profiles that reflect real Web services usage in the industry. The first profile proposed is WS-I Basic (XML Schema 1.0, SOAP 1.1, WSDL 1.1, UDDI 1.0). The development of additional or updated WS-I profiles depends on the continued evolution and maturity of Web services specifications and standards, along with additional work in message extensibility, binary attachments, routing, correlation, guaranteed message exchange, signatures, encryption, and transactions.

Summary

Interoperability via evolving open standards is the cornerstone of Web services. That is why WS-I is crucial for ensuring the continued deployment and success of Web services technology within and between enterprises. The momentum of vendors and the cross-industry commitment behind WS-I demonstrate that the Web services community is maturing and focusing on customer needs. WS-I will speed the worldwide adoption of Web services by providing critical interoperability guidance and testing materials that work across multiple platforms.

Customers implementing Web services want their investment to comply with the existing standards-based model that enables interoperability and fast time to market. WS-I will provide clarity, guidance, and direction concerning Web services, which customers are requesting as they move into the Web services model of computing.

IMPORTANT STANDARDS FOR AUTONOMIC COMPUTING

We need to ask the following question: "If open standards are important, which standards need to be included for success in autonomic computing?" This can be answered by the comparison in Table 9.2.

Note that at the very bottom of Table 9.2 is the indication that new standards are needed as autonomic computing evolves. IBM will continue to leverage the open standards that exist today and move to develop enhanced standards where needed in the future.

Let us briefly review each of these standards:

The Distributed Management Task Force, Inc. (DMTF) is the industry organization that is leading the development, adoption, and unification of management standards and initiatives for desktop, enterprise, and Internet environments.

The Common Information Model (CIM) is a model for describing overall management information in a network/enterprise environment. CIM is comprised of a Specification and a Schema. The Specification defines the details for integration with other management models, while the Schema provides the actual model descriptions.

The Internet Engineering Task Force (IETF)[2] is a large open international community of network designers, operators, vendors, and researchers concerned with the evolution of Internet architecture and the smooth operation of the Internet.

The Policy Core Information Model (RFC3060) is the standard that presents the object-oriented information model for representing policy information developed jointly in the IETF Policy Framework WG and as extensions to CIM activity in the DMTF. This model defines two hierarchies of object classes: structural classes representing policy information and control of policies, and association classes that indicate how instances of the structural classes are related to each other.

The Simple Network Management Protocol (SNMP) is an application layer protocol that facilitates the exchange of management information between network devices. It is part of the Transmission Control Protocol/Internet Protocol (TCP/IP) protocol suite. SNMP enables network administrators to manage network performance, find and solve network problems, and plan for network growth.

Two versions of SNMP exist: SNMP version 1 (SNMPv1) and SNMP version 2 (SNMPv2). Both versions have a number of features in common, but SNMPv2 offers enhancements, such as additional protocol operations.

The Organization for the Advancement of Structured Information Standards (OASIS) is a not-for-profit, global consortium that drives the development, convergence, and adoption of e-business standards. Members themselves set the OASIS technical agenda, using a lightweight, open process expressly designed to promote industry consensus and unite disparate efforts.

Table 9.2   Mapping Open Standards Against Core Autonomic Capabilities

	Solution Install	Common System Administration	Problem Determination	Autonomic Monitoring	Policy-Based Management	Complex Analysis	Trasaction Measurements
Distributed Management Task Force, Inc. (DMTF) Common Information Model (CIM)			•	•			•
Internet Engineering Task Force (IEF) Policy Core Information Model (RFC3060) Simple Network Mangement Protocol (SNMP)			•	•	•		
Organization for the Advancement of Structured Information Standards (OASIS) Web Services Security (WS-Security) Web Services Distributed Management (WS-DM)			•		•		•
Java Community Process Java Management Extensions (JSR3, JMX) Logging API Specificaiton (JSR47) Java Agent Services (JSR87) Portlet Specification (JSR168)		•	• •	•	•	•	• •
Storage Networking Industry Association (SNIA) BlueFin			•	•			
Global Grid Forum (GGF) Open Grid Services Architecture (OGSA) Open Grid Services Infrastructure (OGSI) Web Services Common Resource Model (WS-CRM)			• • •	• •	•	• •	• • •
The Open Group Application Response Measurement (ARM)			•	•			•
New Autonomic Computing Standards (to be developed)	•	•	•	•	•	•	•

OASIS produces worldwide standards for security, Web Services, XML conformance, business transactions, electronic publishing, topic maps, and interoperability within and between market-places.

Web Services Security (WSS) describes enhancements to SOAP[3] messaging in order to provide quality of protection through message integrity, and single message authentication. These mechanisms can be used to accommodate a wide variety of security models and encryption technologies.

Web Services Distributed Management (WSDM) is a standard way of using Web services architecture and technology to manage distributed resources.

The Java Community Process is an open organization of international Java developers and licensees whose charter is to develop and revise Java technology specifications, reference implementations, and technology compatibility kits.

The Java Management Extensions (JSR3, JMX) specification will provide a management architecture, APIs, and services for building Web-based, distributed, dynamic, and modular solutions to manage Java-enabled resources. JMX™ technology provides tools for building distributed, Web-based, modular, and dynamic solutions for managing and monitoring devices, applications and service-driven networks.

The Logging API Specification (JSR47) is a specification for logging APIs within the Java platform. These APIs will be suitable for logging events from within the Java platform and from within Java applications. It is envisaged that:

- It will be possible to enable or disable logging at runtime.
- It will be possible to control logging at a fairly fine granularity, so that logging can be enabled or disabled for specific functionality.
- The logging APIs will allow registration of logging services at runtime, so third parties can add new log services.
- It will be possible to provide bridging services that connect the Java logging APIs to existing logging services (e.g. operating system logs).

Where appropriate, the logging APIs will also support displaying high-priority messages to end-users.

Java Agent Services (JSR87) are a set of objects and service interfaces to support the deployment and operation of autonomous communicative agents. The specification is based upon the Abstract Architecture developed by FIPA, the Foundation for Intelligent Physical Agents. This Abstract Architecture defines how agents may register and discover each other, and how agents interact by exchanging intentional messages which are grounded in speech-act theory and first-order predicate logic.

The specification defines two kinds of entities:

- Java classes for objects corresponding to the various elements of ACL (agent communication language) and SL (content language), as well as FIPA agent names and descriptions.
- Java interfaces corresponding to the agent services for agent registration, discovery, and communication.

It is intended that the service interfaces may be implemented in terms of a number of different technologies, including both existing Java standards and proprietary systems. (In this respect, the specification is similar to previous specifications such as JMS, the Java Message Service.)

The Portlet Specification (JSR268), to enable interoperability between portlets and portals, will define a set of APIs for portal computing addressing the areas of aggregation, personalization, presentation, and security.

The portlet specification will define the different components for portal computing, their interaction, life cycle and semantics. These components will comprise—but not be restricted to—portlets, deployment descriptors, and portlet-related APIs. In addition, APIs for vendor extensions, APIs for security, user customization, and layout management will be considered.

Also, it will define the minimum set of possible window states for a portlet, such as normal, minimized, and maximized, and the valid state transitions and portlet modes (such as view, edit, help, configure) per the markup language.

The Storage Networking Industry Association (SNIA) is a registered standards and nonprofit trade association dedicated to "ensuring that storage networks become complete and trusted solutions across the IT community." [4] SNIA has the following goals:

- Accelerate new technology development and the evolution of standards.
- Define and adhere to smart, collaborative, rigorous methods.
- Collaborate with the IT community to address real business issues.
- Deliver materials, programs, and services to inform and educate.
- Evangelize for acceptance among vendors and IT professionals.

The BlueFin standard will allow IT managers to connect multiple vendors' products into a storage area network (SAN) and manage them all with a common set of tools. HP and IBM continue to support BlueFin in SNIA, most recently participating in a breakthrough demonstration of heterogeneous SAN management using BlueFin technology.

BlueFin employs technology from the WBEM initiative that uses the Managed Object Format (MOF) to describe system resources based on a CIM, or view of physical and logical system components. WBEM includes a data model, the CIM, an encoding specification based on XML, and a transport mechanism based on HTTP.

Global Grid Forum (GGF) is a community-initiated forum of more than 5,000 individual researchers and practitioners working on distributed computing, or grid, technologies.[5] GGF's primary objective is to promote and support the development, deployment, and implementation of Grid technologies and applications via the creation and documentation of "best practices"—technical specifications, user experiences, and implementation guidelines.

GGF efforts are also aimed at the development of a broadly based Integrated Grid Architecture that can serve to guide the research, development, and deployment activities of the emerging grid communities. Defining such architecture will advance the grid agenda through the broad deployment and adoption of fundamental basic services and by sharing code among different applications with common requirements.

Grid technologies provide the foundation for a number of large-scale efforts utilizing the global Internet to build distributed computing and communications infrastructures. As common grid services and interoperable components emerge, the difficulty in undertaking these large-scale efforts will be greatly reduced and, as importantly, the resulting systems will better support interoperation.

Open Grid Services Architecture (OGSA) is a grid-computing initiative. The purpose of the OGSA Working Group (WG) is to achieve an integrated approach to future OGSA service development via the documentation of requirements, functionalities, priorities, and interrelationships for OGSA services. Topic areas scoped and analyzed are common resource model and service domain mechanisms, but the precise set to be addressed will be determined in early discussions.

The output of this WG will be an OGSA architecture roadmap document that defines, scopes, and outlines requirements for key services. It is expected that the development of detailed specifications for specific services will occur in other WGs (existing or new).

Open Grid Services Infrastructure (OGSI) is another important grid-related initiative. The objective of the OGSI Working Group is to review and refine the OGSI specification and other documents that derive from this specification, including OGSA infrastructure–related technical specifications and supporting informational documents. In this specification, an attempt is made to define the minimal, integrated set of extensions and interfaces necessary to support definition of the services that will compose OGSA.

OGSI version 1.0 defines a component model that extends WSDL and XML Schema Definition to incorporate the concepts of:

- Stateful Web services
- Inheritance of Web services interfaces
- Asynchronous notification of state changes
- References to instances of services
- Collections of service instances
- Service state data that augment the constraint capabilities of Standard ML (SML) Schema definitions

OGSA is introducing Web service common resource models (WSCRM) for use in grid space. Examples are MDS discovery services and the resources they operate on. Each grid approach has a different resource model and a specific protocol for talking to the resources. The goal is to assure common models that can publish to a registry, and can support different binding protocols.

Open Group is a non-profit consortium focusing on best practices and process-based XML content for e-business and application integration. The mission of the Open Applications Group is to define and encourage the adoption of a unifying standard for e-business and application software interoperability that reduces customer cost and time to deploy solutions.

The mission of the Open Group is to achieve the creation of boundaryless information flow by:

- Working with customers to capture, understand, and address current and emerging requirements, establish policies, and share best practices.
- Working with suppliers, consortia, and standards bodies to develop consensus and facilitate interoperability, and to evolve and integrate specifications and open source technologies.
- Offering a comprehensive set of services to enhance the operational efficiency of consortia.
- Developing and operating the industry's premier certification service and encouraging procurement of certified products.

The Application Response Measurement (ARM) API defines function calls, which can be used in an application or other software for transaction monitoring. It provides a way to monitor business transactions, by embedding simple cells in the software, which can be captured by a software agent supporting the ARM API.

NEW STANDARDS FOR AUTONOMIC COMPUTING

The journey to a fully autonomic IT infrastructure is one of evolution. That journey has now begun. As the technology evolves and matures, new standards will become apparent and will need to be developed. It is a requirement for success that all interested parties participate in the development process. Such parties include the following:

- Independent software vendors (ISVs)—The software companies, large and small, that must adopt and implement the standards for their products and services.
- Corporate users—The eventual users of the standards now have a chance to guide and recommend features, functionality, and requirements. Their view from the trenches is important to gain the real worldview.
- Standards organizations—As new standards organizations are formed and existing standards bodies adapt to the new requirements, they have much to offer the development process in terms of knowledge of management and implementation of standards.

- Individuals—There is a place for anyone who has an interest and can contribute to the process of standards development. Most standards organizations place their documents on the Internet, so specifications are available for all to review.
- Global users—The final and perhaps most important requirement is that open standards development must not take place in a regional context—for example just in the United States. Global requirements are needed if the true implementation of open standards is to be applied. Open must mean global.

It is up to all of us in IT to be involved in this process. At the heart of the matter is the need to bring together minds from multiple technical and scientific disciplines, as well as different businesses and institutions, to share a sense of urgency and purpose. Although IBM is determined to take on this challenge, one company cannot do it alone.

The age of proprietary solutions is almost over. The key issues moving forward are as follows: How can we design and support open standards that will work? New methods will be needed to equip our systems to deal with changing environments and transactions. How will we create and develop new standards to take previous system experience and use that information to improve the rules?

OPEN STANDARDS AND THE IBM PORTFOLIO

The IBM portfolio of products and services is impressive. IBM strives to lead in the invention, development, and manufacture of the industry's most advanced information technologies, including computer systems, software, storage systems and microelectronics.

With thousands of products—software, hardware, and services—it is vital to IBM's future success that it installs open standards wherever possible, practical, and beneficial for customers.

Table 9.3 shows the IBM products that have open standards at this time.

Table 9.3   IBM Products That Utilize Open Standards

Products/Books/Services	Open Standards Support	Advantages
WebSphere Application Server V4.D *ibm.com/software/webservers*	XML. SOAP, WSDL, UDDI4J	WebSphere Application Server V4.D is the first-to-market SOAP-enables application server, enabling businesses to develop, publish, host, deploy, and manage Web services applications, including UDDI, SOAP, J2EE, and WSDL

Table 9.3   IBM Products That Utilize Open Standards (Continued)

Products/Books/Services	Open Standards Support	Advantages
DB2 Data Management *ibm.com/software/data*	XML, SOAP	IBM DB2 relational database supports XML and SOAP. IBM DB2 Version 7.2 includes the DB2 XML Extender for conversion of data to XML
WebSphere Studio Applicatin Developer *ibm.com/software/webservers/studio*	XML, SOAP, WSDL	Integrated development environment to build Web services and enterprise applications on J2EE. Includes WebSphere Studio Site Developer
IBM Global Services *ibm.com/services* jStart *ibm.com/softwarebusiness/jstart*	IBM's services arm; supports all standards	Consulting and systems implementation including use of open standards technologies. jStart specifically focuses on Web services projects
IBM Web Services Toolkit (WSTK) *ibm.com/alphawork/stech/web servicestoolkit*	Simple Markup Language (SML), SOAP, WSDL, Reliable HTTP (HTTPR), WS-Inspect, UDDI	Runtime environment, demos, and examples to design and execute Web service applications
Web Services Process Management Toolkit (PMT) *ibm.com/alphaworks/tech/wspmt*	SML, SOAP, WSFL	Business process management technology using open standards Web services technologies including tools and examples
IBM UDDI Registry *ibm.com/services/uddi*	SML, SOAP, UDDI	The IBM Universal Description, Discovery, and Integration (UDDI) registry
Web Services Hosting Technology *ibm.com/alphaworks/tech/wsht*	XML, SOAP, WSDL, HTTPR, WS-Inspect, UDDI	Enables hosting support for Web services within a WSTK environment; Hosting Technology allows for the provisioning and metering of services
Web Services Gateway *ibm.com/alphaworks/tech/wsgw*	SOAP/HTTP, Apache, SOAP, WSDL WSL	Middleware component providing intermediary framework between Internet and intranet environments during Web service invocations

> **N O T E** Open standard development at IBM is continually being
> updated and products will change. Check back with the IBM Web site
> for further open standards developments and announcements.

THE E-BUSINESS ON DEMAND SERVICE PROVIDER BUSINESS

Introduction

This section introduces the IBM e-business on demand/autonomic perspective from a service provider viewpoint. Service providers can be thought of both as business "enterprises," and, in many cases, telecommunications companies, due to the nature of advanced services that telecommunications firms provide. As stated by Alex Cabanes, the IBM Software Group's Industry Marketing Manager:

> "In today's rapidly changing marketplace, the ability of a service provider to sense
> and respond to ever-changing customer demands will determine who survives, and
> who does not. This requires a technology fabric that can adapt on demand to these
> ever changing requirements."[6]

This section addresses service providers and this fabric.

As we have discussed in this book, the IBM Corporation defines e-business on demand as "an enterprise whose business processes—integrated end-to-end across the company and with key partners, suppliers and customers—can respond with flexibility and speed to changing customer demands, market opportunity, or external threat." We have also explored several strategic perspectives of e-business on demand—autonomic computing and grid computing; however, it is key to understand one interesting example of an ecosystem that e-business on demand addresses, in a variety of ways.

While the term e-business on demand originally was used in IBM to define activities in "sourcing" initiatives, today a much broader definition of the term is used to encompass what it takes to be an on demand business in an on demand world. For a business to be capable of providing on demand services, it must respond in real time to its markets and customers. An e-business on demand business must be variable in its ability to provide services, focused on its core differentiating capabilities, and resilient to both internal and external interruption. It is also important that the enterprise have an on demand operating environment, which, as we discussed in previous chapters, is an "open, standards-based, and heterogeneous world, integrated and freely enabled with self-managing capabilities."

The term *ecosystem* will be used in this section to describe a three-part service-enabling environment. This ecosystem includes content providers, a center of the ecosystem where the service providers and carriers operate, which ultimately delivers services to the global consumers with a myriad of pervasive devices. The context of the term ecosystem includes a wide spectrum of types of end users and a variety of consumer telephonic and computing devices. It includes several complex strategies involving flexible hosting and delivery of e-business on demand autonomic processes and information anytime and anywhere, as well as advanced Web services. These e-business on demand ecosystem services deliver information to an environment where end user devices are not dependent on proprietary technologies, but rather receptive to many standards of technological integration techniques, devices, platforms, and business operations.

The service provider e-business on demand ecosystem delivers a diverse set of business capabilities to virtually any market. This is achieved by an open standards (or open source) approach to fortifying and sustaining the on demand operating environment.

The general plight of those delivering advanced Web services to this global ecosystem is consistent around the world. The overall objective is a twofold endeavor, enabling content creators to reach out to more consumers utilizing a myriad of methods to enable this on demand ecosystem. The first part is to enable service providers to provide autonomic solution capabilities to both private and public consumers. These consumers are business enterprise consumers (including government consumers) and private individuals. The second part is something of a byproduct of part one, in the sense that once the service provider or enterprise is capable of providing on demand solutions, they will also need to enable their partners to become on demand businesses, thus fortifying the overall ecosystem. This strategy is being realized by a pattern of trends that are prevalent across almost all industry sectors. Telecommunications service providers (Telcos), as noted through the book, are among the leaders in on demand information and services delivery.

Telcos are often referred to as "service providers." This is in part due to the fact that the telecommunications industry does serve as the primary carrier(s) of network transport of data, thereby placing Telcos in the center of this vast ecosystem, touching the daily lives of almost every one of us. This, however, is changing as key industry "services" leaders are now in the midst of providing a multitude of competing enterprise services, while at the same time utilizing carrier transport media for transmissions of networked data. This is sometimes accomplished through the formation of key strategic "service" alliances between Telcos and businesses—they often work together to provide advanced services.

In the next discussion, we will explore interesting strategy perspectives related to providing New Generation Operations Software and Systems (NGOSS). It is critical to understand these strategic perspectives in light of the critical junctions that service providers struggle to surmount while at the same time maintaining optimal costs and efficiencies.

New Generation Operations Software and Systems

The TeleManagement Forum[7] (TMF) is a nonprofit global organization that provides leadership, strategic guidance, and practical solutions to improve the management and operation of information and communications services. The open membership of over 340 companies includes incumbent and new-entrant service providers, computing and network equipment suppliers, software solution suppliers, and customers of communications services. The TMF has been contributing to the information and communications services (ICS) industry for over 15 years and is the prime manager of the NGOSS initiative.

Before we drive to the detail, let's review some basic facts about NGOSS.

What Is NGOSS?

NGOSS is a business solution framework and architecture for creating the next generation OSS/BSS. The NGOSS program is delivering a framework for producing New Generation OSS/BSS solutions, and is a repository of documentation, models, and code to support these developments. The goal of NGOSS is to facilitate the rapid development of flexible, low-cost-of-ownership OSS/BSS solutions to meet the business needs of the Internet-enabled economy.

What Are the Key Elements of the NGOSS Program?

The NGOSS program is made up of a number of key elements:

- Definition of the next-generation business processes and process models for the information and communication services (ICS) industry
- Definition of the systems framework upon which these business solutions will be built
- Practical implementations and demonstrations of these solutions, through a series of multivendor collaborative projects
- Creation of a resource base of documentation, models, and code to support the TM Forum members in the development of their own new generation OSS/BSS
- Development of industry compliance program to certify solutions and products for compliance to the NGOSS specifications

What Are the Major Business Drivers of Service Providers, Which Have Led to the Need for NGOSS?

- Rapid rollout of new services
- Much easier and more flexible business trading
- Lower total cost of ownership
- Lower cost of change
- Greater range of services
- Improved quality of service
- Improved process flow-through
- Greater process automation
- Greater customer access and control
- More flexible provision of services

What Is the Impact of the Above Business Drivers on NGOSS Design?

- A more open industry-wide framework and architecture
- Choice of implementation technologies to fit the need
- Closer coupling between OSSs
- Management data more accessible/less fragmented
- Customers provided with appropriate views of data
- Automation of business processes
- Systems created with reuseable components—thus potentially lowering costs and providing faster time to market for services
- Increased use of commercial off-the-shelf technologies—which give greater choice, reduced costs, faster implementations, and more skilled developer resources
- Service providers able to co-operate according to individual business needs

What Are the Main NGOSS Design Goals?

- Loosely coupled distributed systems

  o Move away from stand alone OSSs to more of a common infrastructure for management process interaction

- Focusing of corporate data

  o Physically and logically centralized data, providing more integrated views of customer and operational data

- Reuse of application components

  o Functional reuse of business process components
  o Code reuse of software components

- Increased use of object-oriented design

  o For components of OSS functionality as well as modeling managed devices
  o Improved development time, costs, etc.

- Technology-neutral system framework with technology-specific implementations
- Multivendor supply and integration
- General purpose (cost effective) systems access

  o Operational staff low-cost access to data/processes
  o Customer system interoperability to service provider data/processes

- Separation of control of business process flow from business component operation

  o Provides flexibility to rapidly produce new business solutions
  o Allows more reuse of business components across multiple business scenarios

- Workflow automation

  ○ Ability to automate presently manual tasks
  ○ Flexibility to change business process sequence

- Legacy/heritage systems

  ○ Ability to integrate existing systems in OSS infrastructure
  ○ Application of adaptation and wrapping techniques

How Can I Go About Using NGOSS?

- Look at introducing the NGOSS frameworks into your development strategy.
- Service providers should use NGOSS frameworks in their procurement specifications.
- Look for reference implementations of NGOSS, which have been derived from the results of successful NGOSS Catalyst projects.

NGOSS is very important in the service provider e-business on demand ecosystem, the worldwide telecommunications industry, and across many other areas of any vertical industry. The objectives of NGOSS include the simplification and transformation of many types of service providers (not simply Telcos) to establish a more automated, more cost-effective approach to integrating operational support systems.

The TeleManagement Forum (TMF) is the founding organization of the innovative NGOSS approach. The TMF is providing hard-hitting leadership initiatives worldwide, while at the same time providing world-class expertise in the complicated area of NGOSS. This section discusses the many successful steps, concepts, and objectives the TMF has taken towards NGOSS initiatives, and some of the many worldwide partnerships they have established with respect to their many accomplishments.

THE TELEMANAGEMENT FORUM IS THE AUTHOR OF THE NGOSS STRATEGY.

The objectives of NGOSS, worldwide, include the simplification and transformation of many types of service providers OSS/BSS environments to establish a more automated, more cost-effective approach to integrating operational support systems. The IBM Corporation is in partnership with the TMF in support of the NGOSS mission, while leveraging specific deliverables from the TMF. This important work is fundamentally intended for simplification of e-business on demand solution integration elements related to OSS/BSS initiatives.

The TMF is involved worldwide in many strategic and tactical corporate endeavors addressing the complexities of Operational Support Systems (OSS) integration. This complicated systems environment is absolutely key to the Services Provider ecosystem.

For purposes of this discussion, it is important to understand that the TMF works diligently with many worldwide telecommunications firms and other service providers (including IBM) to create standardized processes and architectures, and a common language. These cross-industry integration and simplification initiatives then become key enablers in the reduction of costs targeting the integration of OSS/BSS systems.

Members of the TMF include participants from many vertical industries, but there is a strong presence from many of the world's largest Telcos. It is in the interest of Telcos and cross-industry enterprises, as well as the consumer's interest, that industrial sectors work together to reduce today's excessive costs of integrating and managing complicated OSS solutions. This simplified approach is at the core of the NGOSS strategy. The NGOSS approach to systems development and deployment suggests a strong linkage into the e-business on demand ecosystem—that is, a quicker, more cost-effective, and automated means of systems integration.

The NGOSS initiative (among many other benefits) includes a comprehensive, integrated reference framework for developing, procuring, and deploying operational and business support systems and software. Operational and business support software is a key dependency in the e-business on demand ecosystem for service providers. NGOSS is available today as a toolkit of industry agreed-upon specifications and guidelines that cover key business and technical areas. These key areas include:

- The Business Process Automation elements delivered in the enhanced Telecom Operations Map™ (eTOM)
- The common entities and their standard definitions and relationships delivered in the Shared Information and Data (SID) Model
- The Systems Analysis and Design delivered in the Contract Interface and Technology Neutral Architecture (TNA)
- The Solution Design and Integration delivered in the Components and Technology Specific Architecture (TSA)
- The Conformance Testing delivered in the NGOSS Compliance Tests
- The Procurement and Implementation guidelines delivered in the ROI Model, the RFI Template, and the Implementation Guide documents

The NGOSS solution approach enables all players in the OSS/BSS supply chain to use the elements appropriate for their business, while maintaining the confidence that they will all fit together with a reduced level of skills required, and funding or "integration tax."

The NGOSS-based solutions are strategic and, in several ways, compliment the e-business on demand strategies for service providers. This is based upon the fact that NGOSS utilizes mainstream IT concepts and technologies to deliver a more productive development environment, and thus, a more efficient management infrastructure. NGOSS is prescriptive for only those few "cardinal points" where interoperability is key, while enabling ease of customization across a wide range of functionality. This allows NGOSS-based systems to be tailored to provide a competitive advantage, while also working with an industry's traditional legacy systems.

The value proposition towards e-business on demand here is that NGOSS delivers tangible values to the service provider supply chain by enabling business process automation and nimble operations, reducing costs, and improving customer service. In other words, streamlining of process and autonomic business functions are the key underpinnings.

Major Telcos generally have thousands of discrete business processes they use to run and sustain their operations. To automate a subset of these processes, they have at a minimum many hundreds, and sometimes several thousand, discrete OSS/BSS software applications. Adding further complexity, most processes require integration of multiple applications to achieve end-to-end automation. As a result, the scope of the process automation problem gets large and expensive at a rapidly compounding rate.

While service providers can identify the processes they have today and would like to have, they would like to automate the limiting factor in making these process changes. This limiting factor is the complexity of changing the software systems fast enough to meet evergreen production demands. And because of this multifaceted complexity, changes in the ecosystem are often not cost-effective enough to deliver an attractive return on the investment. As a result, the effort to continuously automate existing processes and to further simplify processes with additional automation is too costly and only occurs on a limited basis. Solving this problem is the foundation for NGOSS.

Clearly service providers understand that if they automate processes, they can reduce operational costs and improve service to end customers, becoming "lean" operators. They know they can become nimble in meeting the needs of customers and deliver easily and affordably the plethora of new technology and service combinations that are becoming affordable to the mass markets. However, exactly how to get from today's status quo to tomorrow's well-integrated, easily changeable, and market-driven business and operations systems is the challenge most of the world's service providers face.

THE PROBLEM NGOSS ADDRESSES IS BOTH COMPLICATED AND COMPLEX.

NGOSS is an industrial effort to identify and automate existing core processes, predicated on the fact that to further simplify these core processes with additional automation is too costly and only occurs on a limited basis. Thus, solving this problem of vast complexity is the foundation for NGOSS, which is a primary mission of the TeleManagement Forum. The innovative solutions evolving from NGOSS involve industrywide participation from service providers and business enterprises throughout the world.

To offer the industry a blueprint for a less expensive, more responsive, and significantly more flexible way of performing business, a group of operators, software suppliers, consultants, and systems integrators have been working on a common framework to deliver appreciably more efficient operations to service providers throughout the world. The work has been coordinated by the TMF and developed by TMF member companies working in multiple, collaborative teams. The NGOSS framework is the impressive result, the product of several hundred person-years of development work.

Automating processes requires a multistep approach, from understanding existing processes to designing how systems will simply integrate. Typical activities include:

- Defining and engineering/re-engineering business processes
- Defining systems to implement processes
- Defining data in a common information model
- Defining integration interfaces
- Defining integration architecture

The elements of NGOSS align directly with the steps in this process automation approach. As a result, NGOSS gives service providers the tools they need to undertake automation projects with confidence.

Business Benefits

As with autonomic computing, process transformation and automation is the cornerstone of NGOSS. Many of the business benefits revolve and intersect around the direct and indirect stages in automating telecommunications operations and other service provider operations. However, global service providers are not the only beneficiaries of the standard language and specifications that NGOSS defines. Large enterprises and other businesses realize this benefit delivered through the adoption of NGOSS approaches.

NGOSS offers service providers tangible business benefits that positively impact the bottom line. These benefits include:

- Having a well-defined, long-term, strategic direction for integration of business processes and OSS/BSS implementation reduces investment risk. When new systems and services are purchased, if they fit in with a well-defined strategy and detailed set of requirements, their longevity is more assured than in an environment with ill-defined definitions.
- Being first to market is important in all competitive environments. Being first to market and not spending a lot of money to be there is a well-known recipe for success. Being nimble and exact is key to preparing for the combined broadband and wireless services onslaught that is approaching.
- Moving to an environment where process definitions, interfaces, and architecture are all standard allows for true competitive bidding environments.

The NGOSS initiative delivers measurable improvements in development and software integration environments. These improvements include:

- The fact that with NGOSS, large portions of process language, requirements, data models, interfaces, and tests are already defined, significantly reducing development costs.
- The utilization of standard building blocks, software modules, and even stand-alone products, which can be built once and sold many times, increasing return on investment with every sale.
- The integration cycles for software with standard interfaces are significantly shorter, reducing costs of bringing a new software system into an existing environment. In addition, integration using NGOSS interfaces becomes a repeatable process, therefore saving time and money on each project while improving success rates.
- The clear definition of "use cases" and requirements becomes easier across service providers/supplier and supplier/supplier partnership relationships. This is by virtue of the fact that when a common language, as provided by the TMF eTOM and the SID, a new and simpler language has now been implemented.

Utilizing NGOSS, ongoing savings are realized across the operational environments, specific to the daily churn of tasks to keep networks running and customers satisfied. These savings include:

- The realization of automation, which in turn enables lower operational expenditures. The NGOSS approach, tackling the tasks of introducing additional automation to operational environments, brings with it a clear blueprint to follow and guidelines to step through the changes. The task may still be large, but much of the work has already been accomplished within the NGOSS elements.
- The realization that once the NGOSS automated systems are in place, making changes in a well-designed, well-understood environment is straightforward. Therefore, reacting to a need to change a service offering, a billing option, or a quality of service requirement, for example, becomes an easy-to-follow process rather than a struggle with significant changes that require many resources and weeks of testing.

NGOSS as a Framework

The NGOSS framework is a sound technical solution developed by industry leaders with hundreds of combined years of Telco, OSS/BSS, and enterprise experience from some of the world's major service provider and vendor companies. Recognizing the need to create a common integration environment for software systems, the TMF member companies have contributed the time of their senior architectural and engineering resources to make NGOSS a success. Additional benefits noted by adherence to NGOSS principles are:

- The NGOSS is real, documented, and ready for consideration by any interested party. The NGOSS components all consist of detailed definitions and are ready for implementation.

- The NGOSS principles and many detailed NGOSS documents draw from existing industry standards and recommendations wherever possible. The NGOSS has engaged the best available resources to create the best possible solutions.

- The NGOSS is defined in such a way that it provides a coherent long-term direction and allows for specifications available to developers and implementers of complex (or straightforward) OSS/BSS systems. Whether a service provider targets strategies on long-term directions or a software supplier is establishing a product road map, the NGOSS provides structure and details to work with toward a common goal.

Utilizing the predefined elements of NGOSS allows development efforts throughout the telecommunications supply chain, and among other enterprises, to focus on solving value-added problems, not defining processes, data models, and architectures.

SUMMARY AND CONCLUSIONS

The real world question is as follows: "What value will open standards present to corporations?" The answer is choice—the flexibility to choose the right systems, the right hardware and software to support the corporation's objectives. Another benefit is the ability to seamlessly integrate new systems into standardized architecture that works with the existing set of mixed hardware, software, protocols, and networks on heterogeneous systems. Any future software that supports open standards that can easily be deployed will gain substantial market share. It makes good business sense.

The evolution and development of open standards is strategic in the next few years as indicated by Figure 9.2. The more systems in an on demand world, the more open standards will be needed.

The adoption of open standards and vendor neutral applications is critical for unleashing power, speed, and innovation in the future economy, and the interest in their development among leading vendors is gaining ground. Open standards have the potential of restructuring the software industry. Advantages include less complexity, ease of use and installation, and the reduction of costs and support, so open standards are rapidly gaining ground in most forward-thinking corporations. The way ahead is to more open and unified systems.

IBM refers to these circumstances as a "threshold moment," a time when the demonstrated need is so urgent as to require a whole new conception of the problem and the solution. IBM's solution, autonomic computing, seeks to alleviate these forces by using examples of automation in nature and in past threshold moments as the foundation for a new model of computing.

Simply put: Open standards convert technology into the universal world of business.

Standards Evolution

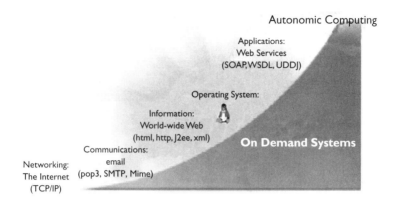

Figure 9.2   In an on demand world, the integration and adoption of open standards is nothing less than vital.

NOTES

1. See *http://www.w3.org/2001/03/WSWS-popa/paper51.*
2. See *www.ietf.cnri.reston.va.us/glossary.html#IETF.*
3. See *www.service-architecture.com/web-services/articles/soap.html.*
4. See *http://www.snia.org/smi/home.*
5. See *http://www.gridforum.org/.*
6. From a speech at WSI meeting, September 2003.
7. For more information on the TeleManagement Forum, refer to their Web site at *http://www.tmforum.org.*

CHAPTER 10

AUTONOMIC IMPLEMENTATION CONSIDERATIONS

INTRODUCTION: TAKE ACTION—BE PREPARED

There are many action items in planning and preparation that corporate IT management can take for the implementation of on demand and autonomic computing. IT management can take the steps necessary to take early advantage of the benefits and savings that will be accrued with autonomic computing. These steps should be considered essential prerequisites that IT management must invest in, rather than waiting for full autonomic technology to be delivered to their doorstep. For IT departments to be successful with autonomic computing will require major shifts in IT organizations, infrastructures, and resources. This work must begin now—for there is much to accomplish. Among the essential steps are the following:

- Assess the overall state of on demand and autonomic computing. Conduct an enterprise-wide complexity study.
- Integrate on demand and autonomic computing into the corporate and IT strategic plan.
- Begin to construct best practices for autonomic development, architectures, and infrastructure.
- Conduct and document a full-scale, corporation-wide complexity reduction study with recommendations for autonomic implementation improvements.
- Review all IT metrics data, service level agreements data, and identify data needed for autonomic implementation.
- Consider restructuring the IT organization to create an internal corporate autonomic group staffed with full-time equivalents (FTEs).
- Map IT services to their underlying processes and begin to monitor end-to-end service levels.
- Focus on improving IT management process maturity.

- Implement a consolidation strategy for servers and storage. Consider introducing workload management.
- Implement automated server provisioning through server configuration management.

Rather than waiting for autonomic computing to become available, these actions can be taken immediately. Incremental benefits can thus be achieved within the current IT organization. Specific, realistic milestones should be put in place and announced in planning documents. As the IT department changes, the costs and benefits can be monitored and documented. IT departments that do not take these essential and necessary steps will become less competitive, and the transition to these newer technologies will be painful and difficult. These IT departments will become prime targets for outsourcing to external service providers who have already adopted and implemented autonomic technology.

IT STAFF OBSTACLES TO ACCEPTANCE

Part of the road map to autonomic success will be the acceptance by all IT staff of the introduction of this new technology. To some, it will be a threat. Others will embrace it with almost religious zeal. To overcome these difficulties, IT senior staff must address the concerns of their subordinates. At least three obstacles to acceptance of autonomic technology spring to mind:

1. Job security concerns
2. Technology maturity
3. Concerns over creating further IT instability

To many data center and operations staff, the promise of full automation and a lights out environment is not new. Many technologies, such as artificial intelligence, case-based reasoning, and rules engines, have promised full automation capabilities. The success rates have been questionable, and many of these technologies have contributed to the overall complexity problem faced in IT architectures today. These are some of the reasons why IT staffers are likely to be skeptical.

Essentially it is a cultural problem whether these obstacles can be eliminated or minimized. Senior IT corporate management must introduce autonomic computing that meets the needs of the corporation.

This IT culture problem is not new. Its roots go back over 20 years. In the early 1980s, I conducted research over a three-year period into improved design methods and higher levels of application development automation. At that time, applications were created over months and years with languages such as COBOL/PL/1 and others. There was a need to design and implement new languages, systems, and design techniques to allow applications to be constructed in days. This research was integrated into a book *Application Development Without Programmers* by James Martin.[1] The book started many trends that resulted in higher productivity, such as fourth generation languages (4GLs), the whole Computer Aided Software Engineering (CASE) era, and eventually Rapid Application Development (RAD) techniques. All of these technologies greatly improved the productivity of application development.

Part of this research concentrated on IT staff and their attitudes toward this new technology. We found that there were major obstacles in terms of resistance to new automation technologies. Some examples of the issues were:

- Conservative IT staff refusing to believe that any new technology is better than the one they are currently using.
- Introducing newer technologies frequently led to further problems.
- IT staff, fearful for their jobs, denigrating new facilities and methods.
- Sentiment existing against pioneering, as pioneers end up dead.

These were the attitudes of IT staff over 20 years ago. While the technology has improved by several orders of magnitude, some of these obstacles to progress have not. It is important that autonomic implementation plans address these issues early on with good communication on progress, plans, issues, and goals. Only then will full implementation be pursued.

One factor that should be communicated clearly to all IT staff is that the full implementation of autonomic computing cannot be introduced quickly. It will take time to move through the five levels towards full autonomic capability.

WHO IS USING AUTONOMIC COMPUTING TODAY?

Many CIOs will ask this question and want the answer before proceeding with the introduction of autonomic computing. There is a need to analyze and map the existing five levels to existing IBM customer environments to determine who is where in the level structure. IBM conducted an internal study of all its customers to determine the autonomic scope in 2004 would be:

- 35 percent are at level 1, Basic
- 27 percent are at level 2, Managed
- 22 percent are at level 3, Predictive
- 14 percent are at level 4, Adaptive
- 2 percent are at level 5, Autonomic

Beginning in 2004, the introduction of autonomic computing will increase by at least 15% a year, as customers move up through the autonomic computing value ladder. The highest growth in predictive and adaptive levels are expected in 2006.

Figure 10.1 illustrates the growth and scale of autonomic computing over the five years from 2002 to 2006. Add to this continuing IBM and industry research and development, resulting in the introduction of newer autonomic products and services, and it adds up to a major new technology of scale, breadth, and scope unlike any that has been introduced before.

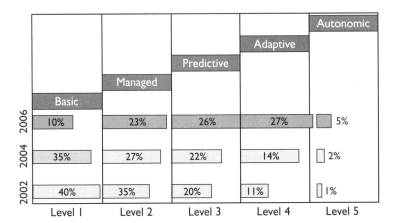

Figure 10.1   Percentages of companies at each of the five levels of autonomic computing, 2002–2006.

EVOLUTION, NOT REVOLUTION

One of the last things a CIO needs is to be told that the latest technology is an IT revolution. Delivering system-wide autonomic computing environments should never be considered in this context. The implementation of autonomic computing is an evolutionary process that requires planning and support with additional processes. The path to full autonomic computing should be carefully planned and implemented. The road map to autonomic computing is achieved through five levels.

1. **Basic level:** This is the starting point for all IT environments. Each infrastructure element is managed independently by IT professionals who set it up, monitor it and eventually replace it.
2. **Managed level:** Systems management technologies can be used to collect information from disparate systems into fewer consoles, reducing the time it takes for the administrator to collect and synthesize information as the IT environment becomes more complex.
3. **Predictive level:** New technologies are introduced to provide correlation among several infrastructure elements. These elements can begin to recognize patterns, predict optimal configurations, and provide advice on what course of action the administrator should take.
4. **Adaptive level:** As these technologies improve and people become more comfortable with the advice and predictive power of these systems, we can progress to the adaptive level, where the systems themselves can automatically take the right actions based on

the information that is available to them and the knowledge of what is happening in the system.

5. **Autonomic level:** The IT infrastructure operation is governed by business policies and objectives. Users interact with the autonomic technology to monitor the business processes, alter the objectives, or both.

Table 10.1 outlines the five levels of implementation.

Table 10.1 The Five Levels of Autonomic Computing Implementation (The purpose is to move from manual Level 1 to automatic Level 5.)

Basic Level 1	Managed Level 2	Predictive Level 3	Adaptive Level 4	Autnonomic Level 5
Multiple sources of system-generated data	Consolidation of data through management tools	System monitors, correlates, and recommends action	System monitors, correlates, and takes action	Integrated components dynamically managed by business rules and policies
Requires extensive, highly skilled staff	IT staff analyzes and takes actions	IT staff approves and initiates actions	IT staff manages performance against service-level agreements	IT staff focuses on enabling business needs
	Great system awareness	Reduced dependency on deep skills	IT agility and resilience with minimal human interaction	Business policy drives IT management
	Improved productivity	Fast and better decision making		Busness agility and resiliency

AUTONOMIC ASSESSMENT

The first step in identifying if autonomic computing is suitable will be to complete an enterprise-wide assessment. The results of this assessment will be used to define the most cost-effective, appropriate autonomic implementation plan to meet corporate goals.

The assessment is performed to measure the potential for introducing autonomic products and services in a corporation and to determine if the corporation is ready to embark on implementation of autonomic capability. It will also define where to focus necessary resources and efforts to gain the maximum benefit. The emphasis is on a business viewpoint, looking at the reasons why autonomic products are needed and how a reduction policy will be crafted and simplicity will be introduced. The expected business value to be gained from complexity reduction or elimination can also be calculated. The result of the overall complexity assessment can be used as the basis for defining corporate complexity goals, complexity reduction adoption strategies, the domains in which to practice simplicity instead of complexity, and the complexity reduction program implementation plan.

Goals

The goal is to perform an autonomic assessment to successfully introduce the technology into a corporation. The purposes are to:

1. Evaluate a corporation's current complexity strategy and the implementation of that strategy in current software projects and various systems groups.
2. Use the results of the assessment to determine a corporation''s needs for autonomic products, the elements of a complexity program to achieve those goals, and the domains in which to focus complexity reduction efforts—for example IT architectures and infrastructure.
3. Recommend actions to take to implement its complexity reduction strategy with autonomic technology.

Instituting the practice of complexity reduction across a corporation is a large, complex task in itself, especially if the ultimate goal is to practice complexity reduction above the project level— that is, across teams, across product lines, and across software groups and organizations. Success requires careful planning, cooperation, and good management practices. To ensure success, a corporation needs to determine how ready, willing, and able it is to practice complexity-reduction driven development approaches and what actions it needs to take to prepare itself to accomplish its complexity objectives and goals.

The assessment will investigate both technical and management/organizational complexity issues. On technical side, some important issues include:

- Identifying and defining core business objects and other kinds of components.
- Defining guidelines and standards for business units.
- Defining the organizational structure and classification scheme.

On the management/organizational side, issues include:

- Defining personnel support for core business objects/components.
- Establishing complexity training programs.
- Establishing the complexity measurement infrastructure (i.e., defining complexity metrics and measurements, corporate complexity policy, complexity incentives).
- Mapping autonomic products and services to business units.
- Defining an implementation plan (first in outline, then in detail).
- Defining resources, roles, and responsibilities for the autonomic implementation team.
- A final road map to success.

Autonomic Assessment Tool

To help corporations understand their current autonomic computing capabilities and map key focus areas to enhance these capabilities as described above, IBM has created the autonomic assessment software tool. This tool measures the level of autonomic function against each of six functional areas within any IT environment.

It analyses against the standard five levels of autonomic maturity—Basic, Managed, Predictive, Adaptive, and Autonomic—to the following key functional areas:

- Security management—The activity of establishing identities and managing security or key business resources.
- User and resource provisioning—The process of changing (adding, moving, or modifying) resources or configurations in all IT environments to enable or enhance the delivery of IT services and to allow users to access or consume these services.
- Performance and capacity management—The activity of managing and maintaining the performance of systems to meet adequate and acceptable levels of business objectives.
- Solution deployment—The activity of planning, testing, and deploying new IT solutions, including all the infrastructure elements needed to support them.
- Availability—The activity of establishing and ensuring consistent and readily available access to business resources.
- Problem management—The process of identifying, analyzing, and resolving issues that impact IT service delivery.

The tool guides users through an interactive question-and-answer dialogue within each of the above areas to determine the exact nature of the IT environment and then give recommendations on autonomic suitability.

The assessment tool provides an evaluation of the corporation. A number of graphs and diagrams are presented that analyze the environment to assist IT management in planning for autonomic implementation. The purpose is to provide an aggregate view of the level of automation currently in place and provide IT management with guidelines to develop higher levels of automation by implementing autonomic technologies.

Example reports include:

Automation Profile

In this example, shown in Figure 10.2, the automation profile is divided into availability, performance and capacity management, security management, solutions deployment, and user administration.

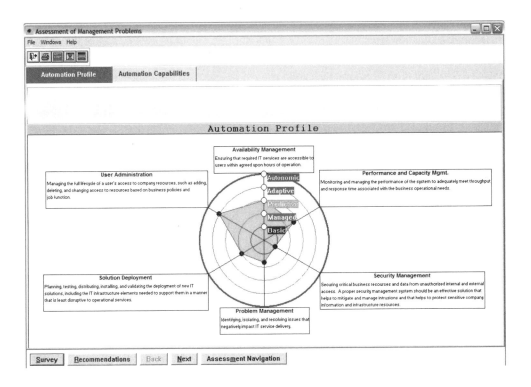

Figure 10.2 Automation profile.

Automation Capabilities Profile

The automation capabilities profile, shown in Figure 10.3, gives an assessment of the process, technology, and skills readiness.

Provisioning Profile

In this provisioning profile example, Figure 10.4, the server and OS, and the identification, storage, application, and network capabilities are analyzed.

AUTONOMIC AND METRICS

The transition to full autonomic computing does not happen in a short time frame. The implementation must be carefully planned and monitored and cannot be solely accomplished by acquiring IBM products. Autonomic computing implementation still requires sound IT project management practices. Other skills in the organization must adapt and change, as new processes need to be introduced to create long-term success. As corporations progress through the five lev-

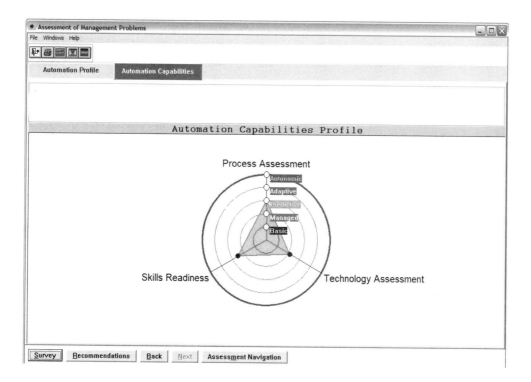

Figure 10.3   Automation capabilities profile.

els, the tools, processes, and skill requirements become increasingly sophisticated. Also the systems will begin to become more closely aligned with the business units.

The Basic level—level 1—represents the starting point for most IT departments and their corporations. The IT department needs to introduce formal measurements and metrics to determine a reference baseline for the introduction of this new technology. If a cost center approach is not being applied, one needs to be introduced. This ensures that the IT resources used are reviewed and measured as an investment.

The Managed level—level 2—is measured by the availability of resources for tasks such as the time it take to solve and close trouble tickets in their internal problem management systems. To improve on these measurements, IT departments must continually seek formal process improvements through existing channels and document their efforts. These channels will mainly be manual processes. This has been the formal approach for almost all IT departments for the last 20 years or more.

At the Predictive level—level 3—IT departments are measured on the availability and performance of the business systems and their return on the investment. To improve at this level, IT

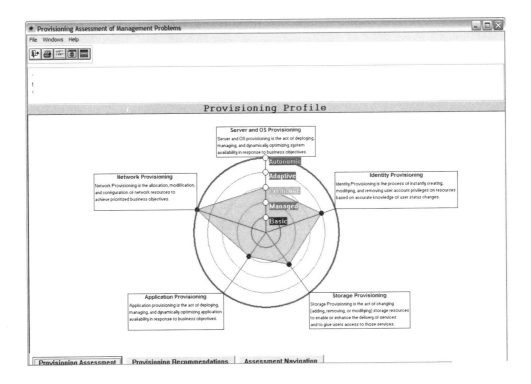

Figure 10.4   Provisioning profile.

organizations must measure and analyze transaction throughput and performance. It is at this level that IT systems are established as a critical role in business success. Predictive tools are introduced for the first time to forecast future expected IT performance. Many of these tools will make recommendations for future performance improvement and enhancements.

At the Adaptive level—level 4—IT resources are automatically provisioned and tuned to provide optimal performance. Business policies are introduced, and can be defined and amended, online. Service level agreements and business priorities will guide autonomic infrastructure behavior. IT departments are measured on their performance such as response time improvements over previous levels and the degree of efficiency as they respond to new problems, and differing workloads and priorities.

At the final Autonomic level—level 5—true autonomic computing is established. Measurements begin to determine how the IT department will make the business more profitable. Extensive financial metrics are available. Advanced modeling techniques are used as well, to optimize the business performance and assist in rapidly deploying new business applications at the same level, which is fully autonomic.

Table 10.2 summarizes the support process needed to make the transition to fully autonomic computing. The road map to success with autonomic computing requires significant changes in processes, skill evolution, more simplified management practices, new technologies and architectures, and implementation of open industry standards. Probably the most important change to be made will be in the IT culture, as there will be fundamental changes in the way systems are managed.

Table 10.2 The Processes, Tools, Skills, and Benchmarks Needed Through the Incremental Delivery Process of Autonomic Computing

	Basic Level 1	Managed Level 2	Predictive Level 3	Adaptive Level 4	Autnonomic Level 5
Process	Informal, reactive, manual	Documented, improved over time, leverage of industry best practices, manual process to review IT performance	Proactive, shorter approval cycle	Automation of many resource management best practices and transaction management best practices, driven by service-level agreements	IT service management and IT resource management best practices are automated
Tools	Local, platform and product-specific	Consolidated resource management consoles with correlation of events, problem management system, automated software install, intrusion detection, load balancing	Role-based consoles with analysis and recommend-ations; product configuration advisors; real-time view of current and future IT performance; automation of some repetitive tasks, common knowledge base of inventory and dependency management	Policy-management tools drive dynamic charge based on resource-specific policies	Costing/financial analysis tools, business and IT modeling tools, tradeoff analysis; automation of some e-business mangement roles

Table 10.2   The Processes, Tools, Skills, and Benchmarks Needed Through the Incremental Delivery Process of Autonomic Computing (Continued)

	Basic Level 1	Managed Level 2	Predictive Level 3	Adaptive Level 4	Autnonomic Level 5
Skills	Platform-specific geographically dispersed with technology	Mulitple platform skills, multiple management tool skills	Cross-platform business system knowledge, IT workload management skills, some business-process knowledge	Service objectives and delivery per resource, analysis of impact on business objectives	E-business cost and benefit analysis, perfomance modeling, advanced use of financial tools for IT context
Bench-marks	Time to fix problems and finish tasks	System availability, time to close trouble tickets and work requests	Business system availability, service-level agreement attainment, customer satisfaction	Business system response time, service-level agreement attainment, customer satisfaction, IT contribution to business success	Business success, competitiveness of service-level agreement metrics, business responsiveness

DEVELOPMENT SOFTWARE

IBM has made available a host of products and software tools to facilitate the introduction of autonomic computing to corporate customers. Below is a summary of what is available at the time this book was written. Interested readers should regularly check with IBM for new announcements and upgrades, as these tools will be improved, withdrawn, or changed over time.

- Software Agent Building and Learning Environment—A Java framework, component library, and productivity tool kit for building intelligent agents using machine learning and reasoning.
- Business Workload Manager—A technology that provides the basis for instrumentation of applications in support of autonomic management.
- Conversation Support for Web Services—A technology that proposes and implements a conversational model of e-business interaction.
- Emerging Technologies Toolkit—A software development kit for designing, developing, and executing emerging autonomic and grid-related technologies and Web services.
- Generic Log Adapter—A rule-based tool that transforms software log events into standard situational event formats in the autonomic computing architectures.
- IBM DLPAR Tool set for the pSeries—A set of tools that enhance the usability of the Dynamic Logical Partitioning feature in AIX 5.2 running on pSeries servers (such as models p690 and p670).

- IBM Grid Toolbox—A grid computing toolbox that includes Globus Toolkit 2.2 with additional documentation and custom installation scripts written for IBM eServer hardware running AIX and Linux.

- Log and Trace Analyzer for Autonomic Computing—An Eclipse-based tool that enables viewing, analysis, and correlation of log files generated by IBM WebSphere Application Server, IBM HTTP Server, IBM DB2 Universal Database, and Apache HTTP Server.

- Manageability Services for Linux—A prototype collection of grid-enabled, on demand manageability services for Linux resources.

- Optimal Grid—A research prototype of grid-enabled middleware designed to hide the complexities of partitioning, distributing, and load balancing.

- Resource Model Composer—A pure Java tool whose visual editor allows generation of a concise specification of an IT resource's syntax and whose engine can generically manipulate the IT resources according to this specification.

- Solution Enabler—A framework for creating and deploying solutions locally or to remote machines with different operating systems.

- Tivoli Monitoring Resource Model Builder—A programming tool for creating, modifying, debugging, and packaging resource models for use with IBM Tivoli Monitoring products.

- Update Tool for Java Applications—A mechanism that enables easy upgrading for users of Java-based desktop applications.

SUMMARY AND CONCLUSIONS

One process in IT we need to improve is that of software implementation. In the past we have been faced with horrendously complex software and are required to make it work quickly in large and sophisticated but equally complex IT architectures. Complexity on top of complexity. Any new approach such as autonomic computing that simplifies this should be welcomed by IT management and the software teams that are charged with implementation. The planning and introduction of autonomic computing must be given the same degree of care and attention as any other software implementation approach. The planning, testing, and, maybe, dual running of autonomic applications may be necessary. Autonomic computing must be implemented in a phased approach. The standard five levels leading to full automation cannot be gained quickly. Depending on the planning approach it might need several years to be fully successful. So plan the plan—and make a start.

NOTE

1. James Martin, *Applications Development Without Programmers*. New Jersey: Prentice Hall, 1981.

GRID COMPUTING— AN ENABLING TECHNOLOGY

WHAT IS A GRID?

Grid computing as we understand it today did not exist is any formal sense five years ago. Since then, it has evolved rapidly and is now an important enabling technology for autonomic computing, among other things. Grid has evolved from being considered a small niche-type academic application technology to a centerpiece of IBM's on demand strategy. All the components of grid computing are in place; processors, storage, networks, and other resources that exist today can be configured to make a grid.

Grid computing has been defined as just an extension of distributed computing; however this is not the case. Rather it can be said that it is an evolution of distributed computing. It has more potential and takes us beyond distributed computing to the next level of sophistication. Simply put, a grid is a powerful, virtual computer system. It consists of multiple processors in a network sharing resources such as software, storage, data, files, printing, and many other peripherals or resources. The term grid was chosen for its similarity to the pervasive electricity power supply industry. The analogy is correct, as both provide services where required.

The basic element of a grid is its computing power, connected by a fast network. Multiple machines from different vendors can be connected together in the grid. In the grid, they do not have to be from the same manufacturer or vendor. They can be geographically dispersed at multiple locations. They can vary in processor speed, memory size, operating system, architecture, types of software and many other factors. Grid computing enables the virtualization of distributed computing and data resources such as processing, network bandwidth, and storage capacity to create a single system, granting users and applications seamless access to vast IT capabilities.

Scalability and speed are important factors in grid computing and a measure of how effective the grid can be. Applications normally run and execute on a single computer. If an application can be spilt and designated to other computers in the grid for execution, it should be faster. For example, if an application or job can be run on two machines with equal-sized processors, the application should finish in half the time. If 10 processors are available, then execution should be completed in one tenth of the time, and so on. Scalability will be an important function for autonomic computing management in a grid network.

A company with 600 grid-enabled desktop PCs can utilize all of them together as one computing platform—suddenly providing it with enough computing capacity to go head to head with many of the world's largest supercomputers. Additional resources, such as applications, storage, bandwidth and data, are also made available.

At its core, grid computing is based on an open set of standards and protocols—Open Grid Services Architecture (OGSA)—that enable communication across heterogeneous, geographically dispersed environments. With grid computing, organizations can optimize computing and data resources, pool them for large capacity workloads, share them across networks, and enable collaboration.

GRID IS IN USE TODAY

Grid computing is used today by many companies across a number of industries. Current IBM customer references for grid include Butterfly.net, a development studio, online publisher and infrastructure provider for massively multiplayer games that connect players on PCs, consoles and mobile devices. Butterfly grid consists of two clusters of approximately 50 IBM xSeries™ servers running in IBM hosting facilities. Specialized game servers and database servers are fully meshed over high-speed fiber-optic lines, enabling transparent routing of players to different servers in the grid. Another current reference for IBM grid computing is the University of Pennsylvania's groundbreaking National Digital Mammography Archive, which gives rapid retrieval of digital patient files from multiple locations in a secure environment. The University of Pennsylvania grid manages this huge volume of data, schedules traffic, and encrypts all image and information transmission using portal systems running almost exclusively on IBM hardware—including 16 distributed IBM Netfinity servers running Linux and Windows 2000. See Figure 11.1 for further illustration.

BENEFITS OF GRID COMPUTING

The business and technology benefits of grid computing are many and varied.

For businesses grid computing can:

- Accelerate time to market
  - Grids help improve corporate productivity and collaboration.

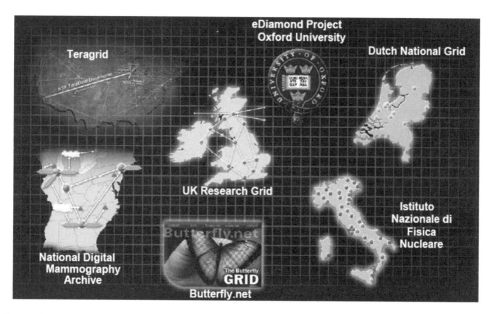

Figure 11.1 Examples of grid computing in use today worldwide.

- Problems can be solved that were previously difficult or unsolvable.

• Enable collaboration and promote operational flexibility

- Grids bring together not only IT resources, but also end users, clients, suppliers, and other interested people.
- Widely dispersed departments and businesses can create virtual organizations to share data and resources.

• Efficiently scale to meet variable business demands

- Grids create flexible, resilient operational infrastructures.
- Rapid fluctuations in customer demand can be addressed—availability on demand is the result.
- Instantaneous access to compute and data resources enables the business to "sense and respond" to needs.

• Increase productivity

- End users can get uninhibited access to the computing, data, and storage resources they need (when they need them).
- Employees are equipped to move easily through product design phases, research projects, and more—faster than ever.

• Leverage existing capital investments

- ○ Improve optimal utilization of computing capabilities.
- ○ Common pitfalls, such as over-provisioning and incurring excess costs, can be avoided.
- ○ IT organizations are freed from the burden of administering disparate, nonintegrated systems.
- ○ The overall IT total cost of ownership (TCO) is reduced.

Grid computing also provides the following technology benefits:

- • Infrastructure optimization

  - ○ Consolidate workload management.
  - ○ Provide capacity for high-demand applications.
  - ○ Reduce cycle times.

- • Increased access to data and collaboration

  - ○ Federate data and distribute it globally.
  - ○ Support large multidisciplinary collaborations.
  - ○ Enable collaboration across organizations and among businesses.

- • Resilient, highly available infrastructure

  - ○ Balance workloads.
  - ○ Foster business continuity.
  - ○ Enable recovery and fail over.
  - ○ Increase workload throughput significantly.

UNDERUTILIZED RESOURCES CAN BE EXPLOITED

Grid computing can take advantage of underutilized computer resources, such as spare processing cycles, free or available disk storage, and even servers and many other types of resources. In most corporations, there are, at times, vast amounts of underutilized computer resources, such as the resources we mentioned above, particularly servers. A desktop PC is a good example of an underutilized resource; the average PC is used for 10 to 20 percent of an eight-hour day. When the workday is over, it stays idle for another 16 hours. This is resource that can be used in a corporate grid. Hundreds of PCs can be connected to the grid, forming a large virtual computer with substantial power and capacity.

Storage is another grid resource. Normally each processor, server, or computer in the grid will make a quantity of storage available. Two types are available: hard disk and dynamic storage. Sometimes this can be a very large amount of storage availability, allowing for very large databases to be stored in multiple locations, thus defeating some of the limitations imposed by certain operating systems. Temporary storage is also needed with some applications, and the grid management software can locate and schedule such storage.

Fast access storage can be used as additional memory for some applications, allowing for increased throughput and quicker processing times if needed.

Servers are another underutilized computer resource, with large amounts of idle time between peak processing times. Servers can be made available to the grid as needed and scheduled for use processing grid applications or jobs. To control priorities and management, rules can set up to control processing. If server utilization rises above a set limit—85 percent, for example—then the grid processing application is passed on to another section of the grid that is not so busy. Grid computing provides the framework to utilize these resources.

WHAT APPLICATIONS RUN ON A GRID?

Certain types of applications have already been very successful using grid computing. Scientific projects, such as the SETI@home project run by the University of Berkeley in California, have been a spectacular success. Here the Internet is used to send small packets of data to over 4 million PC users in a grid. The results are analyzed on the client processor and sent back to Berkley for further analysis, and another packet sent for processing. This project has been running since early 1999 and the statistics are astonishing.

- Since it's start in May 1999 over 4.8 million people have signed on from over 230 countries.
- At any given moment, 475 thousand machines are working fulltime on the problem.
- Results are being returned at a rate of over a 1 million files per day (34 trillion calculations per second, roughly equivalent to a 249-teraHz supercomputer). Each day over 1,000 years of CPU time is used.
- A new participant signs up on the Grid every 58 seconds.
- To date the total CPU time used is approaching 1,900,000 YEARS.

Some observers claim that it is the biggest computing project ever undertaken. No doubt, the success of the SETI@home project has spurred the development of grid computing and illustrated what can be accomplished.

Table 11.1 further illustrates other types of applications that can be used with grid computing. These applications have been successful for a number of years, and much has been learned about the systems design of effective grids. New applications are continuously evolving.

The commercial application of grid computing is in its early stages of development. It requires a different approach to conventional application or systems management. If the application can be split into one or more different subapplications, it can run on a grid. This is not easily achieved and requires considerable skill in system design and segmentation, as well as considerable programming skill to be successful.

Table 11.1 A Sample List of Grid Computing Applications

Grid Computing Application	Application Description
Oil and gas exploration	• Processing data to locate new oil and gas reserves • Seismic analysis
Astronomical data analysis	• Data-processing projects, such as the Search for Extra-Terrestrial Intelligence, or SETI@home, project
New drug development	• Discovering new drug compounds for treatment of cancer, anthrax, AIDS, and other diseases
Motion picture animation	• Making movies and creating special effects, such as rendering
Biomedical applications	• Gene analysis and treating human disorders and disease • DNA/Protein sequencing
Financial Services	• Modeling economic data • Statistical analysis • Portfolio management • Business intelligence • Data warehousing and mining
Consumer services	• Network video gaming
Manufacturing	• New product design and testing • Process simulation • Failure analysis
Energy	• Nuclear bomb testing without explosions • Electricity grid control systems
Other examples	• Collaborative research • Weather forecasting

Many new software tools are needed to convert existing applications to a grid environment. This technology will accelerate as the need intensifies and vendors introduce the much-needed set of software tools to make grid computing applicable for commercial enterprises.

New computation-intensive applications should be designed and written for parallel execution so that they can be easily grid-enabled.

GRID TYPES

Grid computing can provide many corporations with a much-needed technology boost and introduce another paradigm shift in IT resources, by introducing a new service without a large expenditure or increase in budgets. Corporate IT management should evaluate grid computing for internal use within their IT operations. Grids are suitable for data intensive/computational intensive applications, such as business intelligence, data mining, and statistical analysis.

Grids will give outsourcing providers a much need shot in the arm by providing an infrastructure that can meet even the most demanding of clients. Outsourcing organizations are poised to take advantage of the new utility approach and the on demand operating environment. Large hardware companies who also have outsourcing subsidiaries are also prime candidates for this technology.

It is likely that grid computing will evolve into specific industry types or application areas and provide services to clients in those markets.

Three models are developing:

1. Compute grids provide shared access to high performance computing facilities and resources, where the emphasis is on high-end computing capacity.
2. Data grids provide shared access to data/transaction-intensive applications with large databases, file systems, or mass storage.
3. Application grids provide shared access to specific application sectors, such as financial, manufacturing, and health care.

This analysis can be taken further by proposing the types of grids that corporations can implement. Today, many corporations are moving ahead with their grid projects, as the business case and the need are established, and grids can compliment their existing IT infrastructure.

Four types of grids are evolving:

1. Enterprise/corporate—A grid is established as a secure, internal, and private grid drawing on existing resources within a single enterprise.
2. Partner/client/supplier—A designated set of partners, clients, or suppliers share the grid for the business benefit of all. This has particular cost benefits if large number of participants take part.
3. Service/utility—A general all-purpose grid is created that can be made available to all that need it. Clients use the resources and pay for what they use. This is a good example of grid on demand.
4. Educational—Universities and colleges collaborate in a shared pool of resources. Universities have established networks and have been using some of their resources for some years.

IBM prefers to use the following terminology to describe the above classifications.

1. Infra-Grids

  ○ Optimized resources
  ○ Campus or wide area network
  ○ Utilizes excess IT capacity

2. Intra-Grids

  ○ Share resources/networks with external partners
  ○ Designed for specific applications
  ○ Utilizes excess IT capacity

3. Extra-Grids

  ○ External collaboration with clients/partners/suppliers
  ○ Resource and optimization utilization
  ○ Multivendor system integration

4. Inter-Grids

  ○ Sharing of data storage across the public Internet
  ○ Monitored access and security
  ○ Resource sharing and aggregation
  ○ Multivendor hardware/software/network protocols

Figure 11.2 illustrates the relationship of these types of grids

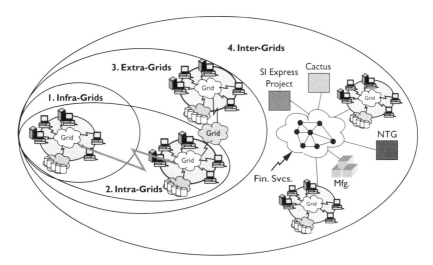

Figure 11.2   The relationship between the four types of grids.

Early adopter companies are already experimenting with elements of on demand computing, sometimes called eUtility computing, selectively outsourcing a portion of their business processes and computing applications, based on the types of grids specified above in the diagram. Several vendors already offer utility-based pricing for server and storage capacity. Web services and grid protocols are gaining credibility, even at a time when technology spending is mostly confined to essentials.

The rapid development of grid computing in the next few years will drive spending to new levels. Estimates range from spending in 2004 of $350 million to growth in 2009 to over $5 billion, with corporate grids being the leading type of grid implementation.

SOFTWARE AND LICENSES

It is likely that a grid will have many different types of machines, architectures, and operating systems. Each will be cataloged by the grid management software and made available as resources for use by participants. The grid may have software installed that is too expensive to install on every processor. The jobs that require this software can be directed to the particular machine where this software resides for successful execution. This is a function that autonomic computing could manage within the self-configuring functionality. If the software licensing fees are considerable, then significant savings, or at least a discount due from the grid licensing arrangements, can be had.

Software licensing can track where the software is installed and where concurrent copies are installed. Some vendors will object to the software grid licensing approach and inject code to prevent this from happening. Agreement is needed on a standardized approach; this is a function that autonomic software can manage.

GRID AND OPEN STANDARDS

As with autonomic computing, grid computing is based on an open set of standards and protocols that enable communication across heterogeneous, geographically dispersed environments in a seamless fashion. As we have already identified in Chapter 9, the importance of open standards for new technologies, such as autonomic computing and grids, cannot be overemphasized.

Grid computing is open standards-based technology. It uses SOAP (Simple Object Access Protocol), a standard for establishing the ground rules of communication interfaces; WSDL (Web Services Description Language), a standard to describe the services used in the network; and XML (Extensible Markup Language) for the common format/syntax language for sharing information. Together these standards, interfaces, and formats enable application data and content to be easily shared in a grid that is comprised of cooperative, yet disparate systems.

There are four standards bodies creating open standards for grid computing:

1. Global Grid Forum (GGF)

The GGF is a community of 5000+ individual researchers and practitioners working on distributed computing, or "grid" technologies. GGF's primary objective is to "promote and support the development, deployment, and implementation of Grid technologies and applications via the creation and documentation of "best practices"—technical specifications, user experiences, and implementation guidelines.

For the latest information see their Web site at *http://www.ggf.org/ home.php?div=about.*

2. Open Grid Services Architectures

The purpose of the OGSA Working Group is to achieve an integrated approach to future OGSA service development via the documentation of requirements, functionality, priorities, and interrelationships for OGSA services. Topic areas that expect to scope early are a common resource model and service domain mechanisms.

The output of this group will be an OGSA architecture roadmap document that defines, scopes, and outlines requirements for key services. It is expected that the development of detailed specifications for specific services will occur in other groups (existing or new).

For the latest information see their Web site: *https://forge.gridforum.org/projects/ogsa-wg.*

3. Open Grid Services Infrastructure (OSGI)

The objective of the OGSI Working Group is to review and refine the OGSI specification and other documents that derive from this specification, including technical specifications related to OSGA infrastructure and supporting informational documents.

The OGSA defines the mechanisms for creating; managing and exchanging information among entities called *Grid Services.*

For the latest version of the specification, see their Web site: *http://www.gridforum.org/ ogsi-wg/.*

4. Common Resource Model (CRM)

The draft CRM specification proposes a model of manageability for manageable resources. Manageability defines information that is useful for managing a resource. Manageability is those aspects of a resource that support management specifically through instrumentation of the resource to allow management tools to interact with the resource. Management is the active process of monitoring, modifying, and making decisions about a resource. Management also includes the capabilities that use manageability information to perform activities or tasks associated with managing IT resources. The draft CRM specification describes how the management interface of the manageable resources is exposed through Web services.

For the latest version of the specification, see their Web site: *http://www.gridforum.org/ Meetings/ggf7/BOFS/CRM%20Working%20Group%20Home%20for%20BOF1.htm.*

GRID AND AUTONOMIC COMPUTING

Grid computing and autonomic computing can be considered complimentary technologies. Both are evolving, being developed, and implemented at the same time. The technologies are utilizing many of the same components, such as Web services, applications, networks, open standards, and storage. The configuration, deployment, maintenance, and management of existing networks is and has always been a complex endeavor. Growth and rapid implementation of new business applications have fueled even more complexity, which is reaching the point where these systems become unstable and almost unmanageable.

The skill requirements for managing these complex environments are extensive and can include detailed knowledge of the network topology, distributed data behavior, load balancing, performance tuning, and system optimization. As we identified earlier in this book, highly skilled IT systems administrators are hard to recruit and even harder to keep. They are expensive, but very necessary, resources. Many have already reached the limits of what they can manage today. With system complexity increasing, the need to introduce self-managing systems such as autonomic computing is becoming a paramount priority.

This analysis can be taken a step further by introducing the prediction that grid computing will only gain widespread acceptance in the global marketplace by integrating autonomic functionality. Grids need self-managed, self-configuring systems within the networks to manage their devices and resources with little or no human intervention.

Many of the following features will be included:

- System configuration management—The OGSA CRM is used to model the system and its resources. Generated events are handled according to user set policy.
- Job execution management—This covers time-, priority-, and space-based scheduling of jobs. In case of application failure, jobs are retried based on applicable policy and priority.
- Resource management—Dynamic and flexible resource management is essential. At the same time, resource isolation between different jobs is crucial, not only for access control but also to ensure that there are no unexpected performance dependencies.
- Infrastructure management—Backup and recovery, failsafe mechanisms, restart procedures, storage allocation and maintenance, and report printing and distribution are all necessary to infrastructure management.
- Clustering features—To handle resource failures and provisioning, features for adaptive resource allocation should be provided to enable autonomic management. The actual behavior should be based on client-specified policies.

- Infrastructure services—Some of these services are end-user management, accounting and billing management, pay as you go/pay what you use, system logging, and tracing.
- Security management—This provides a single sign-on authentication service, with support for local control over access rights and mapping from global to local user identities and security profile handling.
- Grid monitoring—This is an integrated information service distributed across the grid to monitor resources that provide information about the state of the grid infrastructure. The services should be based on the Lightweight Directory Access Protocol (LDAP).
- Network management—This provides an interface to TCP, UDP, and file data I/O. It should support synchronous and asynchronous interfaces, multithreading, and integrated GSI security.
- Provide services—A service that implements a variety of automatic and programmer-managed data movement and data access strategies, enabling programs running at remote locations to read and write local data.
- Workload management—This can be described in three tiers:

  o Integration: The need to manage HTTP, IIOP, JMS, and other requests as they move through the enterprise.
  o Load balancing: Managing the workload based on the resources available at any given time.
  o Failure identification: Describing and documenting what went wrong, and mentioning all of the resources involved.

RECOMMENDED READING

For more information and in-depth view of grid computing please read Craig Fellensteins' book *Grid Computing*.

CHAPTER **12**

AUTONOMIC DEVELOPMENT TOOLS

INTRODUCTION

IBM has released a number of software development tools and technologies that can be used by IBM customers to create their own autonomic software. These tools represent what can be considered the first wave of autonomic development tools. As we indicated previously, there is much to be done in making the transition to autonomic culture, and it is best to start now.

THE IBM EMERGING TECHNOLOGIES TOOLKIT

The IBM Emerging Technologies Toolkit (ETTK) is a software development kit for designing, developing, and executing emerging autonomic and grid-related technologies and Web services. The ETTK provides an environment in which to run emerging technology examples that showcase recently announced specifications and prototypes from IBM's emerging technology development and research teams. In addition, it provides introductory material to help developers easily get started with development of autonomic technologies, Web services, and grids.

The tools can be downloaded from the IBM Web site and contain the following:

- There are two separate downloads: the ETTK Autonomic Computing Track and the ETTK Web Services Track. The ETTK Autonomic Computing Track contains the infrastructure, samples, and documentation for programmers creating their own autonomic programs. The ETTK Web Services Track contains Web services and grid computing infrastructure and samples. Either or both of these technology tracks may be downloaded, depending on one's particular interest.

- Preinstalled environment (Xerces, Xalan, SOAP, Grid, IBM Grid Toolbox, etc.). Also, instructions and configuration utilities for using ETTK with the WebSphere SDK for Web Services, WebSphere Application Server, and Jakarta Tomcat.
- Client-side APIs for interfacing with a WSDL document or a UDDI registry; and APIs for publishing and binding Web services.
- Autonomic Logging demo.
- IBM Grid Toolbox infrastructure and demos.
- Demonstrations that can be used to test ETTK: Publish a service, and then use a client that communicates with the UDDI registry to find the Web service and invoke it.
- A set of utility Web services: User Profile, Metering, Accounting, Contract, and Notification. Provided is a composite demonstration, which makes use of these utility services and of Web Service Level Agreement (WSLA), Web Services Management Middleware, and Service Domain technologies.
- Technology previews of security functions, such as WS-Security, systems management, and SOAP technologies.
- Documentation about the Web Services Architecture, WS-Inspection, and WSDL specifications.

The ETTK Autonomic Computing Track contains the infrastructure, samples, and documentation for programmers creating their own autonomic programs. It contains the following technologies:

- Self-Healing/Optimizing Autonomic Computing Demo implements two aspects of autonomic computing: self-healing and self-optimizing. The self-healing behavior detects when a running application stops and takes the appropriate actions to get it to run again. The self-optimizing behavior is demonstrated when the average response time of the running applications falls below a preset threshold: Actions are taken to create additional applications in order to distribute the load appropriately. Also, idle applications holding system resources are removed.
- Autonomic Manager Toolset (AMTS) aids in the creation of autonomic managers that can enable self-managed systems. Autonomic managers are implemented as OGSI-compliant grid services. The AMTS includes a policy engine, the framework necessary to act as a grid service, and a rich set of supporting classes. The AMTS also provides sample autonomic managers and many coding examples.
- AMTS Thermostat Sample is a tutorial example of how to construct a policy-driven autonomic manager. It is a simple, illustrative device-control application that demonstrates use of a large swath of the AMTS, including the grid support, the policy engine, and the sensor/effector framework.
- Generic Log Adapter for autonomic computing is a rule-based tool that transforms software log events into standard situational event formats in autonomic computing. The adapter is an approach to providing a producer proxy for the early participation of soft-

ware groups in the autonomic computing architecture. The Adapter consists of two main components, a Rule Builder and Configuration tool, which are used to generate parsing rules for a product's log file(s) and configuration of the Adapter. The Adapter runtime environment converts the logs into the standard situation formats for the autonomic computing architecture and forwards them to any consumer/management tools capable of consuming the output. Furthermore, the Adapter provides a plug-in architecture for customization with required functionality external to the users' software.

- Common Base Event (CBE) Data Format is a proposed data open standard for facilitating effective intercommunication among disparate enterprise applications that support logging, management, problem determination, autonomic computing, and e-business functions within an enterprise environment. Through XML-encoded events specified though a well-defined schema, CBE encapsulates properties common to events used by these technologies while allowing several extension mechanisms to support the widest possible range of data. In this release of the toolkit, Version 1.0a of IBM's Java implementation of a CBE API is introduced. This new release includes the first full implementation of the CBE schema, in addition to many new classes and methods for better facilitating the use of CBE. CBEs are used in the Self-healing/Optimizing Autonomic Computing Demo.
- ReGS Autonomic Logging Demo: The Reporting Grid Services (ReGS) specification is a set of core services that provide for logging, tracing, and monitoring of applications. It will be one of the components that the autonomic computing environment will use for providing these services.

The ETTK Web Services Track contains the following technologies:

- The WS-Policy demo has been extended to illustrate a typical usage scenario. The demo illustrates how the developer of a service can specify general requirements that are combined with application server configuration to generate WS-Policy documents. WS-Policy documents are intended to be the interoperable format for stating specific service policy requirements. The demo continues to show how policy is obtained and interpreted when invoking a service, and the consequences of following or ignoring policy.
- Web Services Integration demonstrates the ability to easily combine existing Web services into new execution flows that can be run as a single process. It provides a simple Web-based user interface that allows users to create new flows from selected toolkit services and run them immediately.
- Web Services Failure Recovery (WSFR) is a self-healing framework for Web Services Hosting Environments (AXIS). A WSFR environment is composed of multiple nodes (application servers) that host, monitor, and cause persistence of the state of locally deployed Web services. Information about the environment itself and all deployed Web services is maintained in an entity known as DNA (Distributed Network Agreement),

which is shared among all nodes participating in the environment and is maintained in a repository. In the event of a Web service failure, the nodes communicate in order to recover the failed service, with its last known state intact, at another node in the environment. An administrative GUI is provided that allows users to configure the environment and to create, load, and view the current DNA.

- The IBM Grid Toolbox is a set of components that can be used together or independently to develop grid applications and programming tools. The IBM Grid Toolbox is based on the Globus Toolkit^{TM} 3.0 (GT3). (Globus Tookit is a trademark held by the University of Chicago.) Grid computing, which usually involves problems requiring large amounts of processing cycles or access to large amounts of data, applies resources from many computers in a network toward a single problem. Grid computing allows devices to be virtually shared, managed, and accessed across an enterprise, industry, or workgroup. In addition to the infrastructure, we have included additional grid samples and demos.

- Managing a grid is a challenging and complicated task. The Grid Software Manager is a standard J2EE-based Web application that can be deployed with the IBM Grid Toolbox, simplifying the management of the toolkit's core OGSA infrastructure. By exploiting the toolkit's built-in management grid services, an administrator is able to use the Grid Software Manager to monitor the grid runtime environment, interact with running grid services, and manage and view the runtime logs.

- WS-Reliable Messaging (WSRM) is a recent specification that defines a protocol for reliably delivering Web service messages between applications. In the WSRM demo, several scenarios illustrating some of the various features of WSRM are included.

- JMX Bridge is a tool that creates a WSDL-defined Web service for managing a class of resources. Current implementation acts as a bridge to JMX MBeans. Either an MBean (MBeanInfo) or XML description of an MBean is read as the description of the managed resource. The tool generates an associated Java class, WSDL, and a deployment descriptor.

- WSDLDoc is a tool that allows developers to generate HTML documentation detailing the structure and operation of Web services from WSDL documents. The tool itself has been rewritten to provide better performance, extended documentation, and flexibility in the manner in which documentation is generated (written either to a disk or to a Java object). In order to provide greater flexibility, WSDLDoc has been so designed that it can be embedded in applications.

- Service Domain previews the middleware technology that enables customers to easily implement "On Demand" Software Access, providing broker and marketplace services to enable robust Service-Oriented Architecture. Since its introduction, it has evolved into two modular and complementary layers: the Service Domain layer and the "On Demand" Service Grid virtualization layer. New features and enhancements have been added in this release to provide interactive configuration of service policy rules, including service definitions and selections, Hosting Environment selection, front-end integration, soft contractual bindings for service consumers and suppliers, third-party Billing and Rating application support, online management, change management, interoperations, simplification of programmatic access capabilities, etc.

- UML-to-BPEL mapping Demo includes a UML Profile that defines the manner in which automated business processes can be modeled using UML tools (such as Rational Rose and Rational XDE), and an Eclipse tool that can translate UML models into BPEL4WS (Business Process Execution Language for Web Services) documents. The generated BPEL can be executed by the BPWS4J BPEL runtime environment. In this new release of the demo, the translation tool has been much improved and now fully supports the UML profile, which has also been updated.

- eBusiness Demos illustrate technology related to business processing. The demos vary from simple transaction management to orchestration of Web services. Some example eBusiness Demos include the following:

  - Reputation Protocol: A "proof-of-concept" implementation that provides third-party assurance to Web services through the use of the ARIES (Assured Reputation Information Exchanged Securely) framework. The demo shows the generation, communication, and verification of reputation and assurance information in online transaction environments.

  - Utility Services Demos illustrate how utility services work together; they provide the basis for future utility services that might be shipped in the toolkit. This demo uses several utility services, such as management service, notification service, metering service, and contract service; and it enables them to be used with a real business service (the Stock Quote Service and Address Book Service examples, which are shipped with the toolkit). It is designed to show how to extend a Web service by adding common provisioning services that most business infrastructures will need.

  - WS-C/WS-Transaction/BPEL4WS demos: WS-C/Tx defines an extensible infrastructure for managing transaction flow between various business components. Building on this, BPEL4WS simplifies the modeling of businesses interactions through the definition of flows, which describe how these interactions take place and the relationships among the involved partners.

  - Web Service Security demos, because security is so critical to the success of Web services, illustrate some of the security-related technologies currently being developed for Web services. Some of the security demos include Digital Signature, Encryption, Federated Identity, and WS-Policy.

The ETTK evolved from the package known as the Web Services Toolkit (WSTK). With the renaming of the WSTK package to ETTK, the scope of technologies included within the package has been expanded. The ETTK provides two separate tracks that can be downloaded independently.

The new toolkit assembles related technologies from various IBM development and research labs. The demos and functions of the ETTK run on both Linux and Windows operating systems. Version 1.1.1 contains a WS-Policy demo, Self-Healing/Optimizing Autonomic Computing demo, Autonomic Computing Toolset, Common Base Event Data Format, Web Services Integration, Web Services Failure Recovery, and IBM Grid Toolbox infrastructure, along with a Grid Software Manager, WS-Reliable Messaging demo, and a JMX Bridge.

How Does It Work?

The basic software components needed to experiment with and create Web services and autonomic and grid-related programs are provided with the ETTK. Included is an architectural overview of autonomic technologies, Web services, sample programs, utility services, and some tools (such as ReGS Autonomic Logging demo, XML Parser, and UDDI client APIs) that are helpful in developing and deploying autonomic and grid programs and Web services. The toolkit also includes a fully functioning SOAP and grid infrastructure. ETTK includes a fully functioning SOAP engine (Apache AXIS), and grid (IBM Grid Toolbox) infrastructure.

The IBM Emerging Technologies Toolkit can be used with any operating system that supports Java SDK 1.3.1 or 1.4; it has been tested on Windows and Linux.

AUTONOMIC COMPUTING AND OPEN SOURCE

The Open Source movement today owes much of its creation to a few key individuals. Often in cultural revolutions, particularly in high-tech areas, one person's groundbreaking idea is transformed into a major movement. In the high-tech industry, an entrepreneur starts with an idea, which then becomes a major movement. This happened with open source.

There is a considerable debate and argument over who originated the open source movement. For example, many say it dates back to 1977, when Bill Joy originated the UNIX and BSD (Berkeley Software Distribution) license at the University of California at Berkeley. This first distribution included the Pascal system, and, in an obscure subdirectory of the Pascal source, the editor ex. Bill acted as the distribution secretary, and sent out about 30 free copies of the system for collaboration.

Others say it was Richard Stallman. In 1984, Richard Stallman was a programmer in MIT's Artificial Intelligence Laboratory in Boston, Massachusetts. One day, he was having difficulty adding some new software features to one of the printers in the lab. He called the manufacturer and asked if he could get access to the source code of the printer driver. Naturally, the company refused. Back then, as now, major software corporations did not make source code readily available. This was the straw that broke the camel's back for Stallman. He was not able to solve his problem, and abandoned the effort. Shortly after, he left MIT and set out with a stern resolve to create a collaborative software development world, a world where software could be shared and all programmers everywhere could contribute their ideas, share code, and add code to software projects. The source code would be made available to anyone. The Open Source movement was born. But like most cultural movements, it took a long time to reach saturation point—about 20 years. Only in the last few years has it suddenly become very popular.

Without the Internet, the entire Open Source movement would be invisible and would have only a fraction of its current impact. Early shareware and freeware was distributed via bulletin boards before the Internet, but the ability for communities to share information and work together as part of a global community has been the provenance of the Internet.

More importantly, despite Microsoft, IBM, and other proprietary software suppliers' rapid involvement, the Internet started life as openly as possible, with shared code as the normal mode. The original U.S. Defense contracts for the Internet had as part of their goal the linking together of very different proprietary hardware and software architectures that resided in defense companies and universities worldwide. By design, therefore, the software of the Internet had to be open and not only shareable, but also designed to add modules rapidly and easily. Communities of bright developers all over the world became involved and worked together to solve problems. It is this community that has spawned and inspired the players working in the Open Source movement.

Today, the Internet is full of open source software in heavy commercial use. Without open source, there would be no Internet. Some of the most popular open source products in use today are briefly described here by categories:

Operating Systems

- LINUX is the most used Unix-like operating system on the planet. Versions have run on anything from handheld computers and regular PCs to the world's most powerful supercomputers. Linux is widely distributed among different vendors.
- FreeBSD, OpenBSD, and NetBSD are all based on the Berkeley Systems Distribution of UNIX, developed at the University of California, Berkeley. Another BSD-based open source project is Darwin, which is the base of Apple's Mac OS X.

Many of the router boxes and root DNS servers on the Internet that keep the Internet working are based on one of the BSDs or on Linux. Microsoft keeps BSD boxes hidden behind the scenes, in order to keep their Hotmail and MSN services working—a fact not generally known. Not surprisingly, most of the software on top of the operating system that keeps the Internet humming is also open source.

Internet

- Apache runs over 50 percent of the world's Web servers.
- BIND is the software that provides the DNS (domain name service) for almost the entire Internet.

- Sendmail is a popular email transport program widely used on the Internet.
- Mozilla, the open source redesign of the Netscape browser, is retaking the ground lost by Netscape in the "browser wars." It added functionality, stability, and cross-platform consistency that is not available from any other browser.
- OpenSSL is a standard for secure communication (strong encryption) over the Internet.

The TCP/IP DNS, SSL, and email servers are especially interesting because they're "category killers"; not only are they extremely capable and robust, they're so good that no commercial competition has ever been successful at replacing them as the most widely used product on their respective categories.

Programming Tools

- Perl, Zope, and PHP are popular engines behind the "live content" on much of the World Wide Web.
- Powerful high level languages like PYTHON, Ruby, and Tcl/Tk owe much of their success and prevalence to the active community of developers that use them and continue their development.
- The GNU compilers and tools (GCC, Make, Autoconf and Automake, and others) are arguably the most powerful, flexible, and extensible set of compilers in the world. Almost all open source projects use them as their primary development tools.

Developer tools are especially well represented, because without open source programming tools, open source software would require proprietary tools to build and maintain it. There are literally hundreds of thousands of popular open source packages, covering every imaginable category of software, and more are being developed every single day. Why? Because free open source software is such a compelling idea that once people begin to understand it, most people want to learn to use, promote, and make their own open source software to share with others. You can also make money using open source software to deliver products and services to your customers.

In a recent survey by *CIO* magazine, IT executives said, "The greatest benefits from using open source are lower total cost of ownership, lower capital investment and greater reliability and uptime compared to their existing systems."[1] IT executives report that open source provides greater flexibility and control, as well as faster and cheaper application development. All things being equal, many of IT executives surveyed said they "would choose open source for a new implementation over a proprietary vendor solution." The difference between open and proprietary software—and its deeper strategic and corporate philosophical implications—is something that is barely acknowledged in mainstream conversation, let alone analyzed in probing ways.

THE IBM COMMITMENT TO OPEN SOURCE

IBM was quick to recognize the value of open source, forming alliances with distributors, contributing to the open source community, and enabling IBM products and services for many opens source products. IBM believes this investment will benefit service providers as they continue to look for effective alternatives like Linux for their IT infrastructures and e-business applications.

In 2001, IBM announced a donation of $40 million worth of software tools to the public domain in a move to create an open source organization aimed at developers. An organization called Eclipse will make available some of IBM's software programming tools to developers to create applications for e-businesses and Web services. More than 150 of the leading open source companies, such as Linux distributors Red Hat and SuSE, along with Merant, QSSL, and Rational, are a part of the Eclipse community.

IBM has made a strong push into the open source sector in recent years. Open source and free software represent a challenge to Microsoft and its ubiquitous Windows operating system software, which can cost businesses thousands of dollars a month to license. Open source applications are generally considered lower-cost alternatives.

This demonstrates IBM's commitment to open source software. It also shows that IBM understands that to reach business developers to create open source applications, it has to let them adopt software tools for open source to be successful in major enterprises.

Also, convincing developers inside of large organizations or developers that create software for large organizations to use open source tools is critical.

Shortly after Eclipse, IBM said it would invest $1 billion in Linux across all product lines: PCs, portables, servers, and mainframes. For IBM, Linux represents a single operating system that can span a range of disparate hardware, from wristwatches to the company's multimillion-dollar supercomputers. IBM also sees Linux and open source giving it a competitive edge for developer talent over Sun Microsystems and its proprietary Solaris operating system. By seeding the market with tools for building open source software, IBM gains a large base of developers building applications that can run on its servers. The company could also benefit by offering to its customers programs built under the open source development model, in which thousands of programmers can collaborate on writing and debugging software.

The Eclipse announcement marks another step in the company's open source strategy. Eclipse-based tools run on both Linux and Windows, which allows developers to create a single application, rather than going through the hassle of creating software in Windows and transferring it to Linux, according to IBM. Eclipse is an open universal platform for tools integration based on J2EE. The platform enables developers to work with tools from different vendors in an integrated, portal-like environment, making it easier for technology producers and consumers to create, integrate, and use software tools.

The hope for Eclipse is that with tools that work directly on both operating systems, Linux developers can more easily turn to the more abundant software tools available for Windows, helping to increase the number of available Linux applications. IBM said that more than 5,000 individual developers from 63 countries are participating in the Eclipse open source community.

AUTONOMIC COMPUTING WITH OPEN SOURCE

The prospect of future autonomic software products is intriguing. But is fits well into the open source model. To be successful, it must have the basic open source infrastructure as a foundation of tools, open standards, and support. Those with the interest and expertise in autonomic computing can share their knowledge with each other and the community freely and efficiently. It will also accelerate the development of products.

There are several examples of first wave autonomic open source products under development under the Eclipse framework, such as in the following areas:

- Problem Determination tools for integration into self-healing and self-protection aspects of autonomic computing.
- Autonomic Monitoring tools for the collection of system management data used in self-optimizing.
- Heterogeneous Workload Management tools to manage workloads and resources across multiple vendor networks and machines. These are used in self-optimizing.
- Complex Analysis tools for analyzing many aspects of the impact of data interactions.

A few selected examples follow.

PROBLEM DETERMINATION—A LOG AND TRACE ANALYZER FOR AUTONOMIC COMPUTING

The Log and Trace Analyzer for Autonomic Computing is an Eclipse-based tool that enables viewing, analysis, and correlation of log files generated by IBM WebSphere Application Server, IBM HTTP Server, IBM DB2 Universal Database, and Apache HTTP Server.

This tool makes it easier and faster for developers and support personnel to debug and resolve problems within multitier systems, by converting heterogeneous data into a common event model and by providing a specialized visualization and analysis of the data. The Log and Trace Analyzer for Autonomic Computing works with ISV application plug-ins.

The following runtime operating systems are enabled:

- WebSphere/Apache/IBM HTTP Server: All 32-bit runtime environments on which WebSphere Application Server 4.x or 5.0 is available.
- DB2 UDB: All runtime environments on which both WebSphere Application Server 4.x or 5.0 and DB2 UDB 8.1.x are available.

How Does It Work?

It provides a consolidated environment that deals with logs and traces produced by various components of a deployed system. This technology links these two sets of tools (tracing and logging) and helps bridge the gap between determination of problems and debugging of applications and middleware. By capturing and correlating events from end-to-end execution in the distributed stack, this tool allows for a more structured analysis of distributed application problems that facilitates the development of autonomic, self-healing, and self-optimizing capabilities.

HETEROGENEOUS WORKLOAD MANAGEMENT: BUSINESS WORKLOAD MANAGER PROTOTYPE

Business Workload Manager (BWLM) Prototype is a technology that enables instrumentation of applications with Application Response Measurement (ARM) in order to monitor the performance of transactions across a distributed environment. This ARM-based performance information will be used by BWLM to monitor and adjust the allocation of computing resources on an ongoing, split-second basis. Planned functions include the ability of BWLM to detect changes in its environment and decide which resources (system, network, and load-balancing patterns) to adjust in order to enable a network of systems to meet end-to-end performance goals. When middleware (or, in this prototype, an application) is instrumented with ARM, it will be able to take advantage of products such as BWLM and participate in IBM's autonomic computing initiative.

The prototype allows one to observe and build upon the instrumented application using the ARM 4.0 (preapproval version) standard to handle workload management for better transaction flow across systems and applications. This technology will provide significant value in understanding response times and transaction flow for the following:

- Improved service-level management based on performance policies.
- Determining where transactions hang.
- Active workload management for better capacity use.
- Understanding bottlenecks for better capacity planning.

The prototype demonstrates instrumentation of an application (in this case, a PlantsByWebsphere EJB) using ARM APIs, which could otherwise have been achieved by instrumenting middleware, such as WebSphere. The use of service classes to define performance policies is also shown.

In addition to the prototype, there is a BWLM demonstration (which was posted previously). The BWLM Demo includes a simulation of BWLM's administrative user interface, which is used to show how performance policies are set, to locate performance bottlenecks, and to see how the software optimizes workloads by reallocating resources.

> **N O T E**   The goals of the demo are to communicate workload
> management concepts and to show some of the functionality planned
> for the product. Indeed, the BWLM Demo shows capabilities and
> functions that are not part of the prototype. The prototype is an
> example of instrumentation of an application so that it exploits a
> subset of BWLM capabilities.

How Does It Work?

The preapproval ARM 4.0 standard supports both C and Java applications and will allow developers to instrument applications so that they collect performance data.

This technology is intended to drive the first significant ARM instrumentation in commercial middleware. This basic prototype will feature the following:

- Administrative application
- Management server and BWLM agent for collecting ARM data
- Simple reporting:

    ◦ Server class reporting
    ◦ Service class drill-down reporting
    ◦ High-level server statistics

In the BWLM Demo, the user interface in no way reflects the look and feel of the user interface that will be provided with the actual product; the goals of the demo are to communicate workload management concepts and to show some of the functionality planned for the initial release.

THE SOLUTION ENABLER

The Solution Enabler is a framework for creating and deploying solutions locally or to remote machines with different operating systems. The framework helps to simplify the creation and deployment of software solutions by capturing detailed knowledge of a solution package deployed through a common installer.

A prime objective of the Solution Enabler is to effectively encode information about configuration and customization into a solution package, thus minimizing the need for detailed knowledge of the solution components during deployment. Now more than ever, the Solution Enabler's Eclipse-based plug-in, the Solution Developer, facilitates the encoding of this information. In addition, non-Eclipse command line utilities are included. Once packaged into a specific solution, the Solution Enabler, can be deployed by using the common installer interface provided.

The Solution Enabler 2.2 deployment environment employs a push model deployment approach. The Deployer interface is invoked using a central administration station called a staging server to initiate installation to target machines. Each target machine must have the IBM Installation Agent (IIA) installed (except in the case of local deployment). A security key is used to authenticate connections from the staging server to the target machines. The IIA listens for communication from an authenticated staging server and executes the staging server installation request. Thus, deployments are pushed from one central server to one or many target machines, providing a consistent installation interface across operating systems for disjointed software products.

How Does It Work?

The programmer defines the components, integration steps, topology, and tasks necessary for a solution. All this information may then be encoded in the Solution Enabler's XML wrappers using its Solution Developer tools or build-time environment. The Solution Developer provides the option of creating a solution project, which creates the necessary structure. For each component in the solution, the programmer will develop an application wrapper and one solution wrapper to outline all components in the solution, as well as any desired default configuration or deployment tasks. These wrappers provide input to the application and solution factory builders, which validate the wrappers against each applicable schema to generate a specific solution.

The Solution Enabler file is opened in the deployment interface, which presents a flowchart of tasks associated with deploying the solution. These tasks may be deployable tasks (that is, Install DB2, Deploy WebService on WAS, etc.) or manual tasks indicating that the user needs to perform some operation. A deployment wizard steps the user through the necessary panels in order to collect information specific to each task in the solution deployment. This information includes the host names for the machines the user wants to target for the task, application configuration information (destination path, user ID, etc.), and the media installation image for the application. Once all the necessary information is collected, the deployment wizard will present the option of deploying the solution.

The information collected on the staging server is transmitted to the target machine and used in the native installation program of the solution component. The installation image of the solution components is compressed into a JAR file. During deployment, these files are used to execute the installation of the solution component. If deployment is to a remote target machine, the necessary files are sent to the target machine, and installation of the component is executed. Upon completion of deployment, the target machine's agent returns a message to the deployment server reporting the installation results.

SOFTWARE AGENTS

In this last example in this chapter, we need to review and understand the significance of software agents in an autonomic environment. This technology is one of the key and core technologies that drive true autonomic functionality.

Software agents—or, to use a standard industry term, agents—can be defined as autonomous, problem-solving computational entities capable of effective operation in dynamic and open environments. Agents are often deployed in environments in which they interact, and maybe cooperate, with other agents (including both people and software) that have possibly conflicting aims. Such environments are known as multiagent systems. Agents can be distinguished from objects (in the sense of object-oriented software) in that they are *autonomous* entities, capable of exercising choice over their actions and interactions. Agents cannot, therefore, be directly invoked like objects. However, they may be constructed using object technology.

Agents provide designers and developers with a way of structuring an application around autonomous, communicative elements, and lead to the construction of software tools and infrastructure to support the design metaphor. In this sense, they offer a new and often more appropriate route to the development of complex systems, especially in open and dynamic environments. In order to support this view of systems development, particular tools and techniques need to be introduced. For example, methodologies to guide analysis and design are required, agent architectures are needed for the design of individual components, and supporting infrastructure (including more general, current technologies, such as Web services) must be integrated.

Agent Technologies

Agent technologies span a wide range of specific techniques and algorithms for dealing with interactions with others in dynamic and open environments. These include issues such as balancing reaction and deliberation in individual agent architectures, learning from and about other agents in the environment and user preferences, finding ways to negotiate and cooperate with agents and developing appropriate means of forming and managing coalitions. Moreover, the adoption of agent-based approaches is increasingly influential in other domains. For example, multiagent systems can provide faster and more effective methods of resource allocation in complex environments, such as the management of utility networks, than any human-centered approach. Similarly, the use of agent systems to *simulate* real-world domains may provide answers to complex physical or social problems, which would be otherwise unobtainable. Examples include the modeling of the impacts of climate change on various biological populations or modeling the impact of government policy on the economic or global landscape.

Attributes of Agents

- Adaptability—Agents must be able to work on multiple platforms, networks and software operating systems—and at the same time be able to solve technical problems by themselves without input from the owner.
- Mobility—An agent should be able to roam networks and the Internet according to decisions made internally by itself about where to find data to achieve its predefined goals. It must be able to interact and negotiate with other agents in multiple networks and environments.
- Transparency and accountability—An agent must be completely transparent to the owner/user if required—but it must have features for logging where it has been, what it

has done, and who it contacted and when. And it must produce this information on demand.

- Rugged—If an agent is required to traverse Web sites, and networks—large and small—it must be rugged, able to deal with errors, low resources, underpowered servers, incomplete data, and so on. It should be able to solve as many problems as it can without human intervention.

- Self-starters—Agents must be able to start and stop based on their own criteria, deciding to gather information on their own based on the owners' priorities. The required frequency may be as soon as possible, hourly, daily, weekly, monthly, or whenever. The agent must have the ability to decide when to start/stop and when to deliver its results and through what interface.

- User-centered—The agent must act in the best interests of its owners and the preferences that have been set for it. It must carry out its duties as prescribed without deviating.

The schematic in Figure 12.1 illustrates these attributes in the triangle of information.

1. The user describes/collaborates with the agent.
2. The agent interacts with the information sources or applications.
3. The agent delivers the results to the user.

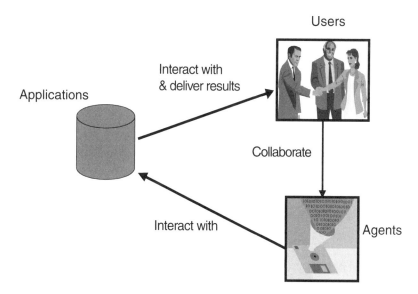

Figure 12.1   Software agents—a simple schematic.

Mobile Agent Systems

Many researchers and programmers in the autonomic community see agents as programs roaming corporate networks in search of specific code or the Internet to collect business-related data in order to help users to buy goods or implement platform-independent code-on-demand, for example. This need for mobile agents is acknowledged and builds on European strengths, where much of this work has been done. But mobility brings added security problems. The research effort concentrates on how to guarantee termination, security, and exactly once protocols. To protect against malicious hosts, agents should contain time limit validity and electronic money with an expiration date. A key issue that needs to be addressed here is *administrability* of mobile agent systems—e.g., authorization policies. This has been a major reason why mobile agents have not yet been taken up by the mainstream. Note also that hosts, as well as agents, need to be self-protected.

One of the commercial application areas in which the added value of mobile agents is very high is large-scale distributed or decentralized system integration with highly adaptive and dynamic business logic. Existing solutions are generally centralized, pulling everything onto one platform, limiting the complexity and changes that can be handled. A decentralized agent approach divides and conquers complexity by pushing a large part of the business logic out to source systems so that monitoring and aggregation can be done on each. This distributes workload and increases robustness because local processing can be performed independently of other systems, resulting in fewer and more relevant interactions with these systems, at a higher level of abstraction. In turn, mobility, mainly single hop, is the answer to the increasing need for flexibility and adaptability in business logic. Agents can easily be deployed to source systems, carrying new database drivers, code to interact with new application or file types, or new data processing rules. Software is updated at the component level at runtime, proving a level of dynamism and flexibility that goes far beyond current release policies. Agent communication and behavior capabilities complete the picture, being very well suited to high-level service—based on the decentralized implementation of business logic—and for adapting and handling change in the on demand environment. A nice property of the dynamic, component-level approach is that it naturally fits step-by-step system integration, with each step resulting in added value for the business.

This is a particularly significant advantage in the current economic climate, in which many companies have seen megaprojects fail.

AUTONOMIC AGENT TECHNOLOGY

Agent Building and Learning Environment (ABLE), a core IBM autonomic computing technology, has enhanced rules function, new Eclipse-based tooling, and major enhancements to the agent platform, including life cycle services, security, and persistence. ABLE is a Java framework, component library, and productivity tool kit for building intelligent agents using machine learning and reasoning. The ABLE framework provides a set of Java interfaces and base classes to build a library of JavaBeans called *AbleBeans*. The library includes AbleBeans for reading and writing text and database data, for data transformation and scaling, for rule-based inferencing using Boolean and fuzzy logic, and for machine learning techniques, such as neural networks, Bayesian classifiers, and decision trees. Developers can extend the provided AbleBeans or implement their own custom algorithms. Rule sets created using the ABLE Rule Language can be used by any of the provided inferencing engines, which range from simple if-then scripting to lightweight inferencing to heavyweight AI algorithms using pattern matching and unification. Java objects can be created and manipulated using ABLE rules. User-defined functions can be invoked from rules to enable external data to be read and actions to be invoked.

How Does It Work?

Core beans may be combined to create function-specific JavaBeans called AbleAgents. Developers can implement their own AbleBeans and AbleAgents and plug them into ABLE's Agent Editor. Graphical and text inspectors are provided in the Agent Editor so that bean input, properties, and output can be viewed as machine learning progresses or as values change in response to methods invoked in the interactive development environment.

Application-level agents can be constructed from AbleBean and AbleAgent components using the ABLE Agent Editor or a commercial bean builder environment. AbleBeans can be called directly from applications or can run autonomously on their own thread. Events can be used to pass data or invoke methods and can be processed in a synchronous or asynchronous manner.

The distributed AbleBeans and AbleAgents are as follows:

Data beans:

- AbleImport reads data from flat text files.
- AbleDBImport reads data from SQL databases.
- AbleFilter filters, transforms, and scales data using translate template specifications.
- AbleExport writes data to flat text files.
- AbleTimeSeriesFilter collects periods of data for use in predicting future values.

Learning beans:

- Back Propagation implements an enhanced back propagation algorithm used for classification and prediction.
- Decision tree creates a decision tree for classification.
- Naive Bayes learns a probabilistic model for classification.
- Radial Basis Function uses radial basis functions to adjust weights in a single, hidden-layer neural network for prediction.
- Self-Organizing Map clusters data using Gaussian neighborhood function.
- Temporal Difference Learning uses reinforcement learning for time series forecasting; gradient descent is used to adjust network weights.

Rules beans inferencing engines include:

- Backward chaining.
- Forward chaining.
- Forward chaining with working memory.
- Forward chaining with working memory and Rete-based pattern matching.
- Predicate logic.
- Fuzzy logic.
- Scripting.

Agents:

- Genetic search manipulates a population of genetic objects, which may include Able-Beans.
- Neural classifier uses back propagation to classify data.
- Neural clustering uses self-organizing maps to segment data.
- Neural prediction uses back propagation to build regression models.
- Script uses rule sets to define its init, process, and timer actions.
- JavaScript names JavaScripts to run when the agent's init, process, or timer actions are called.

SUMMARY AND CONCLUSIONS

As we indicated earlier in this chapter, these tools represent the first wave of autonomic development tools, and their acceptance and success in the corporate trenches has yet to be determined. However, it is a start in the right direction. One observation made is that these tools are themselves complex to use—which may defeat the overall objective of reducing IT complexity that autonomic computing was introduced to eliminate. It may increase the complexity of developing autonomic applications—but will lessen the complexity of operations and support. There is a learning curve to master as well—how long that curve is remains to be seen. This may be an issue that clearly needs to be analyzed and probed much more deeply to determine if it is significant.

Other challenges for the autonomic development tools include:

1. A set of development methodologies is needed—repeatable processes that can help developers construct custom autonomic software with quality, performance and reliability in mind.
2. Training is lacking—although there are many online or downloadable tutorials available, there is very little classroom training announced. The design and construction of autonomic software is new and there are specific methods and knowledge that must be understood by developers.

3. New Technology is coming—expect the tools and software to be significantly developed and enhanced over the next few years, as new features, products, and enhancements are created by IBM with feedback from customers.

For more information on the tools and software discussed in this chapter, please see the following Web sites:

- *Eclipse.org* is an open consortium of software development tool vendors that has formed a community interested in collaborating to create better development environments and product integration
- The main IBM site is located at *http://www.alphaworks.ibm.com/eclipse*
- The main IBM site for autonomic development tools is located at *http://www.alphaworks.ibm.com/autonomic.*
- Starting points for open source sites include the following:

  - *http://www.opensource.org*
  - *http://www.apache.org*
  - *http://www.linux.org*
  - *http://www.freebsd.org*

NOTE

1. See *http://www.cio/archive/091503/index.html.*

CHAPTER **13**

INDEPENDENT SOFTWARE VENDORS

CHALLENGING TIMES FOR SOFTWARE VENDORS

While designing, constructing, marketing, and selling software has never been easy, tomorrow and in the future it will be more difficult and demanding. There are many reasons and shifts in the marketplace that demand attention from all software vendors to protect their future—not just independent software vendors (ISVs), but all software vendors, large and small. Customers, technology shifts, and business pressures all contribute to these changes, so we will examine all of them.

Customer demands and issues include the following:

- Greater efficiency—more performance for less money
- Greater return on investment (ROI)
- Flexible licensing and larger discounts on sales
- Longer life cyles for software—customers take longer to replace their software.
- Increased support without the increase in costs
- Guarantees on rapid error-free deployment

The business pressures on corporations buying software include the following:

- Stalled markets and recession
- Shrinking IT budgets—less money to do more
- Increased competition, prices, and product offerings
- Reduced staffing levels—requests for higher IT salaries
- IT complexity at every turn

Finally, the technology factors listed below compound this problem further.

- Introduction of major technology shifts every few years
- Greater shift to Web services and new styles of e-commerce
- Transition to open standards, less complexity
- Time limits on the utility if any technology product
- Underestimation of the importance of market research as a tool for software vendors—"know your market"
- Demise of long development cycles—rapid, iterative products win the day
- Variance in software developer productivity—some developers provide productivity in quantum proportions

The business of creating new software, services and products in this new environment is difficult at best. It is more difficult if software vendors lack the necessary resources such as marketing, finance, and research and development to enable products to reach the marketplace.

So part of the answer to the question "How can we survive?" is to learn to cooperate and collaborate. Form alliances and partner with other organizations in mutually beneficial relationships.

Software vendors and ISVs can learn much from other industries that have learned to cooperate and collaborate with one another for the greater interest of all parties. Numerous examples are now legend.

- Banks cooperate on ATM withdrawals, which saves all banks money in facilities. They could cooperate on ATM deposits as well, as they do in the United Kingdom and Australia.
- The large newspapers *USA Today* and the *Chicago Tribune* cooperate with joint distribution and printing, even as they compete for readers and advertisers.
- FedEx and the U.S. Postal Service cooperate on mail carriage, and FedEx locates some of its boxes at post offices.
- Amazon.com and Toys 'R Us cooperate on an e-commerce infrastructure, because the toy retailer does not need online capability most of the year.

THE NEW ISV AGENDA

So, it is clear to many software organizations in the marketplace that modern strategies must be implemented to meet the new on demand business environment. What is also clear is that all software vendors alike must learn to co-operate and partner together for the benefit and profit of all concerned. Communication and collaboration together with partnering will lead to many strategic and tactile benefits:

- Maximizing customer value and satisfaction
- Building new long-term revenue streams/profit models
- Managing the market and expectations
- Balancing short and long-term business flow
- Reduced sales cycles—shorter time to contracts

- Ensuring quality on-time delivery of products and services
- Reducing business expenses and increasing profits
- Reducing the risks to the customer
- Penetrating new business markets

This list is compelling and makes good business sense. IBM's strategy focuses on the thousands of ISVs that are important to them either because they are key to a given brand or because they are important niche or local ISVs. The IBM strategy is to go after the broad spectrum of ISVs with a much stronger value proposition. There is a lot of energy now throughout IBM going into these efforts. IBM will aggressively seek out these ISVs and communicate the value to them of partnering with IBM. Then it is possible to go and make money together in the marketplace with autonomic computing. With partners, it is a good business to be in.

ISVS DRIVE THE AUTONOMIC MARKETPLACE

Independent Software Vendors (ISVs) are starting to drive the acceptance and adoption of auto-nomic computing. The need for Intelligent Management software that integrates and automates is the fundamental message underpinning the movement in which ISVs play a leading role. They achieve this by partnering with IBM in building the essential applications for the e-business on demand arena. Designed for the IBM infrastructure and systems management products that are already enabled, ISVs will be arming their mutual customers with applications that are part of a complete autonomic environment.

Autonomic computing is in a state of rapid development, and ISVs are catalysts, helping this technology reach market maturity. To further autonomic adoption—first by innovators, then by the early majority, and finally by the masses—ISVs play a critical role in the proliferation of this and nearly all new technology initiatives. ISV acceptance of autonomic computing as a whole, as well as IBM's strategic direction, is critical for its penetration into the marketplace. ISVs must develop and enable their mainstream enterprise solutions for autonomic computing in order for their customers to begin to reap the benefits of this self-management technology.

To develop their solutions, ISVs will be able to leverage the IBM's investment in already-enabled software, servers, and available services. For example, the Tivoli software is one "super-glue that binds" autonomic computing across IBM brands and product families:

- eServer (xSeries, iSeries, zSeries, pSeries)
- Software Group (DB2, Lotus, Tivoli, WebSphere)
- Personal and Printing Systems Group (desktop, ThinkPad, IntelliStation, printing)
- Storage Systems Group
- IBM Global Services
- Peripherals and Options

EARLY ADOPTERS AND IBM

Building on leading IBM solutions, ISV partners will be able to establish a strong leadership position for themselves with early market entry of their autonomic solutions. Through the entire life cycle of the technology, early adopting ISVs can build a strong customer base and establish solid reputations as pioneers in the field.

Working with IBM, early adopter ISVs will help define industry standards, as well as gain early access to the technology. Through the PartnerWorld for Developers program, ISV members will have codevelopment and comarketing opportunities, technical support, application testing, and validation at IBM Solution Partnership Centers, as well as intensive Web-based, self-guided education offerings.

ISVs that have existing applications with autonomic products qualify for unique program offerings, like Ready for Tivoli. Ready for Tivoli is the official program through which selected Business Partner products are designed, tested, and validated for seamless integration with Tivoli solutions.

A SAMPLE LIST OF ISVs

The many ISVs that have joined with IBM to support the autonomic computing effort include:

PeopleSoft

PeopleSoft is a leading Internet applications company and major software developer with offices in the United States and around the world.

PeopleSoft Inc., Worldwide Headquarters
4460 Hacienda Drive
Pleasanton, CA 94588-8618

See more information at *http://www.peoplesoft.com/corp/en/public_index.jsp.*

Legato

Legato delivers worldwide enterprise software solutions and services to customers on a global basis.

Legato Inc.,
2350 West El Camino Real
Mountain View, CA 94040

See more information at *http://legato.com/index.cfm.*

Crystal Decisions

Crystal Decisions is a provider of business intelligence software, services, reporting, analysis, and information delivery products.

Crystal Decisions, Inc.
895 Emerson Street
Palo Alto, CA 94301-2413

See more information at *http://www.crystaldecisions.com/*.

Tripwire

Tripwire is a provider of software that reduces operational risks and ensures the security and availability of networks.

Tripwire, Inc.
326 SW Broadway, 3rd Floor
Portland, OR 97205

See more information at *http://tripwire.com/*.

Talking Blocks

Talking blocks provides Web services management systems to integrate and manage Web service deployments.

Talking Blocks, Inc.
120 Montgomery Street, Suite #1370
San Francisco, CA 94104

See more information at *http://www.talkingblocks.com/index.htm*.

J. D. Edwards

J.D. Edwards, which has now merged with PeopleSoft, provides a range of enterprise-wide software and services.

J.D. Edwards Corporate World Headquarters
One Technology Way
Denver, CO 80237

See more information at *http://www.jdedwards.com/*

Brio Software

Brio Software is a provider of business performance software and other enterprise software.

Brio Software, Inc.
4980 Great America Parkway
Santa Clara, CA 95054

See more information at *http://www.hyperion.com/news_events/brio/*

Adobe

Adobe creates software for graphics, layout, and video applications for the home and office.

Adobe Systems Incorporated
345 Park Avenue
San Jose, CA 95110-2704

See more information at *http://www.adobe.com/main.html.*

Their support, endorsing autonomic computing, sends a clear message to the industry that IBM's strategy is right on target. Today's customers are asking their ISVs for total solutions that reduce risk. While many ISVs only sell software, they are finding that working with a hardware solutions partner such as IBM accelerates the sales process, reduces risk, saves time and money, speeds up the implementation of delivering total solutions to their customers, and improves customer satisfaction.

TOOLS AND TEMPLATES

The technologies IBM introduced to ISV developers along with the technology map include the following:

- Log and trace tool—Designed to locate problems, it frees up time for systems administrators by eliminating the manual task of tracking down the cause of a system problem by putting the log data from different system components into a common format. IBM expects this tool will help bridge the gap between identifying glitches and debugging affected applications and middleware.
- ABLE (Agent Building and Learning Environment) Rules Engine for Complex Analysis—ABLE is a set of learning and reasoning components built with software agents that, through the use of special monitoring software, can capture and share individual and organizational knowledge.
- Monitoring Engine providing Autonomic Monitoring capability—Developed by IBM's Tivoli brand, this technology detects resource outages and potential problems before they impact system performance. The monitoring engine features self-healing technology to allow systems to quickly recover from situations.
- Business Workload Management for Heterogeneous Environments—This tool helps isolate the causes of bottlenecks in the system through response time measurement, reporting of transaction processing segments, and dynamic learning of transaction

workflow through servers and middleware. This technology will begin to roll out in the IBM Tivoli Monitoring for Transaction Performance product. Chapter 15 will have more on the autonomic workings of IBM's Tivoli product.

AUTONOMIC COMPUTING BUSINESS PARTNER INITIATIVE

IBM is already working to make autonomic computing systems a reality with the introduction of advanced technologies across the IBM portfolio of products and services. These exciting developments in autonomic computing technologies are delivering to customers computing systems that are more self-managing, resilient, responsive, efficient, and secure.

Because business partners are an integral part of making this vision a reality, IBM announced the autonomic computing Business Partner initiative. As part of this initiative, IBM offers technical consultation that will provide a high-level exchange on design and architecture topics to qualified business partners who are in the process of building similar autonomic computing solutions.

Among the offerings are:

- Marketing and sales support
- Education and certification
- Technical support
- Incentives
- Financing
- Relationship management and membership communications

As a link connecting IBM and its customers, the global network of reselling and ISV partners is crucial to the successful delivery of any technology.

As Figure 13.1 shows, there are many benefits to be gained by becoming an IBM business partner.

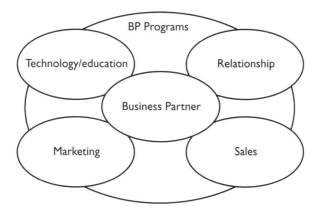

Figure 13.1   The benefits of the IBM Business Partner initiative.

If ISVs want to extend their products and become major players to be reckoned with in the global market, they have to make use of strategic alliances. These alliances need to be made with organizations, such as IBM, that dominate the marketplace. Other industries, such as transport, airline, and building and construction, that are only now realizing the benefits of partnering and alliances could have used this lesson. These industries recognize that few organizations have the skills or resources to meet the demands of their market.

The software sector needs to acknowledge this too. With the convergence of the IT, telecommunications, and content markets, new alliance business models—which will be a mix of technology, regulation, competition, globalization and skills—need to emerge.

AUTONOMIC ALLIANCE WITH CISCO

IBM and Cisco announced a set of open software technologies designed to increase the end-to-end intelligence and responsiveness of the global IT infrastructure—representing a major advancement in the development of "self-healing" computing systems and networks.

IBM and Cisco are working on a set of proposed technologies and standards to create a common language to detect, log, and resolve system problems. Cisco intends to integrate these technologies into its products and services. Together the system and network enhancements will help to enable a self-healing enterprise infrastructure.

Pioneered in the development labs of both companies, the new problem determination technologies are envisioned as the basis for a standardized exchange of problem determination data across the IT enterprise. These new technologies lay the foundation for systems and networks to detect, analyze, correlate, and resolve IT problems and automatically diagnose the root cause of problems in complex systems. Customer data centers have a large set of products with diverse and often proprietary instrumentation, which makes end-to-end analysis difficult or impossible.

Adapting an architected, standards-based design will result in an infrastructure that helps enable delivery of end-to-end problem determination and problem remediation.

"Given the pressures on budgets, time, and skills, our work on standards based technologies for problem determination will make it faster and easier to improve availability and reduce downtime in their IT infrastructure."[1]

The new technologies are part of the commitment of both IBM and Cisco to develop and drive open standards. The two companies are working across the industry to develop an open standards approach. IBM has submitted a Common Base Event (CBE) format, which is envisioned as the basis for standardized exchange of problem determination data via Web services, to the OASIS Standards Body.

Once problem determination tools and processes are implemented, enterprises have the ability to diagnose problems more quickly—often before they happen—reducing downtime and the associated revenue losses.

Building and implementing networked self-healing systems into the enterprise environment is a gradual process, one IBM has already begun helping the industry to undergo, by developing a common approach and terminology to architecting autonomic computing systems. IBM is also working with the business partner community, providing ISVs with the latest technologies as well as supporting them in bringing new applications to market with these latest capabilities, all built around open standards.

One of the factors contributing to the complexity in problem determination is the multitude of ways that different parts of a system report events, conditions, errors, and alerts. Today, even simple e-business solutions may contain as many as 25 to 40 logging mechanisms. These log files contain a variety of content formats because systems are built using disparate pieces and parts, often with products from multiple vendors. Technology developed by the IBM Research Division has been crucial in overcoming these difficulties by providing a way to automatically learn the format of log files, thereby reducing the time required to process and develop interfaces to new log data (often from days to hours).

The network has always played a pivotal role in enabling companies to automate their business processes. As the network increases in strategic value, the intelligence of the network becomes the determining factor in customer success. Cisco continues to lead in the creation of integrated intelligent networks through the delivery of faster, smarter, longer-lasting systems, services, products, and technologies. During this process, businesses can expect to see value on numerous levels, including a reduced total cost of ownership, and improved availability and productivity.

IBM and Cisco have a global strategic alliance, which offers customers a whole new horizon. The two companies draw on their strengths in Internet infrastructure, e-business systems, networks, and services to deliver end-to-end Internet business solutions to enterprises and service providers.

THE ACQUISITION OF THINK DYNAMICS

IBM's decision to acquire Think Dynamics, a privately held company headquartered in Toronto, Canada, was a bold move in its autonomic computing strategy. Think Dynamics' software capability accelerates a critical element of IBM's strategy to help customers respond more quickly to changing business needs—such as peaks in demand and potential system failures—by dynamically allocating the right computing resources at the right time to the processes, minimizing human error in the process.

To achieve an on demand operating environment, the system must be integrated, virtualized, and automated. For automation to be effective across the whole environment, it must be able to provide high availability, optimize the use of resources, secure the infrastructure, and provision resources as required by the business needs. To make this automation successful, the system must choreograph or orchestrate the changes across many disciplines. The automation blueprint in Figure 13.2 defines for customers how they can achieve this automated, on demand operating environment.

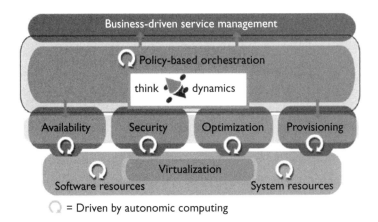

Figure 13.2   Think Dynamics enhances IBM automation computing by providing a way for customers to define their path to automate their environments to achieve on demand. With Think Dynamics, they have the ability to use a wider range of provisioning automation capabilities to maximize the utilization of their existing IT assets to achieve that goal.

This type of automated systems management tied to business needs is known as "orchestrated provisioning" and is a key component of IBM's e-business on demand. Orchestrated provisioning allows customers to respond quickly to business requirements, thus freeing up a company's IT staff to focus more on its core business needs. Based on autonomic technology, orchestrated provisioning obtains real-time feedback on the state of the IT environment, checks the status against business policies, and makes changes by dynamically reallocating a broad variety of computing resources—including servers, middleware, applications, storage systems, and network interfaces—in an orchestrated and coordinated manner.

Think Dynamics capability is unique in the industry in that it is based on key open standards, such as Web services, which allow customers to automatically and dynamically provision resources based on the unique policies and processes of their business. The Think Dynamics products are built on open technologies such as J2EE, XML, and SOAP, which make them easy to integrate with IBM's products as well as third-party systems-management products. By acquiring a leading provider of provisioning software, IBM will bring customers a platform-agnostic solution that further unlocks the value of an on demand infrastructure.

Think Dynamics capability changes the business response from "just in case" provisioning, where expensive resources, such as backup systems for disaster recovery, sit idle "just in case" they are needed, to "on demand" provisioning, in which resources that support lower-priority work can be dynamically reallocated to meet higher-priority needs in minutes. The result for customers will be an on demand capability that aligns IT more closely with business priorities, reducing costs through increased efficiency and better utilization of current IT investments

For example, a bank running an online financing promotion within a traditional IT environment might need to begin preparing months in advance for the potential surge in Web traffic. IT personnel would identify and manually prepare servers, middleware, and other technology to manage resources according to IT policy, which dictates that when an IT system reaches its defined utilization threshold, additional resources must be brought online to balance the workload. Orchestrated provisioning can automate this process, eliminating guesswork. Sensing that a server has reached its peak utilization level, Think Dynamics capability would locate and deploy the appropriate resources and begin sharing the workload. Additional resources would be deployed as needed, and then redeployed back to their normal state when the promotion ends and Web traffic decreases.

In addition, Think Dynamics capability supports heterogeneous environments, so it works with companies' existing IT infrastructures, enabling them to transform themselves into on demand businesses in a straightforward and evolutionary fashion. Think Dynamics capability also supports clustering capabilities, like WebSphere clustering, which enable the dynamic addition of Web services across a cluster of WebSphere servers.

The ability to automatically manage IT resources will help customers get more value out of their technology investments. With the acquisition of Think Dynamics, a leader in IT resource provisioning, IBM promises to be at the cutting edge of this technology.

The incorporation of orchestrated provisioning capabilities will enable organizations to more rapidly achieve the promise of utility computing—accessing processing power and applications where and when a customer needs them. Customers may choose to build it on their own, have IBM build it for them, or leverage IBM utility services on an ongoing basis to provide their company IT and business functions on demand. This capability will be supported via IGS' Utility Management Infrastructure (UMI), which allows companies to begin benefiting from utility computing today by enabling them to integrate and run e-business processes and related applications on a dynamic, consolidated infrastructure.

Think Dynamics will be integrated into IBM software products and leveraged throughout the IBM portfolio of products. In the first instance, expect that Think Dynamics products will be available through IBM Tivoli software, with others to follow.

The combination of Think Dynamics and IBM's products should bring great benefits to IBM customers. It's a leap forward for changing the management of IT resources from a reactive, over provisioning approach that wastes resources to a proactive approach that provisions and delivers just the right amount of resource, when it's needed. As Forrester Research summed up the deal: Small Buy, Big Impact.[2]

SUMMARY AND CONCLUSIONS

IBM is an undisputed leader in hardware/software, services and infrastructure, and core applications but relies on ISVs to achieve vertical market dominance and new market penetration. By enabling ISVs with an integrated platform and open standards information architecture in its autonomic development environment, IBM and its partners can provide horizontal- and vertical-market solutions to the small, medium, and large enterprise. This has to be good news for all concerned.

To create new, long-term business requires major shifts in technology, like autonomic computing. Major companies such as IBM develop these new technologies; thereafter alliances and business partner programs create the future profits. The large companies like IBM are entrenched in their positions due to their enormous financial stability, marketing clout, large customer base, and sales and distribution networks. In this environment, it is difficult for small, or even medium, size ISVs to compete.

The president of Tripwire, a leading ISV, sums up the value of the relationship with IBM.

> "Tripwire shares in the IBM vision of a future in which IT is more reliable and the lives of IT professionals more livable. We believe autonomic computing provides the means to make that vision a reality, and we are proud to partner with IBM in this endeavor."

> —W. Wyatt Starnes, founder and CEO of Tripwire, Inc.[3]

NOTES

1. Remarks by Mike Loughram. IBM Press Release, October 10, 2003.
2. Forrester Research TechStrategy Brief, May 2003
3. See comments in article, *http://www-306.ibm.com/autonomic/pdfs*.

CHAPTER 14

OTHER VENDORS

INTRODUCTION

G lobal sales for autonomic computing systems and other similar approaches are going be very large. From large enterprise-wide products and services to smaller additional software products that will be added to existing products, customers can expect a wide range of products that will fit their requirements from all vendors. This—together with the growing problem of IT complexity, the need to simplify operations, and to reduce staffing and costs—will accelerate the need for enterprise solutions of all kinds. For large, medium, and small businesses, the problems are the same—complexity, costs, and staffing. This means that many software vendors will develop and produce products to meet and solve these needs. The purpose of this chapter is to briefly review some of the other vendors who have entered the market or are in the process of developing products.

Including IBM, there are four vendors whose products are leading the development and implementation of autonomous computing. The others are:

- Sun Microsystems—N1
- Hewlett-Packard—Data Center Utility
- Microsoft—Dynamic Systems Initiative

Other vendors will no doubt enter the market as and when they judge it necessary. This means that there will be broad, and growing, industry support for autonomous computing. The need to unify new hardware and software while harnessing industry-based standards for maximum penetration and satisfying customer needs is the driving force. The end result is a new generation of dynamic autonomous computing systems provided by a variety of vendors. This has to be good for corporations and their IT organizations. It is also about choice, which was referred to in Chapter 4.

When IBM announced its autonomous computing initiative, it mentioned that, as large as IBM is, with all its resources, financial strength, and research facilities, it could not go it alone. IBM referred this as the Grand Challenge—defined as:

> "A problem that by virtue of its degree of difficulty and the importance of its solution, both from a technical and societal point of view, becomes the focus of interest to a specific scientific community.
>
> "We call on our academic colleagues to drive the exploratory work in autonomic computing. We propose that the research community recognize it as an important field of academic endeavor. We also call on our partners at government labs to collaborate on crucial projects in this area. We plan to fund a regular stream of academic awards and fellowships to support research in this area and we call on others in the IT industry to do the same."[1]

IBM needs the support of the entire IT industry to focus its priorities on autonomic computing and acknowledge that we all must cooperate in developing the necessary standards and software to make this a reality. However, this is not easily achieved.

SUN—N1

N1 is Sun's vision for the next-generation data center. Sun's N1 manages widely distributed computing resources, such as servers, storage, software, and networks, and enables them to operate as a single entity.

In September 2002, Sun Microsystems, Inc., unveiled the road map for N1. By automating away the complexity associated with managing technology, business and IT managers will be able to optimize the utilization, efficiency, and agility of their data centers. N1 builds on over 20 years of Sun knowledge and R&D in system architectures to deliver what will be the cornerstone of the next generation of Sun's systems strategy. Such network-centric computing innovations as NFS (Network File System), Dynamic System Domains, Java technology, Solaris, and the Sun ONE Grid Engine software will help Sun to deliver the benefits of the N1 architecture to its customers.

N1 is focused on allowing companies to use their resources on added value projects and doing more with less. N1 is an evolution of the system that will have an impact on the data center. In the N1 world, customers can expand their IT resources to a larger scale, increase utilization rates exponentially, and deploy new services in shorter timeframes than with traditional approaches, without having to keep an army of systems administrators working on maintaining the network.

N1 Road Map

The N1 architecture enables utility computing, where customers "pay as they grow," and brings a new level to the way businesses manage technology. This is a long-term strategy and Sun will be rolling out N1 products to the market in a phased approach, according to the following road map, which is also illustrated in Figure 14.1:

1. **Phase 1—Virtualization (2002 on):** This first phase provides the basic infrastructure for N1. Here, customers will begin transforming individual computers, network elements, and storage systems into an aggregated pool of resources. The system allocates, monitors, and meters the usage of these resources.
2. **Phase 2—Services Provisioning (2003 on):** In Phase 2, administrators specify the business service definition for a service, such as eBanking, and N1 takes care of provisioning the resources required from the virtual computer created in Phase 1.
3. **Phase 3—Policy-Automation (2004 on):** Finally, in Phase 3, application service level objectives are automatically maintained by N1. Policies that reflect business requirements and priorities are defined and used to manage applications and their required network-wide resources. For example, the eBanking service set-up in Phase 2 can be set to give priority access to "VIP" clients.

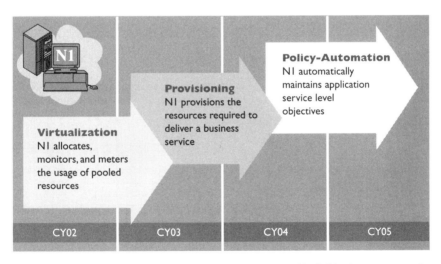

Figure 14.1   Sun's N1 product road map lays out the delivery of individual components from now until end of 2005.

Let us discuss each element of the road map in slightly greater detail:

Virtualization is the real-time pooling of heterogeneous computing, storage, and other network resources—a critical part of the N1 strategy. Virtualization simplifies network-centric computing by fostering a "wire once, reconfigure logically" capability. With N1, administrators need only cable their networks a single time. N1 manages the relationships between virtualized storage, computing, and network resources, and enables system administrators to assign selected resources to a specific application or business.

Once physical resources have been pooled, the next phase is to map business services onto the virtual resource pool. This is the provisioning level of the N1 architecture. The N1 Provisioning Server will play a key role here by creating logical server farms. The software captures all service requirements—network topology, processor types, software, and storage—describes them in software, and then implements the design from pooled resources. Once the server farm is created, the service can be mapped onto it. The software monitors its health and availability to help assure that the service is meeting the business's needs.

Policy and automation make up the third level of the N1 architecture. With policy-based automation, a customer can create a rule defining performance objectives for a given service. Based on set policies, N1 will manage the corporate environment, adding and removing resources as needed to maintain a particular service level objective.

N1 virtualization and provisioning technology offers a new and innovative method for simplifying the deployment and management of complex computing resources. With N1, the focus is not on the individual servers and storage systems. Rather, N1 is all about managing an IT infrastructure as a smoothly integrated whole. It's about making the data center behave as a single, unified system.

N1 is designed to reduce management complexity and cost, increase datacenter resource utilization, improve infrastructure responsiveness and agility, and ensure investment protection.

The N1 architecture:

- Makes datacenters work like systems.
- Unifies heterogeneous resources into "pools."
- Up-levels operation to business service.
- Enables policy-driven services and utility computing.

With N1, IT management and administration functions begin to operate in a shared real-time mode. In the past, an application had a dedicated server and set of storage assigned to it. Because applications aren't designed to share resources, nor can they predict what the user load will be at different times, each instance of an application needed to have its own excess capacity to handle peak usage loads.

N1 allows data center resource capacity to be shared by any number of services. So if one service requires additional capacity, while at the same time another requires less, N1 handles it. It's automatic.

N1 also enables administrators to manage a much larger number of systems because they manage the service, not the underlying resources. With N1, system administrators are now free to focus on maintaining service-level quality and implementing new competitive features. All of this adds up to increased business agility, reduced complexity, streamlined management, increased resources, and lower costs.

Conclusions

N1 is a bold effort by Sun, with a long-term vision for the new computing system infrastructure of the future and its customers. With such a fundamental set of changes in the specification, design, deployment, and operation of computing systems, N1 is a vision to be realized and adopted in phases when available.

MICROSOFT—DYNAMIC SYSTEMS INITIATIVE

In Redmond, Washington on March 18, 2003, Microsoft Corp. announced their Dynamic Systems Initiative (DSI). This initiative proposes to unify hardware, software, and service vendors around a software architecture that enables customers to harness the power of industry-standard hardware, and brings simplicity, automation, and flexibility to IT operations. The dynamic systems enabled by this software promise to streamline IT operations and lower costs for the enterprise datacenter and make datacenter capabilities accessible to a much broader array of businesses. The unifying software architecture centers on a System Definition Model (SDM) embedded in operating systems, which provides a common contract between development, deployment, and operations across the IT life cycle.

The SDM is an XML-based standard that captures and unifies the operational requirements of applications with datacenter policies, serving as an explicit contract between development, deployment, and operations across the IT life cycle. Tools supporting SDM will give IT managers the ability to explicitly define datacenter standards and policies for development, and will give developers the ability to encode operational requirements into their applications at design time. In the datacenter, the operating system's support of SDM will enable IT professionals to automatically provision and dynamically change applications, along with their underlying resources, as workload or business needs change.

The components of the SDM will include:

- Automated Deployment Services—A provisioning and administration tool.
- Windows System Resource Manager—Dynamic systems resource management.
- Volume Shadow Copy Services—A Virtual Disk Service. Storage virtualization.
- Network Load Balancing—Dynamic load-balancing for managing transactions.
- Windows Server Clustering—Giving high-availability and scalable services.
- Virtual Server—Virtual machine technology for consolidation and migration.

The concept is a milestone in Microsoft's Dynamic Systems Initiative (DSI) and represents the Microsoft's long-term collaboration with Hewlett-Packard to enable customers to harness the power of industry-standard hardware, maximize the value of their information technology systems, and achieve new levels of simplicity and automation.

MICROSOFT, HP, AND THE DYNAMIC DATA CENTER

In addition to the main DSI announcement Microsoft announced a few weeks later that it would showcase a concept of a Dynamic Data Center (DDC), jointly developed with Hewlett-Packard. The DDC features a combination of HP servers, software, storage, and networking hardware connected based on prescribed network architecture. Microsoft software dynamically assigns provisions and centrally manages the DDC resources. The software driving the DDC will enable customers to automatically deploy a distributed application; provision the associated server, storage, and networking resources required for that application; and dynamically allocate resources to grow and shrink based on business and workload demands.

The Dynamic Data Center concept is the result of more than a year of collaborative efforts between Microsoft and HP in support of the DSI and the underlying SDM. The SDM, a fundamental building block of the DSI architecture, is a live standard, the operational requirements of applications with datacenter policies.

Collaborating around the SDM, both Microsoft and HP contributed innovations throughout the DDC development process. The Windows Server™ Group at Microsoft first developed a prototype of a future version of Automated Deployment Services (ADS)—a server provisioning and administration tool for Windows Server 2003—extending its support for the SDM. This future version of ADS will enable centralized provisioning and management of a prescribed set of industry-standard servers, storage, and networking hardware.

HP contributed innovations in hardware, including prototypical development of an Authenticated Identity for its ProLiant servers to better enhance server boot security. HP also developed prototype SDM-enabled software providers, which allow Microsoft's software to provision and manage HP ProLiant Servers, HP ProCurve switches, and HP StorageWorks disk arrays. Microsoft also collaborates with HP due in part to HP's expertise in datacenter innovation.

Microsoft will integrate two products and create a new management software facility and product suite called the Systems Center. The Management of Operations (MOM) product, an event and performance monitoring tool, and the Systems Management Server (SMS), which provides resourcing and deployment services, will be combined into the new product. The Systems Center will be used to automatically manage everything from desktops and laptops to PDAs to full-scale applications and servers. The Center will provide a set of tools for application management, performance management and trending, and capacity and resource management.

TRUSTWORTHY COMPUTING

Although not directly related to self-managing software, Microsoft's Trustworthy computing initiative is worth a review in terms of its scope and potential for creating reliable systems. However, on closer analysis, the Trustworthy Computing initiative does have similar functionality to autonomic computing. In January 2002, Bill Gates issued a call to action challenging all of Microsoft's 50,000 employees to build a Trustworthy Computing environment for customers that is as reliable as the electricity that powers homes and businesses today. Software security is an ongoing challenge. Viruses, worms, trap doors, and other security problems are experienced throughout the industry on a daily basis. To address these facts, Microsoft has made Trustworthy computing a key initiative for all its products. Trustworthy Computing is a framework for developing devices powered by computers and software that are as secure and trustworthy as the everyday devices and appliances in use at home such as water, electricity, and the telephone. The basic redesign of Microsoft's products is a step toward making this vision a reality.

Resilient technology is crucial to building secure computing environments, but technology alone cannot completely answer the threats as they evolve. Well-designed products, established and effective processes, and knowledgeable, well-trained operational teams are all required to build and operate an environment that provides high levels of security and functionality.

The Think Tank

Microsoft management and leading academic security and privacy research scientists from around the world have established a Trustworthy Computing Academic Advisory Board. The board was formed to advise the company on security, privacy, and reliability enhancements in its products and technologies, so that Microsoft can obtain feedback on product and policy issues related to its Trustworthy Computing initiative. The board is composed of leading research scientists and privacy policy experts, each with a significant track record in his or her field of expertise, who meet regularly to review progress and set objectives.

Goals for Trustworthy

The four goals defined by Microsoft are straightforward and direct, as shown in Table 14.1.

Microsoft has created a framework to track and measure its progress in meeting the goals and objectives of Trustworthy Computing: such as secure by design, secure by default, secure in deployment, and communications. Table 14.2 summaries the scope and progress of this initiative so far.

The goal of *secure by design* is to eliminate all security vulnerabilities *before* product ships and to add features that enhance product security. Secure by design requires:

- Building a secure architecture—Bank buildings are designed around security requirements. Their architecture is a direct consequence of the need for a bank vault and other

Table 14.1 The Four Goals for Trustworthy Computing

Goals	The Basis for a Customer's Decision to Trust a System
Security	The customer can expect that systems are resilient to attack, and that the confidentiality, integrity, and availability of the system and its data are protected
Privacy	The customer is able to control data about themselves, and those using such data adhere to fair information principles
Reliability	The customer can depend on the product to fulfill its functions when required to do so
Business integrity	The vendor of a product behaves in a responsive and responsible manner

Table 14.2 A Summary of the Trustworthy Computing Initiative and the Progress Made So Far

SD Communications	What Does It Mean?	Progress to Date
Security by design	• Secure architecture • Security aware features • Reduce vulnerability in codes	• Secutiry training for Microsoft engineers • Security code reviews • Threat modeling
Secure by default	• Reduce surface attack area • Unused features turned off by default • Only require minimum privileges	• Office XP SP1: VBScript off by default • No sample code installed by default • IIS off by defaul in Visual Studio Net
Secure in deployment	• Protect, detect, defend, recover • Manage • Process: how-to's, architectural guides • People training	• Deployment tools (MBSA, IIS Lockdown) • Created STPP to respond to customers • PAG for Windows 2000 security
Communications	• Clear security commitments • Full member of the security community • Microsoft Security Response Center	• MSRC severity rating • Free virus hotline • MSDN security guidance for developers

ancillary security features. Software can be designed for security in the same manner. Microsoft is now designing and building products around security from the start.

- Adding security features—Microsoft is extending product feature sets to enable new security capabilities.
- Reducing the number of vulnerabilities in new and existing code—Microsoft is improving its internal development process to make developers more conscious of security issues while designing and developing software. This includes training and peer review of code.

The key approach of *secure by default* is for Microsoft and other software vendors to ship products that are more secure by turning off services that are not required in many customer scenarios and by reducing the permissions that are granted automatically. These efforts minimize the "surface area" available for attack. Making a conscious decision to invoke these services increases the likelihood of their being appropriately managed and monitored.

Secure by design and secure by default are very important, but they apply only when products are being created. *Secure in deployment* is equally, or even more, critical because the operation of computers and network systems is an ongoing activity. Therefore, Microsoft is stepping up support for customers to help them with these five distinct, but closely related activities:

- Protecting systems by ensuring that the right people, processes, and technologies are in place to help ensure that data is accessible only to trusted users, and that systems are configured properly and updated as needed to assist in keeping unauthorized users out. Network protection is like locking the doors of your home to keep out intruders.
- Detecting attempted intrusions, violations of security, operational problems, unexpected behavior, or prefailure indications. Detection is analogous to arming your home alarm so you're alerted to potential danger.
- Defending systems by taking automatic corrective action when a security violation occurs or is suspected. Defense is like calling in the police during an attack. This is the same objective as autonomic computing
- Recovering computers that have been compromised, are suspect, or have failed depends on having the right systems and processes in place to restore a machine and its data to a last known good state while minimizing its downtime. Recovery is like calling the insurance company to take care of damage after a break-in. In IT, this means having backup systems in place that enable quick restoration of infected systems to a previously known good state.

Communications are also important: Vendors should clearly and often communicate their objectives, progress, and long-term strategy so that customers are aware of the issues and plans. In addition, there are other communications practices that can be implemented quickly and easily, such as:

- Getting accurate information and software patches distributed quickly when vulnerabilities are discovered.
- Helping customers understand how to enhance system security with tools and prescriptive guides.
- Being constantly vigilant and providing warning of new attacks and new best practices that evolve in response to threats and changes in technology.

Trustworthy Summary

Trustworthy Computing is a bold initiative on Microsoft's part. It is inherent to autonomic computing, and several objectives overlap. The concept of providing computing that is as trusted and reliable as the utility industries, such as electricity, gas and, the telephone, is indeed praiseworthy, necessary, and attainable. Achieving these high standards will not be easy and, like autonomic computing, is another grand challenge that the entire industry must embrace.

HP—THE ADAPTIVE ENTERPRISE

Hewlett-Packard's approach to autonomic computing is embraced in its Adaptive Enterprise strategy, as illustrated in Figure 14.2. HP's vision for this approach is to provide tools, services, and products that deliver IT service levels that match the flow of real-time business activities or changes whenever needed—during excessive load times and when there are lulls in business activity. HP Adaptive Management offerings are comprised of products that enable IT management to implement an adaptive infrastructure that is agile and can be swiftly changed as the business needs change. There is a dynamic link between the IT infrastructure and the business process. They are closely aligned and mapped together.

The Adaptive Enterprise model is designed around the following policies.

1. All IT resources are shared, not isolated or compartmentalized into specific departments, business units, or lines of business, as they are today. The "silo" approaches of the past cannot be tolerated any further.
2. Business priorities are the determining factor for the allocation of IT resources.
3. Service levels and detailed system expectations are defined preciously, and this will drive the business services.

Corporations must respond in the on demand environment, given the global marketplace and the volatility of the economic landscape. HP responds to this challenge with the Adaptive Enterprise approach—establish an IT environment that can change quickly or respond to the market or clients. It should be able to deal with a number of demands such as:

- Mergers and acquisitions, the integration of new businesses.
- Dynamic changes in the global marketplace.
- Totally new business models.

- Fluid relationships with clients, partners, or suppliers.

The Adaptive Enterprise is designed to provide business benefits that include:

1. **Better Quality Service**—Through agility, senior IT management can meet the demands of the business and meet the terms of service level agreements.
2. **Simplification**—Establishing a standard architecture that can adapt and change quickly leads to greater overall simplified systems, procedures and operations.
3. **Reduced Risk**—If the total environment is simplified and streamlined, the risks of deployment of new applications and implementation are reduced.
4. **Business Costs**—Budgets will be reduced and the total cost of ownership will be lower.

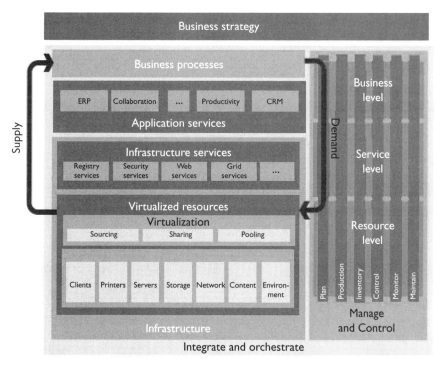

Figure 14.2 The HP reference architecture named Darwin. Each business segment is defined and managed with interaction with the levels. The business applications interface through the infrastructure services that provide all the elements, such as Web services and security, that call the resources needed—printers, storage, servers, and so on. On the right of the diagram, the management and control elements are provided at three levels—the business level, the service level, and the resource level. Each level has layers, such as plan, provision, inventory, control, monitor, and maintain.

Sharing IT resources eliminates underutilized or overdeployed pockets of resources; it spreads the load and smooths out any components. Sharing resources across lines of business can help corporations become much more agile, respond to threats or opportunities quicker, and be more responsive to existing customers. Further, sharing IT resources will reduce the costs by simplifying the task of managing those resources. It means few managers are needed to manage.

The HP vision for the Adaptive Enterprise is build around the HP Darwin Reference Architecture, shown in Figure 14.2. This architecture includes the basic elements for an agile or adaptive infrastructure and includes HP software solutions, services, and products.

INTEL—PROACTIVE COMPUTING

Another project of note is Intel's research into proactive computing. A new era of computing is on the horizon. In this new era, billions of computing devices will be deeply embedded within our physical environment. These tiny sensors and actuators will silently serve us, acquiring and acting on a multitude of data to improve our lives and make us more productive. However, today's model of interactive computing, whereby individuals interact one-on-one with computers, inputting commands and waiting for responses, will not scale to the new environment.

The interactive computing model is already showing its limitations, as we begin to confront the challenges of dealing with multiple computers, from desktop and laptop systems to cell phones, PDAs, and a growing variety of consumer electronic devices. When we each have hundreds or thousands of devices to deal with, it will be impossible for us to interact directly with each one. Intel proposes that the time has come to transition from interactive to *proactive* computing. Proactive computers will anticipate our needs and take action on our behalf. Instead of serving as glorified input/output devices, humans will be freed to focus on higher-level functions.

Intel has identified three steps that are essential to making proactive computing a reality. The first is *getting physical*—connecting billions of computing devices directly to the physical world around them so that human beings are no longer their principal I/O devices. The next step is *getting real*—having computers running in real time or even ahead of real time, anticipating human needs rather than simply responding to them; early examples include airbags and antilock brakes. The third step is *getting out*—extending the role of computers from the office and home into the world around us and into new application domains.

Small, inexpensive, low-powered sensors and actuators, deeply embedded in our physical environment, can be deployed in large numbers, interacting and forming networks to communicate, adapt, and coordinate higher-level tasks. As we network these micro devices, we'll be pushing the Internet not just into different locations but deep into the embedded platforms within each location. This will enable us to achieve hundredfold increases in the size of the Internet beyond the growth we're already anticipating. And it will require new and different methods of networking devices to one another and to the Internet.

Increased access to data is a necessary, though not sufficient, condition if we are to obtain greater productivity gains from human endeavors. As we move up the stack and integrate data from the world around us, we must learn to deal with uncertainty. The physical world does not exhibit the deterministic behaviors computer scientists have come to know, model, and love.

Anticipation

In the era of proactive computing, software will anticipate our needs. Excess computation and communication capacity will be harnessed to fetch and manipulate information, producing answers before they are required—much as a chess champion predicts his opponent's moves many steps into the future. We see glimpses of anticipation today, both in the speculative execution features of Intel's processors and in some of the most advanced Web proxy engines. Intel's project is related to the emergence of a new genre of machine learning tools that is firmly grounded in statistical methods. Systems such as those under development by Stanford, University of Washington, and Carnegie Mellon University exploit uncertainty to support new software techniques, a key stepping stone to anticipation.

Once proactive computing has learned to manage uncertainty and can get computers to anticipate needs, the next challenge is bridging the gap between anticipating those needs and acting on them. The difficult step is not so much in determining the action to be taken, but to develop the feedback and control mechanisms essential to the stable operation of any closed loop system. Today, most systems rely on human beings to close the loop and provide stability, placing human beings under intolerable stress.

Figure 14.3 summarizes the research challenges facing this project.

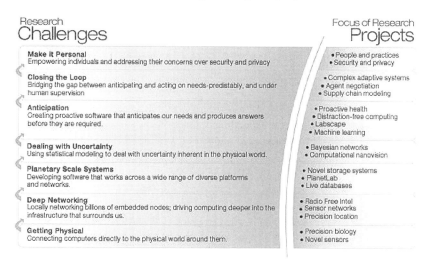

Figure 14.3   A summary of the Intel Proactive Project.

AUTONOMIC ALLIANCE WITH CISCO

We briefly discussed the alliance between IBM and Cisco in Chapter 3. IBM and Cisco are collaborating on a set of open software technologies designed to increase the end-to-end intelligence and responsiveness of the global IT infrastructure—representing a major advancement in the development of "self-healing" computing systems and networks. IBM and Cisco are working on a set of proposed technologies and standards creating a common language to detect, log, and resolve system problems.

Cisco started developing its own version of autonomic computing and called it the Adaptive Services Framework (ASF). It soon became apparent to senior Cisco management that there was a good deal of synergy and overlap with IBM's autonomic computing projects, and it made good sense to think about a joint venture.

ASF is a series of proposed interfaces and formats that allows customers to interact with service providers. ASF enables automation detection, diagnosis, and rectification of a wide range of systems problems and support services. ASF is leveraged on autonomic aspects of self-configuring, self-healing, self-optimizing, and self-protecting and is being developed along the same processes. Cisco intends to integrate these technologies into its products and services. Together, the system and network enhancements will help to enable a self-healing enterprise infrastructure.

Pioneered in the development labs of both companies, the new problem determination technologies are envisioned as the basis for standardized exchange of problem determination data across the IT enterprise. These new technologies lay the foundation for systems and networks to detect, analyze, correlate, and resolve IT problems and automatically diagnose the root cause of a problem in complex systems. Customer datacenters have a large set of products with diverse and often proprietary instrumentation, which makes end-to-end analysis difficult or impossible.

Building and implementing networked self-healing systems into the enterprise environment is a gradual process, one IBM has already begun helping the industry to undergo, by developing a common approach and terminology to architecting autonomic computing systems.

One of the factors contributing to the complexity in problem determination is the multitude of ways that different parts of a system report events, conditions, errors, and alerts. Today, even simple e-business solutions may contain as many as 25 to 40 logging mechanisms. These log files contain a variety of content formats because systems are built using disparate pieces and parts, often with products from multiple vendors. Technology developed by the IBM has been crucial in overcoming these difficulties by providing a way to automatically learn the format of log files, thereby reducing the time required to process and develop interfaces to new log data (often from days to hours).

The network has always played a pivotal role in enabling companies to automate their business processes. As the network increases in strategic value, the intelligence of the network becomes the determining factor in customer success. Cisco continues to lead in the creation of integrated intelligent networks through the delivery of faster, smarter, longer-lasting systems, services, products, and technologies. During this process, businesses can expect to see value on numerous levels, including a reduced total cost of ownership, and improved availability and productivity.

The two companies draw on their strengths in Internet infrastructure, e-business systems, networks, and services to deliver end-to-end Internet business solutions to enterprises and service providers.

Today's Network Challenges

On the networking side of IT, increased complexity has resulted in many significant challenges, especially in network software products, protocols, and services. This is caused by the rapid implementation of thousands of network products and features in combination with high transaction rates in multiple vendor environments. One basic problem is the understanding of how these products work and behave, and the results that they give. ASF can address this problem by providing a range of tools, from simple network management to advanced monitoring, and analysis of problems and behavior. ASF is the superglue that joins the front and back end systems together.

Figure 14.4 describes the logical progression of the Adaptive Networking Progression.

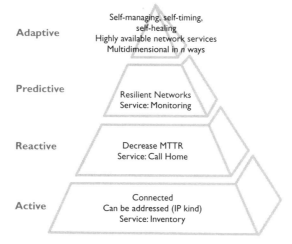

Figure 14.4 The stages of Cisco's Adaptive Networking Progression. Note the similarity to the levels of autonomic computing.

The four levels can be described as follows:

1. The first level is the active stage. Here the network has the capability of addressing and communicating with devices and protocols.

2. At the reactive stage, the network can react to problems and take steps for remediation. ASF is considered to be reactive at this stage.

3. At the predictive stage, the network is monitoring and making intelligent decisions according to predetermined service level agreements.

4. The last stage, adaptive, builds on the previous three stages, so the network can be optimized, automated, and self-managed.

The Adaptive Network Framework—Principles

The Adaptive Network Framework (ASF) consists of a number of principles, which have the characteristics of elements, rules, ontologies, and methodologies. The basic core functionality includes:

- Mechanisms for diagramming models of the network, devices, and servers in an autonomic format.
- Common Event Format, for events from a device to an adaptive or autonomic manager or network management system as well as those shared between agents and the network management system.
- A common format to analyze events and discard unwanted events.
- A common format that can describe symptoms and problems based on actual network events.
- Standardized message formats for exchange with operational autonomic or adaptive elements.
- Widespread adoption of industry-based open standards.

Conclusions

The development of autonomic management products in the network arena is needed. The timing of this joint venture is significant as this work is resulting in both products and services for both companies can only benefit the IT industry. This venture brings together two large vendors who have substantial resources to make it a success. We need to see more joint cooperation between other major vendors in the self-managing market.

OTHER MANAGEMENT SOFTWARE

Autonomic computing is in a state of rapid development, and other products from vendors are catalysts to help this technology reach market maturity. To further its adoption—first by innovators, then by the early majority, and finally by the masses—other software vendors play a critical role in the proliferation of this and all new technology initiatives.

The acceptance of autonomic computing as a whole, as well as IBM's strategic direction, is critical for its penetration into the marketplace. Vendors interested in providing other software tools must develop and enable their mainstream enterprise solutions for autonomic computing in order for their customers to begin to reap the benefits of this important new technology. Table 14.3 is a list of vendors by categories that are currently developing or have released software in the autonomic arena.

Table 14.3 Software Vendors Providing Autonomic-Type Software and Products

Software Type	Company Name
Distributed Load Balancing Software	• Cisco Systems
	• F5 Labs
	• Nortel
	• Radware
	• Resonate
	• Array Networks
Virtual Provisioning Software	• Egenera
	• Ensim
	• VM ware
Service Assurance Software	• BMC Software
	• Computer Associates
	• HP
Server or Service Provisioning Software	• Blade Logic
	• Centerun
	• Configuresoft
	• HP
	• Marimba
	• Microsoft
	• Moonlight
	• Novadigm
	• ON Technology
	• Opsware
	• Peakstone
	• Symantec
	• Veritas
Storage Provisioning Software	• ApplQ
	• Creekpath
	• EMC
	• Softek
	• EMC
	• Softek
	• Interscan
	• HP
	• Veritas
Workload Management Software	• Aurema

SUMMARY AND CONCLUSIONS

When a major vendor introduces a major new technology, it is normally an interesting event. It is the subject of much scrutiny in the media. Many analysts and reporters examine it for accuracy, fit to current business models, competitive fit to the marketplace, and so on. With every major new technology, decisions and opinions—whether good or bad—are always shaped.

What is particularly interesting is when the majority of major vendors introduce the same technology—albeit with different names and terminology. This has to be significant for IT senior management, CIOs, and the IT industry in general. Vendors are increasingly becoming customer-centric—providing real world solution solutions to meet the needs of the customers. This is the fundamental approach for autonomic computing, providing solutions that have real and definable business value, reducing costs and complexity, and providing self-management systems.

NOTE

1. Remarks made in IBM document, *http://www.research.ibm.com/autonomic/research/ papers/AC_Vision_Computer_Jan_2003.pdf.*

CHAPTER 15

THE TIVOLI MANAGEMENT SUITE— AUTONOMIC FEATURES

INTRODUCTION

To gain a better understanding of the autonomic features of the Tivoli Management Suite, you'll need some background information. IBM's Tivoli software suite consists of an underlying infrastructure containing a growing set of Tivoli and third-party management software applications that can utilize this framework to manage heterogeneous systems and applications in a consistent manner. Tivoli provides a standardized management interface to different operating systems and services. This allows administrators to manage users, systems, databases, networks, and applications from one interface and provides a streamlined way to automate and delegate routine time-consuming tasks.

A corporate IT infrastructure contains a large number of resources to manage. These resources can be network components, operating systems, databases, Web servers, Intranets, middleware, and off-the-shelf or custom applications. The foundation of the Tivoli Enterprise architecture is distributed object-oriented software called *Tivoli Framework*. Most of the applications of the Tivoli Enterprise suite use the services included in the framework. This means that when a major function in the framework is improved, these Tivoli applications can take advantage of the improvement. The Tivoli Framework also serves as a single point of integration for Tivoli and third-party applications. In addition to the framework, Tivoli Enterprise provides a suite of management products in the disciplines of deployment, availability, operations, and security management. These are often called the fundamental Tivoli management applications or the Tivoli core applications.

Tivoli provides software products in four distinct areas, namely:

1. Security—Providing access to the right resources at the right time.

2. Configuration and operations—Managing the change and complexity of your e-business infrastructure.

3. Performance and availability—Monitoring and optimizing the performance of your e-business infrastructure.

4. Storage management—Protecting and maximizing the integrity and availability of all business data.

The scope of systems management is wide-ranging and covers many product lines within IBM and third-party vendors. Figure 15.1 illustrates this coverage of the IBM portfolio of products and services.

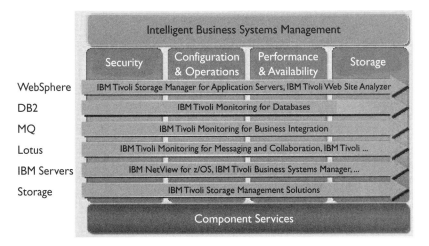

Figure 15.1   Coverage of IBM Tivoli products across the IBM portfolio of products and services.

When autonomic computing is integrated with Tivoli software products it provides solutions that:

- Increase responsiveness through provisioning by creating self-configuring systems.
- Ensure better business continuance with availability management through self-healing systems.
- Increase service delivery using workload management solutions that create self-optimizing systems.
- Protect corporate information and resources with security management solutions that foster self-protecting systems.

Now let us review the autonomic features—self-configuring, self-healing, self-optimizing, and self-protecting—of Tivoli in more detail.

SELF-CONFIGURING

Any corporation can greatly increase its responsiveness to both customers and employees by utilizing the autonomic capabilities of self-configuring systems. With this facility in place, systems can dynamically adjust and configure themselves to adapt to a changing environment. This can be achieved with the minimum of human intervention. The deployment of changes can take place rapidly with no disruption of service to customers. The periodic swings in business cycles are a prime example. Take the retail sector during holiday seasons. Peaks are experienced at different times at the end of the year. The self-configuring infrastructure can be automatically adjusted to reassign servers to cope with the loads. It seeks out resources that are available and underutilized and assigns them accordingly.

Tivoli software management tools are available to provision a wide range of resources such as systems, applications, and users, and access privileges as well as physical and logical storage. Monitoring and event correlation tools can determine when the changes are needed and initiate the actions. These changes can be implemented rapidly—in minutes rather than days or weeks

The software tools available in Tivoli for self-configuration include:

- **Tivoli Configuration Manager**
  The Configuration Manager automatically configures the IT environment and provides a scanning engine and state engine that can sense when software on a machine is not synchronized with the reference model. It can automatically create a customized deployment plan for each machine in a cluster and execute the sequence of installation in the proper order.
- **Tivoli Identity Manager**
  The Identity Manager automates the user life cycle with the HR and native repositories. It uses automated role-based provisioning for account preparation and creation. The provisioning system communicates directly with access-control systems to help establish the accounts, providing user information and passwords as well as defining account entitlements
- **Tivoli Storage Manager**
  The Storage Manager provides self-configuring tasks to automatically identify and load the drivers for the storage devices connected to the server. Configuration and policy information can be defined once to the storage manager and then populated to other servers automatically. Policy definition and other automated recovery, and logging and administrator defined thresholds are available.

Figure 15.2 illustrates these tools in the Tivoli environment for self-configuration.

The self-configuring aspects of Tivoli can boost productivity and reduce the costs of software configuration. The management of software is a complex and costly task that requires careful automation.

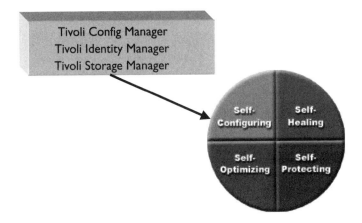

Figure 15.2   The self-configuring software tools in the Tivoli environment.

SELF-HEALING

A self-healing capability can detect the abnormal operation of the system and business processes (either in predictive or reactive mode), then initiate corrective and appropriate action. It needs to achieve this without disrupting the users. Actions such as balancing work load and volume or transactions are examples. The Tivoli software management availability portfolio of software products provides tools to assist in the autonomic monitoring of system health and performance. They also provide metrics from numerous resources to allow the filtering, correlation and analysis of system data. Based on this analysis, autonomic actions can be taken to halt problems—sometimes before they occur. Autonomic features are provided at multiple levels to proactively manage the IT infrastructure.

The software tools available in Tivoli for self-healing include:

- **Tivoli Enterprise Console**
  The Enterprise Console collates error reports, derives the root problem cause, and initiates corrective action. The event server and correlation engine help allow cross-resource correlation of events observed from the hardware, the running applications, and the network devices. Events from the multiple resources can be analyzed in real time to highlight the problems that merit immediate attention versus lower priority events. After a problem is determined, the system takes self-healing actions by responding automatically. As an option, support staff can be included to verify the response.
- **Tivoli Switch Analyzer**
  The Switch Analyzer correlates network device errors to the root cause without user

intervention. It is a level 2 (out of the five autonomic levels) network management solution that provides automated level 2 discovery. It identifies the relationship between devices, including level 2 and level 3 devices, and identifies the root cause of a problem without human intervention. During a network event storm, it can filter out extraneous events to correlate the true cause of the problem.

- **Tivoli NetView**
  NetView® helps enable self-healing by discovering TCP/IP networks, displaying network topologies, correlating and managing events and SNMP traps, monitoring network health, and gathering performance data. Router fault isolation technology quickly identifies and focuses on the root cause of a network error and initiates corrective actions.

- **Tivoli Business Systems Manager**
  The Business Systems Manager collects real-time operating data from distributed application components and resources across the enterprise and provides a comprehensive view of the IT infrastructure components that make up different business solutions. It contains technologies that analyze how an outage would affect a line of business, critical business process, or service-level agreement (SLA).

- **Tivoli Systems Automation S/390**
  The Systems Automation for the IBM mainframe model S/390 manages real-time problems in the context of an enterprise's business priorities. It provides monitoring and management of critical system resources, such as processors, subsystems, the Sysplex Timer, and coupling facilities. It supports self-healing by providing mechanisms to reconfigure a processor's partitions, perform power-on reset on IML processors and IPL operating systems (even automatically), investigate and respond to I/O configuration errors, and restart and stop applications if failures occur.

- **Tivoli Risk Manager**
  The Risk Manager enables self-healing by assessing potential security threats and automating responses, such as server reconfiguration, security patch deployment, and account revocation. This helps enable system administrators who are not security experts to monitor and assess security risks in real time with a high degree of integrity and confidence across an organization's multiple security checkpoints. This product contains technology developed by IBM Research.

- **Tivoli Monitoring for Applications, for Databases and Tivoli Monitoring for Middleware**
  This family of products minimizes vulnerability by discovering, diagnosing, and reacting to disruptions automatically. It provides monitoring solutions and a local automation capability through a set of Proactive Analysis Components. A sophisticated resource model engine allows for local filtering of monitored data, raising events when specific conditions are met. Local rules can be encoded to take immediate corrective action, providing automatic recovery for server failures.

- **Tivoli Storage Resource Manager**
  The Storage Resource Manager automatically identifies potential problems and executes policy-based actions to help prevent or resolve storage issues, minimize storage costs, and provide application availability. It can scan and discover storage resources in the IT environment. It supports autonomic policy-based automation for the allocation of storage quotas and storage space; monitors file systems; and provides reports on capacity and storage asset utilization.

Figure 15.3 summarizes the self-healing products with the Tivoli product suite.

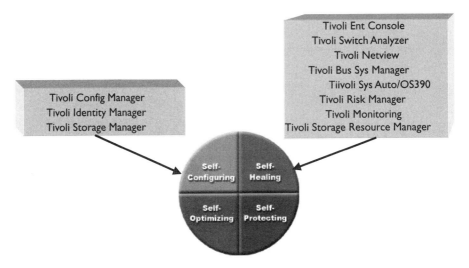

Figure 15.3   A summary of the self-healing products in the Tivoli suite.

Software that can repair itself must be a valuable contribution to future IT operations, data-centers, and corporate applications.

SELF-OPTIMIZING

Self-optimization is the ability of the IT infrastructure to efficiently maximize resource allocation and utilization to provide service for both system users and their customers. In the short term, self-optimization primarily addresses the complexity of managing system performance. In the long term, self-optimizing software applications may learn from experience and proactively tune themselves in an overall business objective context. Workload management uses self-optimizing technology to help optimize hardware and software use and verify that service-level goals are being met. Predictive analysis tools provide views into performance trends, allowing proactive action to be taken to help optimize the IT infrastructure before critical thresholds are exceeded.

Tivoli software products that can be used to implement a self-optimizing environment include the following:

- **Tivoli Service Level Advisor**

  The Service Level Advisor helps prevent SLA breaches with predictive capabilities. It performs trend analysis based on historical performance data from Tivoli Enterprise™ Data Warehouse and can predict when critical thresholds could be exceeded in the future. By sending an event to Tivoli Enterprise Console, self-optimizing actions can be taken to help prevent the problem from occurring.

- **Tivoli Workload Scheduler for Applications**

  The Workload Scheduler for Applications automates, monitors, and controls the flow of work through the IT infrastructure on both local and remote systems. It can automate, plan, and control the processing of these workloads within the context of business policies. It uses sophisticated algorithms to maximize throughput and help optimize resource usage.

- **Tivoli Business Systems Manager**

  The Business Systems Manager has multiple functions within the Tivoli suite, among which is enabling optimization of IT problem repairs based on business impact of outages. It collects real-time operating data from distributed application components and resources across the enterprise and provides a comprehensive view of the IT infrastructure components that make up different business solutions. It works with Tivoli Enterprise Console to enable self-optimizing actions to help prevent poor performance from affecting a line of business, critical business process, or SLA.

- **Tivoli Storage Manager**

  The Storage Manager supports Adaptive Differencing technology to help optimize resource usage for backup. With Adaptive Differencing, the backup archive client dynamically determines an efficient approach for creating backup copies of just the changed bytes, changed blocks, or changed files, delivering improved backup performance over dial-up connections. These technologies allow just the minimum amount of data to be moved to backup, helping optimize network bandwidth, tape usage, and management overhead.

- **Tivoli Monitoring for Transaction Performance**

  Monitoring for Transaction Performance helps customers tune their IT environments to meet predefined service-level objectives. It enables organizations to monitor the performance and availability of their e-business and enterprise transactions to provide a positive customer experience. It integrates with the Tivoli Enterprise Console environment for alerting and proactive management, helping enable optimization of resource usage from a transactional perspective.

- **IBM Tivoli Analyzer for Lotus® Domino™**
  The Analyzer for Lotus Domino contains a Proactive Analysis Component that allows administrators to verify the availability and optimal performance of Lotus Domino servers. It provides intelligent server health monitoring and expert recommendations to correct problems.

Figure 15.4 diagrams the software tools associated with self-optimization of Tivoli.

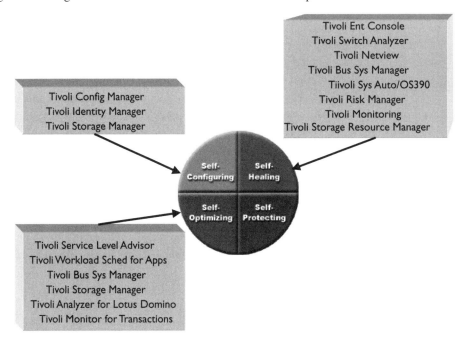

Figure 15.4   The software tools associated with self-optimization of Tivoli.

Currently, optimization is an intensive manual operation requiring great IT skill and diligence. It is a prime candidate for automation and will bring significant benefits to IT shops that embrace it.

SELF-PROTECTING

A self-protecting IT environment must take appropriate actions automatically to make itself less vulnerable to attacks on its runtime infrastructure and business data. These attacks—which often occur on a daily basis—can take the form of unauthorized access and use, malicious viruses that can reformat hard drives and destroy business data, and denial-of-service attacks that can cripple critical business applications. A combination of security management tools and storage manage-ment tools are necessary to deal with these threats. Security management tools can help businesses consistently enforce security and privacy policies, help reduce overall security administration costs, and help increase employee productivity and customer satisfaction. Critical configuration changes and access-control changes should only occur with the right approvals. Tools should detect violations of security policy, and if necessary, automated actions should be taken to minimize risk to IT assets. Tivoli software storage management tools help enable businesses to automatically and efficiently back up and protect business data. Autonomic security and storage solutions provide administrators with a way to create policy definitions and express event correlation and automation knowledge.

Tivoli software products that can be used to implement a self-protecting environment include the following:

- **Tivoli Storage Manager**
  The Storage Manager self-protects by automating backup and archival of enterprise data across heterogeneous storage environments. Scaling to protect thousands of computers running a dozen operating system platforms, its intelligent data movement and store techniques and comprehensive automation help reduce administration costs and increase service levels.
- **Tivoli Access Manager**
  The Tivoli Access Manager family of products self-protects by helping prevent unauthorized access, using a single security policy server to enforce security across multiple file types, applications, devices, operating systems, and protocols. It supports a broad range of user authentication methods, including Web single sign-on, and has the ability to control access to many types of resources for authenticated users.
- **Tivoli Identity Manager**
  The Identity Manager self-protects by centralizing identity management, integrating automated workflow with business processes, and leveraging self-service interfaces to increase productivity.
- **Tivoli Risk Manager**
  The Risk Manager provides system-wide self-protection by assessing potential security threats and automating responses, such as server reconfiguration, security patch deployment, and account revocation. It collects security information from firewalls, intrusion detectors, and other vulnerability scanning tools with security checkpoints. It simplifies and correlates the vast number of events and alerts generated by numerous security point products and quickly identifies the real security threats to help administrators respond with adaptive security measures.
- **IBM Tivoli Privacy Manager for e-business**
  Tivoli Privacy Manager for e-business self-protects by automating many privacy-compliance activities, simplifying the incorporation, monitoring and enforcement of privacy policy into business processes. It can record an end user's opt-in and opt-out

choices according to the policy, can be used to monitor and enforce access according to the privacy policy, and can create audit trail reports.

Figure 15.5 shows the Tivoli products that provide the four facets of autonomic computing.

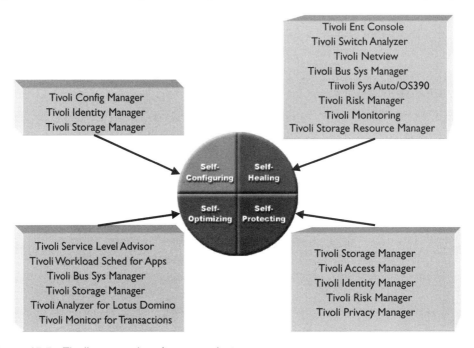

Figure 15.5   Tivoli autonomic software products.

TIVOLI CASE STUDIES AND SUCCESS STORIES

Businesses face difficult decisions in trying to accurately and efficiently allocate IT resources within their enterprise. These days, user demand on a company's IT infrastructure can range from relatively even to spiky and unpredictable. This makes allocating resources difficult and complex. Businesses must find a way to determine appropriate resource size to meet peaks in demand, while avoiding excess capacity and underutilization. What's more, e-business has created the expectation of a "round-the-clock" economy while advances in technology lead customers to demand more and faster services. Increasing competition and decreasing customer loyalty means that businesses can't afford to lag. If you aren't providing the services your customers want and need, they'll look for someone else who is.

A recent IBM study discovered that 69 percent of IBM customers are concerned about ensuring infrastructure reliability and availability to support their business operations. IBM's automated Tivoli technology can help now—allowing companies to manipulate their IT environment in real time, according to predefined business policies. By dynamically allocating capacity across systems to applications where it is needed, utilization is improved, eliminating underutilization and the need to invest in additional capacity. The technology becomes better aligned with your business goals, increasing your company's flexibility and responsiveness. Many Tivoli customers are reaping the benefits of the autonomic computing products with this suite.

HSBC TRINKAUS & BURKHARDT KGAA

HSBC Trinkaus & Burkhardt KGaA is a bank that offers customers in Germany and Luxembourg an array of financial services, including private and commercial banking, corporate investments, and portfolio management. Additionally, HSBC Trinkaus & Burkhardt offers interest and currency management. The company maintains its headquarters in Düsseldorf, Germany with branches in Hamburg, Berlin, Munich, Stuttgart, Baden-Baden, and Frankfurt, and a subsidiary in Luxembourg.

Founded in 1785 as a private bank, HSBC Trinkaus & Burkhardt is today a member of HSBC Holdings PLC, an international financial services organization based in London. The company has 1,500 employees.

Challenge—Proactively Monitor and Manage Complex IT Systems

The availability of mission-critical applications is mandatory to operate in the financial services industry anywhere in the world and crucial in any company to employee productivity. Knowing this, systems administrators at HSBC Trinkaus & Burkhardt made infrastructure management a top priority. By strengthening how the company monitored IT resources and responded to problems, administrators felt that they could make a significant impact on their company's success.

A major area of concern for administrators was monitoring systems across a number of platforms—Microsoft Windows NT®, Microsoft Windows® 2000, Sun Solaris, Linux and z/OS. At the time, administrators had to develop scripts to monitor IT resources under each platform and check the systems frequently for problems. Often, users were the first to report that a problem existed, placing administrators in an awkward position. To make matters worse, administrators typically did not learn of server problems that occurred outside of standard business hours. If a problem arose at night or on weekends, workers were stranded, with no access to IT resources.

The larger issue was there was no centralized event management and no escalation procedure implemented for the distributed platforms. This had to change. Administrators also struggled to manage about 1,300 workstations and 100 laptops running Microsoft Windows NT and Microsoft Windows 2000. The company's previous approach to software distribution did not provide the flexibility and capacity the company needed, slowing the distribution of new application services to users and increasing the workload on administrators. Similarly, the company's lack of an inventory and centralized remote control solution hampered the efforts of help-desk staff, lengthening response time.

With a variety of operating systems and a large number of applications in use, HSBC Trinkaus & Burkhardt began evaluating framework-based solutions that would help increase availability of its mission-critical applications and provide better service to IT users.

Solution—Managing Diverse IT Assets with Tivoli Software

The company selected Tivoli software from IBM, based on its comprehensive approach to infrastructure management and its autonomic management functions. Systemcall Ingenieurgesellschaft GmbH, Düsseldorf, an IBM Business Partner, provided enterprise systems management design and implementation services and trained HSBC Trinkaus & Burkhardt staff on the Tivoli implementation.

Today, administrators use IBM Tivoli Enterprise Console, IBM Tivoli Monitoring, IBM Tivoli NetView for z/OS, IBM Tivoli Configuration Manager, and IBM Tivoli Remote Control. The autonomic features of these Tivoli products, which help IT environments become more and more self-managing and resolve mundane IT issues automatically, are essential in helping administrators effectively manage the company's distributed resources. For example, the self-healing capabilities of Tivoli Monitoring help administrators detect and automatically recover from critical system problems across an estimated 145 servers. These servers are distributed among the bank's branch offices and its headquarters and support everything from office productivity applications, such as Lotus Notes®, to essential banking and financial applications. Tivoli Monitoring 3.7 also helps administrators monitor the company's clustered environment that hosts its trading applications.

Tivoli Enterprise Console integrates alerts from Tivoli Monitoring and Tivoli NetView for z/OS, which gathers event data about mainframe-based applications including IBM DB2, IBM WebSphere MQ (formerly IBM MQSeries®) and proprietary trading applications. Tivoli Enterprise Console also integrates alerts from a third-party network management product. As a result, administrators have a single view to system, application, and network events across both mainframe and distributed environments. Using policy-based rules for escalation management, a self-healing feature of the software, Tivoli Enterprise Console alerts administrators when a problem occurs by a predefined method—from pop-up error messages to email alerts to automatic paging.

The self-healing capabilities of Tivoli software help HSBC to be more proactive in managing their environment. IT staff can monitor distributed applications more easily, correlate events and resolve issues before they affect the end users.

To support configuration and operations management, HSBC Trinkaus & Burkhardt has deployed Tivoli Configuration Manager and Tivoli Remote Control. The company uses Tivoli Configuration Manager to gather hardware and software information on its more than 1,400 PCs through weekly scans. The data is used to support help-desk, software distribution, and software licensing activities. Tivoli Configuration Manager also helps administrators efficiently distribute new software updates, including upgrading employee workstations from Microsoft Windows NT to Microsoft Windows 2000 operating system. Tivoli Remote Control gives help-desk analysts secure, reliable and centralized control over user workstations. Help-desk staff no longer needs to dispatch personnel to branch offices to resolve user problems.

At the same time that HSBC Trinkaus & Burkhardt implemented Tivoli software, the company launched a new enterprise-wide initiative called GEOS™ (Global Entity Online System). GEOS, developed by SDS (Software Daten Service Vienna), is a state-of-the-art software product for high-speed, real-time, straight-through processing of large volumes of securities transactions including online securities account management. This major reorganization optimizes mission critical business processes. In addition, GEOS allows HSBC Trinkaus & Burkhardt to offer transaction banking services to other banks. The insourcing from third parties' securities businesses is key to cost-efficient improvement.

Tivoli software has become a fundamental component of this initiative and is helping administrators understand the impact of IT on bank operations. The company has created a road map of about 200 essential business processes, following each process from initiation to completion across all applications and platforms. Currently, HSBC uses Tivoli Enterprise Console to group and correlate events for each process and provide a comprehensive business view of IT events.

Results—Banking Time and Money

The company is realizing many benefits and cost savings with the implementation of IBM's Tivoli software. For example, enterprise systems management has become much easier, helping improve staff productivity. Project managers can now have more time to proactively plan new projects.

The autonomic features of Tivoli software provide the bank with substantial cost savings and help increase the availability of systems and applications. Take the self-healing features of Tivoli Monitoring. In the past, administrators had to look at each server to see whether it was running or not, and then initiate a fix if necessary. Now, Tivoli software informs administrators when problems arise and, in many cases, automatically tries to recover the system in a failure situation. Likewise, the self-healing features of Tivoli Configuration Manager can automatically reinitiate software distributions that are not successfully completed. Previously, administrators frequently had to redistribute application updates to workstations because of distribution problems.

With the Tivoli Configuration Manager, the bank can distribute software updates to more workstations simultaneously without wasting manpower.

Future—Comprehensive Business Impact Management

HSBC Trinkaus & Burkhardt is currently evaluating Tivoli Business Systems Manager, now that administrators have more than 200 business process event groups to manage through Tivoli

Enterprise Console. Tivoli Business Systems Manager uses daily operational data to build a resource map that illustrates how a specific resource outage affects a particular business process, line of business, or SLA.

The use of the Linux operating system is also becoming more important for HSBC Trinkaus & Burkhardt as it works to consolidate applications running on several UNIX-based systems onto a single system, helping lower hardware costs and boost system performance. Because Tivoli software supports many different platforms, including Linux, the bank can implement new platforms without acquiring new systems management tools.

SANTIX AG

Santix AG is an established systems integrator in Central Europe, delivering IT management and e-business solutions to large national and multinational corporations.[1] The company has teamed with IBM to help its customers integrate business processes and effectively manage their IT infrastructures. As an IBM Business Partner, santix resells the full range of Tivoli infrastructure management solutions and has a long history of success in delivering Tivoli Performance and Availability and Tivoli Configuration and Operations management solutions. Headquartered in Munich, Germany, santix has offices across Germany as well as in Zurich, Switzerland.

Challenge—Helping Companies Meet SLA Requirements

In recent years, the role of IT organizations has changed dramatically. No longer designated as cost centers, IT organizations have become service centers, providing IT support to business units under an service level agreement (SLA) model. Ultimately, Michael Santifaller, president of santix, predicts that sophisticated service and provisioning models will evolve under which IT must customize its offerings for each line of business, and deliver and document rapid response time.[2]

Companies across Central Europe have been turning to santix for robust tools that help them improve the availability and performance of their IT infrastructures and understand the business impact of an IT outage. Now, these companies also want products that provide the comprehensive service reports needed to demonstrate if their IT department is meeting their SLAs.

In Europe, as it is everywhere because of budget constraints, IT executives are also demanding solutions that help them to do more without increasing staff resources. This is an area where autonomic computing can help. Products such as Tivoli employ autonomic computing self-managing capabilities that allow hardware and software to dynamically adapt to their environment and automatically configure, heal, optimize, and protect themselves.

Solution—Managing IT against SLA Using Tivoli Software

To help IT organizations meet SLA requirements and reduce the cost of IT management, santix offers companies an end-to-end service management solution that supports IT administrators across the entire service management life cycle—monitoring, reporting, analyzing, solving, automating, deploying, securing, and controlling. The company provides clients with design, implementation, training, and troubleshooting services to help them leverage industry best practices and realize a rapid return on their investment.

At the heart of santix's offering is Tivoli software from IBM. For example, Tivoli Performance and Availability management solutions, such as IBM Tivoli Enterprise Console®, IBM Tivoli NetView, and IBM Tivoli Monitoring, allow companies to monitor their infrastructure at the component, business system and enterprise levels and, in many cases—through self-healing capabilities—cure problems before they occur. IBM Tivoli Service Level Advisor simplifies and automates the management and reporting of SLAs and provides proactive alerts for SLA violations.

Tivoli software is the foundation of the santix solution. It offers best-of-breed products to help its customers effectively manage IT against their SLAs and provides an open architecture to easily integrate point solutions for asset management and service desk support.

Santix originally became an IBM Business Partner because of IBM's innovative approach to IT management. This innovation relationship has continued and, as proof, highlights the fact that new releases of Tivoli software deliver more out-of-the-box functionality and autonomic capabilities than ever before. For example, the self-optimizing features in the latest version of IBM Tivoli Service Level Advisor include predictive capabilities that can help prevent SLA breaches. IBM Tivoli Service Level Advisor can perform trend analysis based on historical performance data from Tivoli Data Warehouse and can predict when critical thresholds could be exceeded in the future. By sending an event to IBM Tivoli Enterprise Console, self-optimizing actions can be taken to help prevent the problem from reoccurring.

The autonomic capabilities, such as the self-optimizing features of IBM Tivoli Service Level Advisor, help IT departments more efficiently manage IT resources while reducing the workload on administrators.

Other software, such as the Tivoli Data Warehouse, can be a significant advancement in enterprise systems management that helps administrators identify trends, predict business needs, and support predictive management tasks, all critical in meeting end-user requirements. The Tivoli Data Warehouse is an open repository that acts as a central data store for historical data for management applications—both Tivoli and non-Tivoli applications.

Results—Simplified Management, Lower Support Costs

With Tivoli software, santix customers are seeing significant improvements in their IT operations. For example, a large European bank looked to santix to help it both monitor its online banking system and measure the solution's performance against SLA metrics. The online banking system is an important revenue source for the bank, enabling customers to manage account activity and purchase products online. If the system isn't available or is too slow, the bank can lose money.

In response, santix installed IBM Tivoli Monitoring, IBM Tivoli Monitoring for Databases, IBM Tivoli Monitoring for Messaging and Collaboration, and IBM Tivoli Enterprise Console to help the bank increase the availability of its online banking system along with other critical business applications. IBM Tivoli Monitoring for Transaction Performance measures response time and incorporates self-optimizing capabilities that allow the software to tune the environment to meet predefined service-level objectives. IBM Tivoli Service Level Advisor will also help the bank reduce the cost of SLA management and align IT management closely with business needs.

Customers know that SLA management is very complex. IBM Tivoli Service Level Advisor provides a powerful tool that simplifies this task, enables self-optimization of IT infrastructures, and helps to communicate the value of IT to the business. As part of the bank's infrastructure management solution, santix also deployed IBM Tivoli Configuration and Operations management products to help administrators deliver reliable services to end users at a lower cost. For example, IBM Tivoli Configuration Manager reduces the cost of rolling out new software by helping administrators to automate software distribution from a central location. IBM Tivoli Remote Control provides remote support capabilities to reduce the need to dispatch technicians for expensive and time-consuming onsite visits. The bank plans to use the policy-based centralized user administration capabilities of IBM Tivoli Identity Manager, a Tivoli Security management solution, to bring users, systems, and applications online faster and reduce the cost of managing user identities across the enterprise.

Future—Refining SLA Support

Santix IT administrators will continue to see an increasing emphasis on supporting SLAs against business requirements, and santix plans to leverage the IBM Tivoli Business Impact Management solution to help customers in this area. This solution includes IBM Tivoli Service Level Advisor along with IBM Tivoli Business Systems Manager, which groups and correlates resources into business views, and IBM Tivoli Web Site Analyzer, which helps administrators identify performance trends and user traffic patterns so that they can evaluate the impact of their Web-based programs.

Santix can offer companies a clear vision for end-to-end service management and provide clients with products and services necessary to implement this vision. IBM's Tivoli software, with its autonomic capabilities, fits well into this offering, delivering state-of-the-art technology that is unparalleled in the industry.

SUMMARY AND CONCLUSIONS

Companies want to and must reduce their IT costs, simplify management of their IT resources, realize a fast return on their IT investment, and provide high levels of availability, performance, security, and asset utilization. Autonomic computing addresses these issues. This fundamental evolutionary shift in the way IT systems are managed will free the IT staff from detailed mundane tasks and allow them to focus on managing business processes. It can be accomplished through a combination of process changes, skills evolution, new technologies, architecture, and open industry standards. With autonomic computing reducing the demand for the specialized skills currently required to manage these IT initiatives, projects are more likely to be implemented on time and on budget. The incorporation of autonomic technologies will lead to systems that deliver the expected and required quality of service, helping eliminate many configuration problems introduced in today's environments due to human error. It will reduce the outages caused by malfunctions that can now be self-corrected and deliver maximum results and performance by continually optimizing the use of resources.

NOTES

1. For more information, see their Web site at *www.santix.de.*
2. See*www.ibm.com/software/success/cssdb.nsf/CS/KNOK-5KSVGD?OpenDocument&Site=software - 26k*

AC MARKETS AND THE FUTURE

- Small Business and Personal Computing
- Autonomic Research Challenges
- Final Thoughts

CHAPTER 16

SMALL BUSINESS AND PERSONAL COMPUTING

INTRODUCTION

In this chapter, we shall explore several separate, but still important subjects and topics related to autonomic computing, the first of which is small and medium-sized businesses (SMBs) and their potential for applications using autonomic computing. Generally, SMBs do not have dedicated resources to manage their IT operations, but the very necessary computing systems are vital to growth and profits. So, here we can see a substantial opportunity for autonomic computing to provide many of the self-management benefits we have been discussing in the book.

The next topic is personal computing and the market for self-managing autonomic software. Personal computer (PC) owners and users are a substantial market, and again, the need for self-managing self-healing software products is significant.

In the last topic, we touch on the usefulness of software agents. Using agents in autonomic computing is important. They can be used to fetch and search for resources, roaming over private systems, corporate enterprises, or the Internet to meet the requirements of the on demand world.

THE ROLE OF SMALL BUSINESSES IN THE ECONOMY

SMBs are a very important sector of the U.S. economy. For the purposes of simplicity and consistency, we define a small business as having less than 500 employees in all of the industries or business locations in which the firm operates. Eventually some small businesses grow to become large businesses. Importantly, small businesses are a dynamic force in the economy, bringing new ideas, products, technology, processes, and vigor to the marketplace. They fill niche markets and locations not served by large businesses. Large firms, on the other hand, generally provide stability to the economy.

The differences in the small- and large-business workforces are, at least in part, a result of the inherent differences in small and large firms. Small firms are often younger (indeed, they are sometimes recent startups), and more apt to be in industries with lower economies of scale, such as services or technology. Small firms can represent a life stage before economies of scale are reached (or hoped-for future growth is attained), or they can be a stable anchor in the marketplace. These age, location, and industry effects constitute the basic differences between small and large firms. They can lead to different workforce needs and different resources to attract workers of various education levels and occupations.

Small businesses are usually entrepreneurial. The creation of a new business or enterprise is an integral and significant activity in a growing U.S. job market. Just as new establishments are created, some existing ones expand, contract, or dissolve operations altogether. Countries that have the capacity and wherewithal to accommodate high rates of business formation and dissolution will be best positioned to compete in global markets.

SMBs have unique requirements in their business infrastructure, as illustrated in Figure 16.1.

- Multi channel access—SMBs need an on demand business environment and a full range of channels, information requirements.
- Customer-centricity—SMBs concentrate very closely on their customers and need to react, change, and be agile as the market changes.
- Premium services—Those vendors who provide services and products to SMBs need to achieve multiple layers of services—anytime and anywhere. Consistency is the key.
- Best of breed—The products and services that SMBs use in their daily business need to be the best there is.

Small businesses provide a competitive environment and prompt the economy to evolve by introducing new ideas, products, technology, and processes. Small businesses are the stock from which large businesses grow, the first job of many new workers, and an opportunity for their owners to achieve the American Dream. Small firms represent about 99 percent of employers, employ about half of the private sector workforce, and are responsible for about two-thirds of the net new jobs. While small firms contribute substantially to the growth of the U.S. economy, the number of small firms does not change dramatically over time. This is because the process of growth entails some small firms evolving into large firms and some large firms shrinking into small ones.

The statistics, trends, and demographic makeup of the U.S. small business market is both interesting and surprising. Small business effects on the economy can be dramatic. There are an estimated 22.9 million small businesses in the United States: Those businesses:

- Represent more than 99.7 percent of all employers.

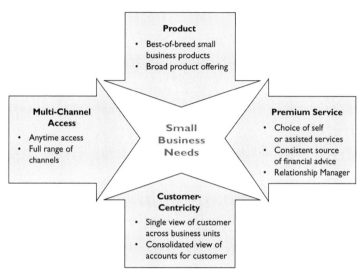

Figure 16.1   Small business needs.

- Employ more than half of all private-sector employees.
- Pay 44.5 percent of total U.S. private payroll.
- Generate 60 to 80 percent of net new jobs annually.
- Create more than 50 percent of nonfarm private gross domestic product (GDP).
- Supplied 22.8 percent of the total value of federal prime contracts (about $50 billion) in FY 2001.
- Produce 13 to 14 times more patents per employee than large patenting firms. These patents are twice as likely as large firm patents to be among the one percent most cited.
- Employ 39 percent of high-tech workers (such as scientists, engineers, and computer workers).
- Are 53 percent home-based and 3 percent franchises.
- Made up 97 percent of all identified exporters and produced 29 percent of the known export value in FY 2001.

Eighty-five percent of small businesses are expected to conduct business via the Internet by the end of the year 2003. Small business information technology-producing industries contributed more than one-third of total real economic growth between 1995 and 1998.

THE GROWTH OF SMALL BUSINESS TECHNOLOGY

Many small businesses now rely on technology and the Internet to sustain and grow their markets, even as they increasingly rely on computers to perform daily duties. This increases their productivity without the need for additional resources.

Small businesses that use the Internet have grown 46 percent faster than those that do not, according to several studies. Some 85 percent of U.S. businesses with fewer than 100 employees are PC users; more than 61 percent of them have Internet access. According to IDC, Internet infiltration by small businesses was high in 2001, with approximately 67 percent accessing the Web; 85 percent are expected to conduct business via the Web by the end of 2003. A private annual business study finds that some 35 percent of small businesses maintained a Web site as of 1998 and one-third of those did business transactions through it. Other estimates say that more than 1 million small businesses had a Web site in 1998, while in 1999 an estimated 2.3 million small businesses (with fewer than 100 employees) were online.

Small business spending on IT has been consistent and increased over the last six years, as indicated by Figure 16.2.

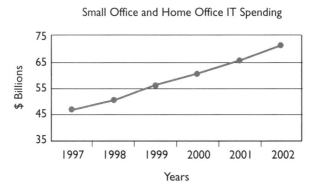

Source: Prepared by the Office of Advocacy

Figure 16.2   IT spending in small business continues to rise—despite economic uncertainty.[1]

This IT spending trend is expected to continue and increase. Worldwide, small businesses are investing in information technology products, accessing the Internet, and conducting commerce online again in large numbers. Small businesses in Europe—specifically Germany, France, and the U.K.—spent approximately $106 billion on IT and telecommunications a year ago, while other small businesses worldwide spent about $450 billion on IT and telecommunications.

IBM AND SMALL BUSINESS

IBM has been supporting and developing solutions for small business since it began as a company and generates substantial sales from this market. However, IBM realizes that the small business market still represents an untapped market worth from $30 billion to $300 billion. Microsoft, which defines a small business as having less than $50 million in revenue, adheres to the lower end of this market estimate. IBM, which considers small to be less than $1 billion in sales, likes the larger number.

IBM has determined that the small business market could mean new sales. This is based on the fact that up to 54 percent of all IT spending will happen in the customer space below 1,000 employees. IBM disclosed that sales to medium-sized businesses accounted for $4.3 billion in revenue, or nearly one-fifth of total sales, in the year's first quarter, up 6 percent from a year earlier last year.

Since 2001, IBM has invested $500 million in the small and medium-business market for development of new IT products. IBM has developed financing packages from IBM Credit for these resellers. This allows IBM to have a discussion about purchase without having to go to a bank, making the process much faster.

IBM's e-business on demand strategy is designed to address the growing dynamic between IT solutions and business strategies. Corporations and their management regard technology as a means to power business evolution to the next competitive level. To compete and win in today's markets, companies must be agile and responsive to customer demands, marketplace shifts, and competitive pressure.

The ability of on demand solutions to leverage existing IT infrastructures with additional integrated services and capacity solutions has implications for corporations of every size. Small to medium-sized businesses can use on demand solutions to gain the economic scale of large companies. Large enterprises can use on demand to become as nimble as small businesses.

Of interest is IBM's Small and Medium-Sized Business Advantage Program. This program is designed to help the IBM partner community of approximately 90,000 customers grow profitability and successfully service this market. The approach that IBM is taking is one of partnership—with IBM and its partners working closely to address this market segment. The program includes some unique elements to help the partners be successful that has different technology and financial considerations. By creating a unique program and set of rules of engagement for this market, IBM has shown that it is serious about penetrating this segment of the market with and for its partners.

SMBS AND AUTONOMIC COMPUTING

The prospect of autonomic technology for small and medium businesses is both intriguing and necessary. One thing small businesses cannot afford or deal with is the issue of IT complexity. The time taken to deal with complexity issues will affect the profitability of most small businesses. As a result, they fail to get the benefits they expected from the technology, which is required to support them and grow their business.

IBM's autonomic computing goal is to make technology take care of the things technology can take care of, freeing people to do the things they do best: thinking about how they can use technology to solve business problems and concentrating on the business. SMB owners do not have a lot of time to deal with IT on a day-to-day basis. They need to concentrate on growing and managing their business. They do not have the finance or the human resources to spend on IT. To be successful, the SMB market is going to need a pretested, pre-integrated autonomic software solution. This solution needs packaged intelligence that automatically modifies or adds resources to the existing SMB infrastructure environments. It needs to adjust the system capacity immediately, streamlining operations, optimizing resources, lessening complexity, and lowering management costs. The vision of autonomic computing as a holistic approach to managing IT is never more relevant than to small business owners.

An Example—Net Integration Technologies Inc.

Net Integration Technologies Inc. (NITI), a software developer, delivers an autonomic computing solution to the small and mid-sized business and enterprise (SMB/SME) market with its autonomic, Linux-based Net Integrator Operating System (NIOS).

NITI is one of the first companies to deliver on the promise of autonomic technology with a complete set of intelligent networking solutions for the SMB market. Its NIOS operating system simplifies deployment and administration for VARs (Value Added Resellers) and boasts self-healing and self-maintenance capabilities in support of its network software.

NITI's Linux-based NIOS-powered servers are self-aware, self-maintaining, self-tuning, and self-healing, greatly reducing the cost and complexity of IT infrastructure. The company also announced the successful launch of its ExchangeIt! collaborative software. ExchangeIt! works with NIOS to provide SMB/SMEs with an affordable and reliable solution.

Millions of businesses don't have the budget or the time to manage what has become an IT infrastructure nightmare with traditional servers. NITI offers out-of-the-box setup in a fraction of the time it takes with traditional servers, bulletproof Linux security, self-healing computing and a system that runs month after month with minimal human intervention. NIOS-powered servers and add-ons like ExchangeIt! answer the call for significant changes in the way computing is managed by small and mid-sized businesses.

Net Integration Technologies' NIOS software and ExchangeIt! groupware provide SMB/SMEs with a complete set of intelligent networking solutions that are secure, easy to deploy, and easy to maintain. Building on top of open source software, such as Linux, and using commercial, off-the-shelf hardware components, the NITI has achieved an autonomic computing environment that conforms to existing networking and open computing standards.

Combining open source Linux software with its own patent-pending technology, Net, NIOS is taking Linux beyond where it is today. NIOS-powered servers automate common setup procedures, streamlining deployment and maintenance. NIOS is self-healing—it is able to recover from routine and extraordinary events that might cause some of its subsystems to malfunction or crash. It is able to discover problems or potential problems, and then find a way to fix these in order to keep functioning smoothly.

The Key NIOS Platform Components

NetIntelligence is an artificial intelligence module that facilitates and employs intuitive auto-nomic features to simplify deployment, installation, and ongoing maintenance. It provides NIOS-powered servers with self-healing and self-monitoring capabilities and offers automatic network discovery, configuration, and real-time optimization. NetIntelligence also provides autoconfiguration of all internal subsystems, including firewall parameters, DNS records, and DHCP parameters.

SystemER enables easy recovery from any type of catastrophic failure into a fully functional state in just two minutes. No other SMB server has ever been able to match this level of recover-ability.

ExchangeIt! is a full-featured collaboration server created for SMBs that is an alternative solu-tion to Microsoft Exchange Server. It provides users with schedule sharing, group schedules, meeting invitations, contact list sharing, group contact lists, task lists, journal sharing, and notes. ExchangeIt! works seamlessly with Microsoft Outlook® and gives SMBs a more manageable and cost-effective alternative to Microsoft Exchange.

TunnelVision is an intelligent Virtual Private Network (VPN) solution. It is a fully automated solution that installs quickly and provides automatic route discovery and propagation across the VPN. TunnelVision also automates the propagation of DNS information across the VPN and can work without static IP addresses.

Expression Desktop is zero-setup, zero-maintenance, networkcentric, Linux-based Microsoft-replacement desktop. Expression provides users with an automatically and fully configured desktop. Expression provides virus-free computing, can run Windows applications, and gives system administrators complete control of the corporate desktop environment.

DoubleVision is a redundant Internet connectivity technology designed to connect multiple high-speed interfaces to NIOS-powered servers. It load shares across multiple Internet feeds from different ISPs, automatically detects network problems, and fails over to back up band-width. DoubleVision has a built-in DDNS capability.

For more information on NIOS, contact Net Integration Technologies Inc., or see their Web page at *www.net-itech.com.*

Small Business Conclusions

The current data indicate that small businesses are embracing electronic commerce and spending significant and increasing amounts on information technology. Small businesses are serving as providers to other small businesses and are a contributing force in the economy. On average, small firms may not be technologically sophisticated, but some are among the most sophisti-cated developers of new technology. And while some small firms are less technologically advanced, they are often, because of their size, in a better position to act quickly to adopt—and make innovative adaptations to—new technologies in the market. E-commerce takes a number of forms—business-to-business, business-to consumer, e-procurement, and e-marketplaces or auction sites. Small businesses participate in e-commerce as a supplier of IT products and services and also as a buyer of IT products and services, mainly to minimize costs and increase sales. E-commerce growth is concentrated in the business-to-business sector. However, business-to-consumer e-commerce is growing gradually and is dominated by larger companies. As this phenomenon continues, small businesses may continue to find more uses for on demand business e-commerce.

The growth of Internet technology among small businesses is expected to expand rapidly as owners become aware of, educated in, and knowledgeable about the potential for process efficiencies and cost savings. Global expansion of the Internet also continues, which will mean new competitive challenges for the U.S. small business sector. Proposals to regulate and tax Internet sales will likewise continue to increase, and small businesses will serve themselves well by staying informed and involved as e-commerce develops.

It is with this backdrop that IBM has committed resources and marketing to this important initiative.

AUTONOMIC PERSONAL COMPUTING

Autonomic computing shares many complimentary objectives and goals with personal computing. While the ubiquitous personal computer has made enormous strides in the development of its technology since it was introduced in the early 1980s, it has grown in complexity to the same extent. Some of that complexity is managed through graphical interface software such as Windows; however, there still remains much to do to make the personal computer more accessible and simplified.

Personal computing has gone through several phases of evolution. From the era of faster processors, bigger storage, and newer operating systems to the times when the PC was treated as a commodity for increasing operational efficiency, there have been many changes.

The goals of autonomic computing and personal computing are similar. The goals they share include:

- Ease of installation and configuration.
- Ease of operation.
- Management of complexity in all its forms.
- Better protection from external threats.
- Solving problems.
- Reduction of cost of ownership.

When autonomic computing is widespread in the personal computing world, many millions of users will benefit worldwide. Of particular note is that autonomic personal computing will bring substantial benefits to less developed countries that do not have an abundance of infrastructure, technical support, and help.

For autonomic computing to make significant improvements in the management of personal computing, it must be addressed in the context of the complete infrastructure environment in which it operates. This means adding autonomic functionality to such areas as the Internet, servers, and networks that the personal computer is connected to. Figure 16.3 depicts this approach. Simply adding autonomic computing to the stand-alone desktop will not provide the needed self-management and support. All the current features of autonomic computing—self-configuring, self healing, self-optimizing and self-protection—will be used in the personal computing world.

Industry analysts believe that 80 percent of the cost of a personal computer is in managing and supporting its own systems after its initial purchase, whereas the purchase price amounts to less than 20 percent of the total cost of owning (TCO) and supporting a PC.

Autonomic computing means a computing infrastructure that adapts to meet the demands of the applications that are running in it. In other words, the software is developed and deployed with applications, and the infrastructure takes care of itself—adjusting automatically as applications and workloads change. The ultimate effect is not only less work for the hardware vendor but also much more effective utilization of the personal computer user's time, hence less frustration and more productivity.

Autonomic Personal Computer Infrastructure

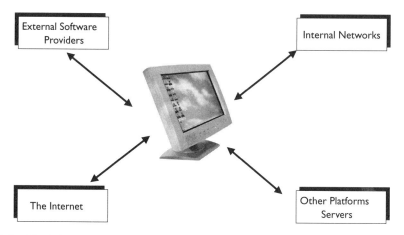

Figure 16.3 The infrastructure of the autonomic PC.

Existing Features

Today's PC-related networks and the Internet already have a number of system management and semiautonomic features that have been successful. Some examples are:

- Plug and play—Certain hardware and software can be installed and configured without the intervention of the user in a transparent fashion. This procedure is designed to enable simple and robust connectivity among stand-alone devices and personal computers from many different vendors. This is a good example of the success of open standards acceptance by the IT industry.
- Optimization—Software such as Norton Utilities can sense the level of disk fragmentation and alert users that performance may suffer if the condition is allowed to continue. Once the user accepts the recommendation, the software will automatically reorganize the placement of data and software applications to improve the access to files and related data.
- Software Updates—Certain operating systems, for example Windows XP, have the capability to sense, receive, and install software updates automatically. Complexity is an inherent issue in personal computers. Windows XP has over 30 million lines of code that must be regularly maintained and updated with fixes, patches, and security enhancements.
- Backup and restore—Operating systems such as Windows XP will save an image of the applications on installation. This is available to users who may need it. IBM has a solution called RapidRestore which saves hidden partition and system information.
- Automatic clock changes—To adjust the time changes for daylight savings twice a year, Windows will automatically request that the personal computer clock be updated.

It should be noted that all these features, while useful and necessary, are semiautonomic because they require user action for complete implementation.

Personal Computing and Self-Protections

The issues with autonomic personal computing security and privacy are similar to the mainstream technology issues that have been identified for some time, namely:

- Authentication
- Authorization and access control
- Intrusion detection
- Definition of autonomic security policies
- Fraud detection and prevention
- User privacy
- Digital signatures (for e-commerce)

Computer viruses pose a serious threat to the security and integrity of the Internet, its applications and data, and its main access device—the PC. The growth in distributed computing along with new technologies, such as document-resident macros, powerful groupware environments, and the Internet itself, have increased the corporate network's vulnerabilities. Computer viruses can cause significant damage in terms of lost work and productivity to the individual directly affected by the virus, the individual's colleagues, and the corporate community as a whole. While the potential for virus attack on stand-alone computers is considerable, there is a significantly more dangerous potential for virus attack with networked computers, due to the speed and ease with which viruses can spread across networks. As a consequence, it is imperative that a virus strategy be adopted and adhered to rigorously. This will reduce the likelihood of a virus outbreak and minimize the risks associated with any virus outbreak.

In 1989, Robert Morris, then a student, wrote and released 49 lines of code that became known as the "Morris Worm." The Morris Worm paralyzed more that half of the Internet, yet mercifully so few of us were connected at that time that the impact on our society and commerce was minimal. Since then, the Internet has grown from primarily a tool of academia and the defense/intelligence communities to a global electronic network that touches nearly every aspect of everyday life at the workplace and in our homes.

The costs of viruses are phenomenal. Take the Code Red virus as an example. This worm virus, released in late 2001, infected thousands of sites and networks. According to the FBI's National Infrastructure Protection Center (NIPC) cleanup costs exceeded $1.2 billion.[1] The FBI worked with experts in the United Kingdom, Australia, and Canada to try to contain the worm's spread. The Code Red program is a worm because it can spread across networks and infect new machines without computer users having to do anything at all. This was only one virus—multiply by the thousands of viruses released each year and the costs are unimaginable.

Viruses can go beyond the personal computer—desktop or laptop. Personal digital assistants are very popular, but the PDA in your pocket could be a pipeline for viruses. A PDA-borne virus could have a double payload—damaging data on the device itself and then using the PDA as a transmission device to spread the damage to notebook and desktop computers, and eventually the network.

The meteoric rise of the Internet in global commerce and its widespread use in communication makes solving information security problems over wide area networks of paramount importance. The building blocks of the Internet are components that are intrinsically not secure, and given their complexity, it is not possible to build secure components. Furthermore, for most applications, the definition of security is ambiguous, and will remain so until security policies are created for the myriad uses of large systems.

Hence, it will be necessary to retrofit flexible security measures into existing systems. One solution is intrusion detection, which involves the detection of activity that threatens a system. The focus of the intrusion detection community has been on *detection*, but the broader problem of response in the face of a detected incident is also being considered.

So, the self-protecting functions of autonomic computing must work in the environment described above. Here are a few examples:

1. One autonomic approach is with policy-driven detection and prevention. Start with a defined policy on how the threats and solutions will be implemented and managed. The policies can be described to the autonomic element. These policies must be clear, concise, workable policies to be implemented on autonomic systems, that will raise inside or outside threat awareness and accountability for organizations, while acknowledging and understanding privacy issues for system monitoring.

2. As new attacks are observed, the signature database must be updated automatically by the autonomic element. This requires abstracting the features of an attack that (1) can be observed from audit logs or network sniffing and (2) relates directly to the ability of the attack to achieve its goal.

3. Can an autonomic system detect previously unseen attacks? Clearly, those systems that match data streams against patterns in a simple-minded way will fail to detect any attack that is not recognized in the system pattern database. Since it is very easy to construct an unbounded number of variants in almost every attack, this may be a serious obstacle to overcome.

4. Autonomic detection must be made safe from attack and able to protect itself. The issue here is whether the autonomic intrusion detection system can be attacked. It will be a target for hackers and egotists wishing to defeat IBM's technology. All previous and existing software for intrusion detection systems seems to be vulnerable to denial of service attacks (e.g., through flooding). The problem is exacerbated as network capacity increases. In general, the problem of protecting an autonomic intrusion detection system seems to require the cooperation of intrusion detection components, perhaps based on the techniques of fault-tolerance and carrying into the realm of autonomic. The problem is somewhat simplified by making it difficult for an attacker to break into an intrusion detection system, much as it is difficult to break into a router that is not intended for general-purpose use. However, providing a remote management capability gives a handle to attack an intrusion detection component.

5. Infrastructure support is another critical development issue that the autonomic community needs to confront. No one product or capability may be able to solve every intrusion detection problem if anomaly detection and internal misuse are included. This means that the community needs to begin to think about architecture for potential damage detection, prevention, and recovery. The architecture may need to use several security tools together across broad groups of networks within an enterprise. Will that architecture be hierarchical, distributed, or something else? Autonomic collaboration may the key. Someone needs to think about autonomic systems engineering of computer security systems, including some areas that are usually avoided, such as cost, maintenance, and usability. This also means that someone needs to think about what an

"ideal" autonomic computer security management scheme would look like and how it would engage with legal and other enterprise-wide system management.

These are just a few of the challenges and opportunities that autonomic self-protecting technology and software must address in the personal computer market.

AUTONOMIC COMPUTING BEYOND THE IT INDUSTRY

The ultimate scope of autonomic computing will go beyond just the IT industry. The technology of autonomic computing is based around sensors. The prospect of expanding this to other areas—particularly the consumer market—is enticing. Sensors are a concept that has been accepted for some time.

Once sensors are placed in everything, computing will truly be pervasive. Everything from cell phone to refrigerators and toasters, the clothes we wear, the cars we drive, and shopping malls that will pick up your preferences as you enter will be available to the consumer. Nor are these the only possibilities.

Smart homes are already a market with products and software services. A smart or intelligent home uses readily available devices, many of which are currently used in home security systems, such as:

- passive infrared sensors
- pressure pads
- magnetic reed switches

This could expand with the installation of a home-based server installed in the basement of a home—near the furnace, water heater, or air-conditioning. This server would perform functions such as polling all the sensors throughout the house—in the refrigerator, say, to order milk, eggs, and cheese automatically when needed. It would turn the house lights on or off, inside or out, as required. It would sense when a new movie is available that meets the needs of the family and download for viewing. Sensors could be placed in the roof of the house—if a leak is detected, the server would automatically locate the nearest repair specialist. Another use would be to sense when the roof needed painting and contact the local painters for a quote. Smart homes have the potential to enable elderly and disabled people to lead independent lives in their own homes. However, the devices and their interactions need to be chosen and designed in such a way that the system as a whole meets the very specific needs of the householder. The list is almost endless, as is indicated by Figure 16.4.

If your local library is technologically efficient, you can already go online to reserve books. But when those books are due to be returned, it may be a different matter. One approach to solving this problem would be to install sensors in the books themselves. The sensors could then send a wireless message to your personal computer indicating when the book should be returned. It can

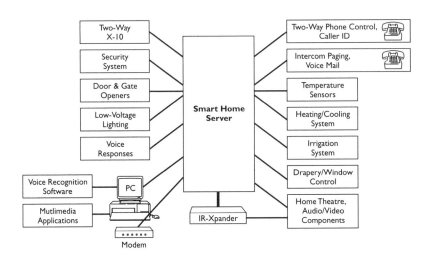

Figure 16.4 A smart home server could have thousands of sensors installed all over the house.

also help locate lost books—perhaps by sending out an audible alarm to help locate the book on your bookshelf.

We are already seeing examples of this technology on the highways. Car owners can purchase prepaid sensors that sit on the windshield or the dashboard of a car. The tollbooths sense and recognize the car approaching then process and deduct the fee from the sensor. The cars no longer have to stop to proceed through tollbooths. Current tests indicate that few cars go slower than 65 miles per hour, and one unit can handle 330,000 vehicles a day. Traffic volume is on the rise everywhere in the United States. The Federal Highway Administration (FHA) forecasts that by the year 2005 there will be 50 percent more vehicles on the road than in 1990.[2] We need more automated methods to manage our highways.

This technology has enormous applications both commercially and in industry. In the retail industry, large companies are already beginning to test the technology with smart shelves. Some retail stores plan to install specially designed shelves that can read radio frequency waves emitted by sensors. The shelves can scan the contents of the shelves and, via computer, alert store employees when supplies are running low or when theft is detected. This makes reordering an on demand process.

Privacy advocates are worried about the ramifications of embedding tiny sensors in all kinds of personal items. Corporations could use the technology to keep consumer belongings under surveillance not only in stores, but also in their homes and on the street. Imagine, for instance, walking down the sidewalk and having a high-tech billboard flash an ad for ketchup at you because it recognized the package of hotdogs in your bag. This scenario—not unlike a scene in the sci-fi film *Minority Report*—is already technically feasible and in operation. Grocery retailer Safeway is testing new in-store shopping cart technology that traces shoppers' steps through its stores and flashes personalized ads at them while they're shopping. Pop-up ads are no longer limited to the Internet.

Sensor Conclusions

Sensor products provide accurate measurement of temperatures in production processes that include chemicals, food, beverages, petroleum, paper, minerals, metals, plastics, rubber, photographs, and pharmaceuticals. Key sectors where sensors are used include the automotive industry, process industries, industrial automation, machinery/equipment, building automation/HVAC, aerospace/defense, medicine, and consumer products. The auto industry is a major user and growth driver for the sensors industry; and process industries also significantly impact this industry.

During the next five years, sensors will find key growth opportunities in high-volume consumer applications and in other core areas, such as process monitoring, control and defense, security, and space industries.

Lower-priced, robust, and compact sensors with customer-centric packaging and electronics have potential to impact various types of consumer products or office automation products. The key to the proliferation of electronic sensors in the smart home and its appliances is to provide very inexpensive sensors that can work effectively with standard server technology.

In addition, with the development of standard wireless communication protocols optimized for sensors, wireless sensor networks are expected to gain acceptance. Momentum is gaining in such applications as machinery health monitoring and predictive maintenance, homeland security, asset management, food monitoring, environmental monitoring, power supplies, utilities, test and development, process monitoring, and medical instrumentation.

SUMMARY AND CONCLUSIONS

The structure of the U.S. economy is extremely diverse and involves the complex interaction of many factors, trends, and economic sectors. This diversity and complexity has resulted in one of the most advanced economies in the world, which has led the way in the development of new technologies. The United States is by far the world's economic superpower—our GDP totaled $10.2 trillion in 2001; assuming international purchasing power parity, this was three times the size of Japan's output, almost five times the size of Germany's and more than seven times the size of the United Kingdom's.[3]

Venture capital activity is beneficial to small enterprise because it provides a source of long-term capital investment. Any increase in venture capital investment is beneficial to small businesses, as it provides another source of financing. A rise in venture capital financing is also indicates increased innovation and entrepreneurship. This money can be made available to purchase new types of technology and services.

As the economy in the 21st century evolves, small business entrepreneurs are now armed with an aggressive IT tools and technology to meet new challenges head-on. Many agree that while the challenges facing small business have changed over the past few years, the long-term view is very optimistic, this despite concerns about the economy. Small business entrepreneurs frequently go on to be heroes of American society. Small businesses also can become larger and bigger businesses.

A vital part of this future will involve what IT technology is used and purchased. The tools that provide the maximum productivity, ease of use, and capacity will have substantial markets in the small business sector.

This chapter illustrates the far-reaching effect that autonomic computing can grow to. While the initial autonomic computing thrust is for corporate IT environment, there are other markets and products that can benefit from the self-managing software systems.

NOTES

1. Graphs courtesy of the Small Business Administration. See *http://www.sba.gov/advo/stats.*
2. For more information see *http://www.nipc.gov/.*
3. For more information see *http://www.fhwa.dot.gov/.*
4. Statistics from the Economist Intelligence Unit, Country Profile, July 31, 2002.

C H A P T E R **17**

AUTONOMIC
RESEARCH
CHALLENGES

INTRODUCTION

Research defines four areas of major importance, given their potential for long-term influence on the future directions in autonomic computing:

1. Autonomic computing describes the next era in computing wherein complexity is either hidden from the user or eradicated by computing systems modeled after the body's self-regulating autonomic nervous system. While IBM will lead the industry in this area, autonomic computing cannot be a proprietary solution and will demand the efforts and active contributions of the IT industry and academic world.

2. E-business describes the rapid transformation occurring in traditional business and economic models as companies large and small (and many entirely new) turn to an online environment to function more efficiently and productively. The transformation will not stop with businesses, but extend to markets, trading environments, and exchanges, altering economics in as yet unseen ways.

3. Pervasive Computing describes the ensuing global environment where computing ceases to be something that occurs only in a specified, restricted space—inside a box on your desktop, for instance—and instead becomes an accepted, readily available utility that occurs in the "ether" of the networked world.

4. Deep Computing defines an expanded method of computing—some would argue a novel approach to thinking—that will marry incredible computational ability with human intelligence in problem solving. Using this approach, companies, educational institutions, and eventually individuals will be able to take the enormous amounts of information that a pervasive computing world will capture and make sense of it.

Autonomous computing will need to draw on all four areas to be successful. IBM has stated that it has reorganized its research division around autonomic computing, giving it priority in research projects.[1]

IBM believes that autonomic computing will require industry-wide acceptance before the technology will have a meaningful impact on corporate enterprises. In 2001, IBM called upon the information technology industry and academic community to rally around autonomic computing and committed to underwrite approximately 50 research projects at universities during the next four to five years to take on the complexity challenge.[2]

RESEARCH CHALLENGES

Virtually every aspect of autonomic computing offers significant research challenges. The life cycle of an individual autonomic element or of a relationship among autonomic elements reveals several challenges. Others arise in the context of the system as a whole, and still more become apparent at the interface between humans and autonomic systems. Briefly, here are some of these issues.

THE LIFE CYCLE OF AN AUTONOMIC ELEMENT

An autonomic element's life cycle begins with its design and implementation; continues with test and verification; proceeds to installation, configuration, optimization, upgrading, monitoring, problem determination, and recovery; and culminates in uninstallation or replacement. Each of these stages has special issues and challenges.

Design, Test, and Verification

Programming an autonomic element will mean extending Web services or grid services with programming tools and techniques that aid in managing relationships with other autonomic elements. Because autonomic elements both consume and provide services, representing needs and preferences will be just as important as representing capabilities. Programmers will need tools that help them acquire and represent policies—high-level specifications of goals and constraints, typically represented as rules or utility functions—and map them onto lower-level actions. They will also need tools to build elements that can establish, monitor, and enforce agreements.

Testing autonomic elements and verifying that they behave correctly will be particularly challenging in large-scale systems, because it will be harder to anticipate their environment, especially when it extends across multiple administrative domains or enterprises. Testing networked applications that require coordinated interactions among several autonomic elements will be even more difficult.

It will be virtually impossible to build test systems that capture the size and complexity of realistic systems and workloads. It might be possible to test newly deployed autonomic elements in situ by having them perform alongside more established and trusted elements with similar functionality.

The element's potential customers may also want to test and verify its behavior, both before establishing a service agreement and while the service is provided. One approach is for the autonomic element to attach a testing method to its service description.

Installation and Configuration

Installing and configuring autonomic elements will most likely entail a bootstrapping process that begins when the element registers itself in a directory service by publishing its capabilities and contact information. The element might also use the directory service to discover suppliers or brokers that may provide information or services it needs to complete its initial configuration. It can also use the service to seek out potential customers or brokers to which it can delegate the task of finding customers.

Monitoring and Problem Determination

Monitoring will be an essential feature of autonomic elements. Elements will continually monitor themselves to ensure that they are meeting their own objectives, and they will log this information to serve as the basis for adaptation, self-optimization, and reconfiguration. They will also continually monitor their suppliers, to ensure that they are receiving the agreed-on level of service, and their customers, to ensure that they are not exceeding the agreed-on level of demand. Special sentinel elements may monitor other elements and issue alerts to interested parties when they fail.

When coupled with event correlation and other forms of analysis, monitoring will be important in supporting problem determination and recovery when a fault is found or suspected. Applying monitoring, auditing, and verification tests at all the needed points without burdening systems with excessive bandwidth or processing demands will be a challenge. Technologies to allow statistical or sample-based testing in a dynamic environment may prove helpful.

The vision of autonomic systems as a complex supply web makes problem determination both easier and harder than it is now. An autonomic element that detects poor performance or failure in a supplier may not attempt a diagnosis; it may simply work around the problem by finding a new supplier. In other situations, however, it will be necessary to determine why one or more elements are failing, preferably without shutting down and restarting the entire system. This requires theoretically grounded tools for tracing, simulation, and problem determination in complex dynamic environments. Particularly when autonomic elements—or applications based on interactions among multiple elements—have a large amount of state, recovering gracefully and quickly from failure or restarting applications after software has been upgraded or after a function has been relocated to new machines will be challenging. David Patterson and colleagues at the University of California, Berkeley, and Stanford University have made a promising start in this direction.[3]

Upgrading

Autonomic elements will need to upgrade themselves from time to time. They might subscribe to a service that alerts them to the availability of relevant upgrades and decide for themselves when to apply the upgrade, possibly with guidance from another element or a human. Alternatively, the system could create entirely new elements as part of a system upgrade, eliminating outmoded elements only after the new ones establish that they are working properly.

Managing the Life Cycle

Autonomic elements will typically be engaged in many activities simultaneously—participating in one or more negotiations at various phases of completion, proactively seeking inputs from other elements, and so on. They will need to schedule and prioritize their myriad activities, and they will need to represent their life cycle so that they can both reason about it and communicate it to other elements.

RELATIONSHIPS AMONG AUTONOMIC ELEMENTS

In its most dynamic and elaborate form, the service relationship among autonomic elements will also have a life cycle. Each stage of this life cycle engenders its own set of engineering challenges and standardization requirements.

Specification

An autonomic element must have associated with it a set of output services it can perform and a set of input services that it requires, expressed in a standard format so that other autonomic elements can understand it. Typically, the element will register with a directory service such as Universal Description, Discovery, and Integration (UDDI) or an Open Grid Services Architecture (OGSA) registry, providing a description of its capabilities and details about addresses and the protocols other elements or people can use to communicate with it.

Establishing standard service ontologies, a standard service description syntax, and semantics that are sufficiently expressive for machines to interpret and reason about is an area of active research. The U.S. Defense Advanced Research Projects Agency's semantic Web effort is representative.

Location

An autonomic element must be able to locate input services that it needs; in turn, other elements that require its output services must be able to locate that element.

To locate other elements dynamically, the element can look them up by name or function in a directory service, possibly using a search process that involves sophisticated reasoning about service ontologies. The element can then contact one or more potential service providers directly and converse with them to determine if it can provide exactly the service they require.

In many cases, autonomic elements will also need to judge the likely reliability or trustworthiness of potential partners—an area of active research with many unsolved fundamental problems.

Negotiation

Once an element finds potential providers of an input service, it must negotiate with them to obtain that service.

Negotiation can be construed broadly as any process by which an agreement is reached. In demand-for-service negotiation, the element providing a service is subservient to the one requesting it, and the provider must furnish the service unless it does not have sufficient resources to do so. Another simple form of negotiation is first-come, first-served, in which the provider satisfies all requests until it runs into resource limitations. In posted-price negotiation, the provider sets a price in real or artificial currency for its service, and the requester must take it or leave it.

More complex forms of negotiation include bilateral or multilateral negotiations over multiple attributes, such as price, service level, and priority, involving multiple rounds of proposals and counterproposals. A third-party arbiter can run an auction or otherwise assist these more complex negotiations, especially when they are multilateral.

Negotiation will be a rich source of engineering and scientific challenges for autonomic computing. Elements need flexible ways to express multiattribute needs and capabilities, and they need mechanisms for deriving these expressions from human input or from computation. They also need effective negotiation strategies and protocols to establish the rules of negotiation and govern the flow of messages among the negotiators. There must be languages for expressing service agreements—the culmination of successful negotiation—in their transient and final forms.

Efforts to standardize the representation of agreements are underway, but mechanisms for negotiating, enforcing, and reasoning about agreements are lacking, as are methods for translating them into action plans.

Provisioning

Once two elements reach an agreement, they must provision their internal resources. Provisioning may be as simple as noting in an access list that a particular element can request service in the future, or it may entail establishing additional relationships with other elements, which become subcontractors in providing some part of the agreed-on service or task.

Operation

Once both sides are properly provisioned, they operate under the negotiated agreement. The service provider's autonomic manager oversees the operation of its managed element, monitoring it to ensure that the agreement is being honored; the service requester might similarly monitor the level of service.

If the agreement were violated, one or both elements would seek an appropriate remedy. The remedy may be to assess a penalty, renegotiate the agreement, and take technical measures to minimize any harm from the failure, or even terminate the agreement.

Termination

When the agreement has run its course, the parties agree to terminate it, freeing their internal resources for other uses and terminating agreements for input services that are no longer needed. The parties may record pertinent information about the service relationship locally, or store it in a database a reputation element maintains.

Other System-wide Issues

Other important engineering issues that arise at the system level include security, privacy, and trust, and the emergence of new types of services to serve the needs of other autonomic elements.

Autonomic computing systems will be subject to all the security, privacy, and trust issues that traditional computing systems must now address. Autonomic elements and systems will need to both establish and abide by security policies, just as human administrators do today, and they will need to do so in an understandable and fail-safe manner.

Systems that span multiple administrative domains—especially those that cross company boundaries—will face many of the challenges that now confront electronic commerce. These include authentication, authorization, encryption, signing, secure auditing and monitoring, non-repudiation, data aggregation and identity masking, and compliance with complex legal requirements that vary from state to state or country to country.

The autonomic system infrastructure must let autonomic elements identify themselves, verify the identities of other entities with which they communicate, verify that a message has not been altered in transit, and ensure that unauthorized parties do not read messages and other data. To satisfy privacy policies and laws, elements must also appropriately protect private and personal information that comes into their possession. Measures that keep data segregated according to its origin or its purpose must be extended into the realm of autonomic elements to satisfy policy and legal requirements.

Autonomic systems must be robust against new and insidious forms of attack that use self-management based on high-level policies to their own advantage. By altering or otherwise manipulating high-level policies, an attacker could gain much greater leverage than is possible in nonautonomic systems. Preventing such problems may require a new subfield of computer security that seeks to thwart fraud and the fraudulent persuasion of autonomic elements.

On a larger scale, autonomic elements will be agents, and autonomic systems will in effect be multiagent systems built on a Web service or OGSA infrastructure. Autonomic systems will be inhabited by middle agents that serve as intermediaries of various types, including directory services, matchmakers, brokers, auctioneers, data aggregators, and dependency managers. They will also be used for detecting, recording, and publicizing information about functional dependencies among autonomic elements—event correlators, security analysts, time-stampers, sentinels, and other types of monitors that assess the health of other elements or of the system as a whole.

Traditionally, many of these services have been part of the system infrastructure; in a multiagent, autonomic world, moving them out of the infrastructure and representing them as autonomic elements they will be more natural and flexible.

Goal Specification

While autonomic systems will assume much of the burden of system operation and integration, it will still be up to humans to provide those systems with policies—the goals and constraints that govern their actions. The enormous leverage of autonomic systems will greatly reduce human errors, but it will also greatly magnify the consequences of any error humans do make in specifying goals.

The indirect effect of policies on system configuration and behavior exacerbates the problem because tracing and correcting policy errors will be very difficult. It is thus critical to ensure that the specified goals represent what is really desired. Two engineering challenges stem from this mandate: Ensure that goals are specified correctly in the first place, and ensure that systems behave reasonably even when they are not.

In many cases, the set of goals to be specified will be complex, multidimensional, and conflicting. Even a goal as superficially simple as "maximize utility" will require a human to express a complicated multiattribute utility function. A key to reducing error will be to simplify and clarify the means by which humans express their goals to computers. Psychologists and computer scientists will need to work together to strike the right balance between overwhelming humans with too many questions or too much information and underempowering them with too few options or too little information.

The second challenge—ensuring reasonable system behavior in the face of erroneous input—is another facet of robustness: Autonomic systems will need to protect themselves from input goals that are inconsistent, implausible, dangerous, or unrealizable with the resources at hand. Autonomic systems will subject such inputs to extra validation, and when self-protective measures fail, they will rely on deep-seated notions of what constitutes acceptable behavior to detect and correct problems. In some cases, such as resource overload, they will inform human operators about the nature of the problem and offer alternative solutions.

SCIENTIFIC CHALLENGES

The success of autonomic computing will hinge on the extent to which theorists can identify universal principles that span the multiple levels at which autonomic systems can exist—from systems to enterprises to economies.

Behavioral Abstractions and Models

Defining appropriate abstractions and models for understanding, controlling, and designing emergent behavior in autonomic systems is the challenge at the heart of autonomic computing. We need fundamental mathematical work aimed at understanding how the properties of self-configuration, self-optimization, self-maintenance, and robustness arise from or depend on the behaviors, goals, and adaptivity of individual autonomic elements; the pattern and type of interactions among them; and the external influences or demands on the system.

Understanding the mapping from local behavior to global behavior is a necessary but insufficient condition for controlling and designing autonomic systems. We must also discover how to exploit the inverse relationship: How can we derive a set of behavioral and interaction rules that, if embedded in individual autonomic elements, will induce a desired global behavior? The non-linearity of emergent behavior makes such an inversion highly nontrivial.

One plausible approach couples advanced search and optimization techniques with parameterized models of the local-to-global relationship and the likely set of environmental influences to which the system will be subjected. Melanie Mitchell and colleagues at the Santa Fe Institute have pioneered this approach, using genetic algorithms to evolve the local transformation rules of simple cellular automata to achieve desired global behaviors.[4] At NASA, David Wolpert and colleagues have studied algorithms that, given a high-level global objective, derive individual goals for individual agents. When each agent selfishly follows its goals, the desired global behavior results.[5]

These methods are just a start. We have yet to understand fundamental limits on what classes of global behavior can be achieved, nor do we have practical methods for designing emergent system behavior. Moreover, although these methods establish the rules of a system at design time, autonomic systems must deal with shifting conditions that can be known only at runtime. Control-theoretic approaches may prove useful in this capacity; some autonomic managers may use control systems to govern the behavior of their associated managed elements.

The greatest value may be in extending distributed or hierarchical control theories, which consider interactions among independently or hierarchically controlled elements, rather than focusing on an individual controlled element. Newer paradigms for control may be needed when there is no clear separation of scope or time scale.

Robustness Theory

A related challenge is to develop a theory of robustness for autonomic systems, including definitions and analyses of robustness, diversity, redundancy, and optimality and their relationship to one another. The Santa Fe Institute recently began a multidisciplinary study on this topic.

Learning and Optimization Theory

Machine learning by a single agent in relatively static environments is well-studied and well-supported by strong theoretical results. However, in more sophisticated autonomic systems, individual elements will be agents that continually adapt to their environment—an environment that consists largely of other agents. Thus, even with stable external conditions, agents are adapting to one another, which violates the traditional assumptions on which single-agent learning theories are based.

There are no guarantees of convergence. In fact, interesting forms of instability have been observed in such cases. Learning in multiagent systems is a challenging but relatively unexplored problem, with virtually no major theorems and only a handful of empirical results.

Just as learning becomes a more challenging problem in multiagent systems, so does optimization. The root cause is the same—whether it is because they are learning or because they are optimizing, agents are changing their behavior, making it necessary for other agents to change their behavior, potentially leading to instabilities. Optimization in such an environment must deal with dynamics created by a collective mode of oscillation rather than a drifting environmental signal. Optimization techniques that assume a stationary environment have been observed to fail pathologically in multiagent systems; therefore, they must either be revamped or replaced with new methods.

Negotiation Theory

A solid theoretical foundation for negotiation must take into account two perspectives. From the perspective of individual elements, we must develop and analyze algorithms and negotiation protocols and determine what bidding or negotiation algorithms are most effective. From the perspective of the system as a whole, we must establish how overall system behavior depends on the mixture of negotiation algorithms that various autonomic elements use, and establish the conditions under which multilateral—as opposed to bilateral—negotiations among elements are necessary or desirable.

Automated Statistical Modeling

Statistical models of large networked systems will let autonomic elements or systems detect or predict overall performance problems from a stream of sensor data from individual devices. At long time scales—during which the configuration of the system changes—we seek methods that automate the aggregation of statistical variables to reduce the dimensionality of the problem to a size that is amenable to adaptive learning and optimization techniques that operate on shorter time scales.

Is it possible to meet the grand challenge of autonomic computing without magic and without fully solving the AI problem? I believe it is, but it will take time and patience. Long before many of the more challenging problems are solved, less automated realizations of autonomic systems will be extremely valuable, and their value will increase substantially as autonomic computing technology improves and earns greater trust and acceptance.

A vision this large requires that we pool expertise in many areas of computer science as well as in disciplines that lie far beyond computing traditional boundaries. We must look to scientists studying nonlinear dynamics and complexity for new theories of emergent phenomena and robustness. We must look to economists and e-commerce researchers for ideas and technologies about negotiation and supply webs. We must look to psychologists and human factors researchers for new goal-definition and visualization paradigms and for ways to help humans build trust in autonomic systems. We must look to the legal profession, since many of the same issues that arise in the context of e-commerce will be important in autonomic systems that span organizational or national boundaries.

Bridging the language and cultural divides among the many disciplines needed for this endeavor and harnessing the diversity to yield successful and perhaps universal approaches to autonomic computing will perhaps be the greatest challenge. It will be interesting to see what new cross-disciplines develop as we begin to work together to solve these fundamental problems.

RESEARCH PROJECTS IN AUTONOMIC COMPUTING

Listed below are a selection of brief descriptions of and links to some of the projects underway at IBM. These projects are at different stages of development or progress. Some of them have already appeared in products. Some are just beginning. This list of projects will grow as new areas of research emerge. Check the main IBM research Web page regularly for updates and new projects announced.

Gryphon: Pub/Sub (Middleware)

This middleware for Publish/Subscribe is used to distribute large volumes of data/content in real time to thousands of clients distributed throughout a large "public" network, such as a wide area extranet or intranet that is too large or complex to be centrally administered to support specific applications.

Gryphon has already been tested and deployed over the Internet for real-time sports score distribution at the U.S. Open, and Australian Open in tennis and Ryder Cup in golf, and for monitoring and statistics reporting at the Sydney Olympics.

See *www.research.ibm.com/gryphon/* for additional information.

HWLM: Heterogeneous WorkLoad Management (Total System)

Workload management, a function of the IBM OS/390 operating system base control program, allows installations to define business objectives for a clustered environment (Parallel Sysplex in IBM OS/390). This business policy is expressed in terms that relate to business goals and importance, rather than the internal controls used by the operating system. The IBM OS/390 ensures that system resources are assigned to achieve the specified business objectives.

See *www.research.ibm.com/journal/sj/362/aman.html* for additional information.

LEO: DB2's Learning Optimizer

LEO is a comprehensive way to repair incorrect statistics and cardinality estimates from a query execution plan (QEP). By monitoring previously executed queries, LEO compares the optimizer's estimates with actuals at each step in a QEP and computes adjustments to cost estimates and statistics that may be used during future query optimizations.

In practice, LEO actually learns from its past mistakes—i.e., accelerating, sometimes drastically, future executions of similar queries—while incurring a negligible monitoring overhead on query compilation and execution.

See *http://www.research.ibm.com/* for additional information.

SMART: Self-Managing and Resource Tuning DB2 (Middleware)

IBM will be building a SMART (Self-Managing and Resource Tuning) database into upcoming versions of DB2. This database is designed to reduce the human intervention needed to run and maintain a database. For example, the user can opt not to be involved and the database will automatically detect failures when they occur (and correct them). The database will also configure itself by installing operating systems and data automatically to cope with the changing demands of e-business and the Internet.

The long-term vision is to offer customers the option of preventative maintenance or zero administration/zero maintenance to reduce the total cost of ownership. LEO is one look at the future of "SMART" databases and how they will operate more effectively.

See *www.research.ibm.com/autonomic/academic/research.html* for additional information.

Storage Tank

Storage Tank is a new file system for storage area networks that is being developed at the IBM Almaden Research lab, located in Silicon Valley in California. Major features of this system include heterogeneous file sharing, policy-based file and storage management, high performance, and scalability. This technology is currently used in IBM's Tivoli's Storage Manager product.

See *www.almaden.ibm.com/* for additional information.

UFiler: Facilitating Enterprise File Access/Sharing

IBM developed and demonstrated the first Web-based enterprise file system solution with the UFiler project. This solution facilitates access and sharing of files that can be geographically distributed over an entire enterprise or the Internet. It allows access to files anytime and anywhere, and files are protected through fine-grained access-control lists. UFiler desktop clients allow applications to access files stored in UFiler as if they were on a local disk. WebDAV integration is prototyped to allow Windows users to access their UFiler files through WebFolder and other WebDAV-enabled applications such as Office 2000. UFiler's automated backup ensures the integrity of user data. Currently UFiler supports AFS and allows existing AFS users to benefit from UFiler's browser interface. Other file systems, such as CIFS or NFS, will be added when they get deployed within IBM on an enterprise scale. UFiler's back-end design includes SAN-based server clustering. Failover and load balancing among servers can be achieved without moving data

See w*ww.research.ibm.com/autonomic/academic/research.html* for additional information.

UNIVERSITY RESEARCH PROJECTS IN AUTONOMIC COMPUTING

IBM Research contributes to university research in a number of ways, including awarding money and equipment grants. The following projects are funded and co-managed by IBM research and other units within IBM. Note that the projects are spread throughout the world.

Berkeley University of California: OceanStore

OceanStore is a global persistent data store designed to scale to billions of users. It provides a consistent, highly available, and durable storage utility atop an infrastructure comprised of untrusted servers. Any computer can join the infrastructure—users need only subscribe to a single OceanStore service provider, although they may consume storage and bandwidth from many different providers. Researchers at Berkeley are exploring the space of Introspective Computing—systems that perform continuous, online adaptation. Applications include on-chip tolerance of flaky components and continuous optimization to adapt to server failures and denial of service attacks as well as autonomic computing.

See *http://oceanstore.cs.berkeley.edu/* for additional information.

Berkeley University of California: Recovery-Oriented Computing

Recovery-Oriented Computing (ROC) project is a joint Berkeley/Stanford research project that is investigating novel techniques for building highly dependable Internet services. ROC emphasizes recovery from failures rather than failure-avoidance. This philosophy is motivated by the observation that even the most robust systems still occasionally encounter failures due to human operator error, transient or permanent hardware failure, or software anomalies resulting from software aging. David Pattersen is a Professor in Computer Science at UC Berkeley working on the ROC project.

See *http://roc.cs.berkeley.edu/* for additional information.

University of Bologna, Italy: Anthill project

Anthill is a framework built to support the design, implementation, and evaluation of peer-to-peer (P2P) applications. P2P systems are characterized by decentralized control, large scale, and extreme dynamism of their operating environment and can be seen as instances of Complex Adaptive Systems, typically found in biological and social sciences. Anthill exploits this analogy and advocates a methodology whereby the desired application properties correspond to the "emergent behavior" of the underlying complex adaptive system. An Anthill system consists of a dynamic network of peer nodes; societies of adaptive agents (ants) travel through this network, interacting with nodes and cooperating with other agents in order to solve complex problems. Anthill can be used to construct different classes of P2P services that exhibit resilience, adaptation, and self-organization properties.

See *http://www.cs.unibo.it/projects/anthill* for additional information.

Duke University: Software Rejuvenation

Software rejuvenation is a proactive fault management technique aimed at cleaning up a system's internal state to prevent the occurrence of more severe crash failures in the future. It involves occasionally terminating an application or a system, cleaning its internal state, and restarting it. Current methods of software rejuvenation include system restart, application restart (partial rejuvenation), and node/application failover (in a cluster system). Software rejuvenation is a cost-effective technique for dealing with software faults that include protection not only against hard failures, but against performance degradation as well. Duke University collaborated with IBM to develop the IBM Director Software Rejuvenation tool.

See *http://www.software-rejuvenation.com/* for additional information.

University College London, England: Bio-Inspired Approaches to Autonomous Configuration of Distributed Systems

Ian Marshall, a visiting Royal Society Industrial Fellow from British Telecom, is working with Lionel Sacks on bio-inspired approaches to autonomous configuration of distributed systems (including bacteria inspired approach). Next generation networks require new control techniques to increase automation and deal with complexity. Active networks in particular will require the management and control systems to evolve extremely rapidly, since users will be continuously adding new applications, services, and virtual configurations. This research is exploring novel ad-hoc distributed control algorithms and architectures derived from biological and geophysical systems and measurements of fabricated systems such as the World Wide Web.

See *http://www-dse.doc.ic.ac.uk/projects.html.*

SUMMARY AND CONCLUSIONS

Since 1945, when IBM set up its first research laboratory hosted in renovated fraternity house near Columbia University in New York City, its management has realized the value of both internal and external research. Indeed it is fair to state that IBM would not be the size and success it is today without continuous innovative research programs that turn ideas and concepts into products, and then substantial profit. IBM has nearly 3,000 researchers worldwide with eight locations in six countries and has cumulatively produced more research breakthroughs than the rest of the entire IT industry combined.

With these enormous sources available to autonomic computing we can expect to see significant new enhancements, products, and services.

Note: Grateful thanks are due to Jeff Kephart of IBM, who contributed much to the discussion on research challenges.

NOTES

1. Statement made at IBM Research Web site. See *http://www.research.ibm.com/autonomic/academic/.*
2. For information see *http://www.research.ibm.com/autonomic/overview/.*
3. For information see *http://www.cs.berkeley.edu/~pattrsn/.*
4. For information see *http://www.santafe.edu/sfi/research/indexResearchAreas.html.*
5. For information see *http://ic.arc.nasa.gov/~dhw/.*

CHAPTER 18

FINAL THOUGHTS

INTRODUCTION

In this final chapter, we shall review some of the topics we have discussed so far and take a hard look at the state of autonomic computing today and where it needs to be in the future. Sir Arthur C. Clarke, noted science fiction writer, futurist, and inventor of the satellite industry is a family friend. Arthur's father and my grandfather were the best of friends in England. A few years ago, Arthur gave me some good advice, *"Beware of anyone who is predicting the future."* So it is with some trepidation that I attempt to review the future of autonomic computing.

The new connected e-business on demand economy is changing the fundamental rules of business, and the fundamental nature of work itself. No longer will the traditional, static, compartmentalized, stovepipe, and hierarchical model of the workplace suffice in a speed-based, agile, flexible, global, and knowledge-based economy. Mobility, speed, simplicity, connectivity, integrated processes, and highly interoperable systems and applications are the emerging drivers of enterprise efficiency, effectiveness and inventiveness.

At the center of the new economy are people—specifically people's skills, intelligence, relationships, and imagination as the currency of *value.* And new hybrid business infrastructures that combine the power of IT with places and spaces newly conceived and adapted for more mobile and collaborative work are proving to be a key ingredient in the electronically mediated workplace.

The fundamental reality is that corporations will be compelled to substantially increase their investment in people to maintain competitive advantage in the connected on demand economy. This increase in IT investment will compel corporations to transform in part—"bricks to clicks"—to shift resources to these incremental investments.

The second fundamental reality is that many traditional workplace locations and settings are incompatible with the highly mobile, wireless, and collaborative style of the knowledge-based workforce. To attract and retain talented employees, traditional workplaces must be adapted for new flexible work styles and expectations. For these reasons particularly, workplace transformation is emerging as one of the key drivers of change in the overall on demand/e-business transformation.

It is the implementation of the major strategies, implementation processes, success criteria, organizational best practices, and performance metrics of workplace transformation. But these alone are insufficient without the commitment and resolve of senior enterprise leadership to embrace workplace transformation as a key imperative in reinventing the enterprise to compete in the new economy.

IT'S ALL ABOUT SPEED

There are examples in this book showing how hard it is to predict the speed of technological advance or its effect on social or commercial life. Space travel. Cloning. Cures for cancer. The search for clean, renewable energy sources. The sense of apprehension in the last days of 1999 arose from the fact that while most experts believed the "Y2K bug" would not shut down computer systems, no one really could be sure.

Several years into the future, when we can look back on the early in the 21st century, we may determine that "speed" is the one word that stands above other possible descriptors for this time.

1. Speed, as in the rate at which new ideas are transmitted to every corner of the globe.
2. Speed, as in the rapidity with which markets change, new markets are created, and old ones abandoned.
3. Speed at which corporate decisions are made or not made.
4. Speed, as in the ever-shortening product to market cycles.
5. Speed at which new technology is developed and implemented.
6. Speed, as in the rollout of new business ventures.
7. Speed, as in the accelerating rate of technological change.
8. Speed at which IT is required to develop and implement new business solutions.
9. Speed kills the competition.
10. Speed is vital to the digital economy.
11. Speed is a new currency.

Speed is also the one word which best describes the key business drivers influencing the management of information systems. Speed in business demands flexibility in management and technology to respond to rapidly changing market conditions. Speed. Flexibility. Responsiveness. We heard these words over and over from senior IT executives. These executives are typically charged with responsibility for helping their organization make effective use of information technology. Speed and time are the new currency of business.

As the balance of power continues shift more rapidly from producers to consumers, the next wave of e-business will surface, characterized by the realignment and redefinition of entire industries. In wave three, enterprises will attempt to build dynamic e-businesses capable of rapidly accommodating and participating in a range of value chains with a variety of new partners. In the process, organizations will face a series of challenges centered on what customers will pay for and how best to align the business to meet their changing demands. This will require launching some major initiatives:

- Migrating existing businesses and operating models to a defensible competitive position.
- Applying brands across multiple businesses and industries.
- Assessing prospective economic opportunities (and threats) from emerging technologies.
- Leveraging next-generation technologies to create competitive advantage.
- Gaining customer acceptance and loyalty.

THE STATE OF AUTONOMIC COMPUTING TODAY

It is pertinent in this last chapter to review how far autonomic computing has come in the technology race and where it needs to go in order to be more successful. We need to take a long hard look at this technology, and I will provide a number of specific recommendations.

The Marketplace and Companies

An increasing number of companies have developed their own autonomic computing projects. Large organizations, such as HP, Sun, and Microsoft, are already developing this technology. The markets follow the latest products and services. It is essential that all companies exchange research ideas. For example IBM, Sun, HP, and other companies in the industry should be exchanging ideas at the research level.

An area where this will be successful is the collaboration in building autonomic infrastructure around grid computing. This is precisely because in order to build a heterogeneous, self-managing infrastructure, you need to have a set of common protocols that run on every system, so that the various systems can collaborate with each other.

You will see more collaboration in the IT autonomic community on security that works across various systems and on self-healing algorithms. For example, workload managers that run across the infrastructure can detect which nodes are having problems and should therefore be taken offline, and route that work to other nodes that are operating well. Because of heterogeneous infrastructure, we need common protocols. Building autonomic capabilities is one of major application areas on top of grid protocols.

Open Standards

Good progress has been made in the development, construction, and assessment of the much-needed open standards for autonomic computing. Industry participation and corporate interest is increasing. All IT vendors must become engaged to keep this momentum going and not let it flounder or become dormant—which is always a risk in the standards. The IT industry is going through major changes. New concepts in technology, such as autonomic computing, Web services, and grid computing, are opening the door to tremendous opportunities for taking business to the next level of profitability. The potential of these technologies to transform business is truly remarkable, and open standards and autonomic software will play increasingly critical roles in this new world. Just as open standards were critical to the emergence of the Internet and the first generation of e-business, they will play a critical role in the next generation of autonomic computing, e-business on demand. In the first generation of e-business, standards allowed heterogeneous systems to communicate with each other and exchange data. This was critical to the development of the World Wide Web, e-markets, e-commerce, and intercompany integration. These capabilities drove cost down and productivity up, while increasing both speed to market and business agility. During the next 10 years, business agility will continue to be the critical business differentiator for businesses and governments, and those that can shift their business strategies quickly in response to market dynamics, emerging opportunities, and competitive threats will prosper as on demand organizations.

THEN AND NOW

Table 18.1 compares the four states of autonomic computing with how we manage today and what it will be like with full autonomic systems.

Table 18.1 A Comparison of Systems, Then and Now

Concept	Current Computing	Autonomic Computing
Self-configuration	Corporate data centers have multiple vendors and platforms. Installing, configuring, and integrating systems is time-consuming and error prone	Automated configuration of components and systems follows high-level policies. Rest of system adjusts automatically and seamlessly
Self-optimization	Systems have hundreds of manually set nonlinear tuning parameters, and their number increases with each release	Components and systems continually seek opportunities to improve their own performance and efficiency
Self-healing	Problem determination in large, complex systems can take a team of programmers weeks	System automatically detects, diagnoses, and repairs localized software and hardware problems

Table 18.1 A Comparison of Systems, Then and Now (Continued)

Concept	Current Computing	Autonomic Computing
Self-protections	Detection of and recovery from attacks and cascading failures is manual	System automatically defends against malicious attacks or cascading failures. It uses early warning to anticipate and prevent systemwide failures

FUTURE RECOMMENDATIONS

The following list is a select number of recommendations and observations that have come to light during the research and writing of this book. These recommendations are not in any specific order—rather they are a list of thoughts, suggestions, and recommendations that may make autonomic computing more functional.

- Develop autonomic tools and technologies on top of existing standards.
- Develop autonomic-based systems using multivendor approaches.
- Develop metrics to assess the relative strengths and weakness of different approaches.
- Provide mature software development methodologies and tools for autonomic-based systems.
- Develop sophisticated yet easy-to-use autonomic environments to include support for design, test, maintenance, and visualization of autonomic-oriented systems.
- Develop libraries of interaction protocols designed for specific autonomic behavior interactions.
- Develop the ability for autonomics to collectively evolve languages and protocols specific to the application domain and the autonomics involved.
- Work toward autonomic-enabled semantic Web services.
- Develop tools for effective sharing and negotiation strategies.
- Develop computational models of norms and social structure.
- Develop sophisticated organizational views of autonomic systems.
- Advance the state of the art in the theory and practice of negotiation strategies.
- Develop an enhanced understanding of autonomic society dynamics.
- Advance the state of the art in the theory and practice of argumentation strategies.
- Develop autonomic-based eScience systems for the scientific community.
- Develop techniques for allowing users to specify their preference and desired outcome of negotiation in complex environments.
- Develop techniques to enable autonomics to identify, create, and dissolve coalitions in multiautonomic negotiation and argumentation contexts.
- Work on enhancing autonomic abilities to include appropriate adaptation mechanisms.
- Develop techniques for autonomic personalization.
- Develop distributed learning mechanisms.

- Develop techniques to enable automatic runtime reconfiguration and redesign of autonomic systems.
- Develop techniques for testing the reliability of autonomics.
- Undertake research on methods for ensuring security and verifiability of autonomic systems.
- Develop and implement trust and reputation mechanisms.
- Engage in related-research standardization activities (e.g., UDDI, WDL, WSFL, XLANG, OMG, CORBA, and other widely used industrial-strength open standards).
- Build autonomic prototypes spanning organizational boundaries (potentially conflicting).
- Encourage early adopters of autonomic technology, especially those who take some risk. Provide incentives.
- Develop a catalogue of early adopter case studies, both successful and unsuccessful.
- Provide analyses and publish reasons for success and failure cases.
- Identify and publish best practices for autonomic-oriented development and deployment.
- Support open standardization efforts.
- Support early industry training efforts.
- Provide migration paths, helping industries protect their investments and smoothly evolve autonomic-based services, solutions, systems, and products.
- Focus on process optimization, intelligent services and added value functionality, rather than on creating new infrastructure.
- Build technology bridges with distributed systems, software engineering, and object technology communities.
- Clearly articulate the relationship between distributed software engineering and autonomic computing.
- Explore and clarify relationships between autonomic theories and abstract theories of distributed computation.
- Build bridges, especially to uncertainty in AI, logic programming, and traditional mathematical modeling communities.
- Begin to teach autonomic computing in colleges and universities.
- Establish and fund an industry-wide Autonomic Institute and establish as participants IBM, Sun, HP, Cisco, Oracle, and all other industry vendors.

CONCLUSIONS

We have now explored the technology and strategy perspectives of autonomic computing. In this book, a full analysis and treatment of many topics of autonomic computing and its operating environment were provided. We have explored the fact that the autonomic computing journey is an evolution, not a revolution, or a temporary state of operations. We discussed that autonomic computing is a state of operational efficiencies, with concepts, methods, and techniques. There are a number of very successful technologies and strategies, along with products and services, which are available, today, to begin the transformation.

Autonomic computing is something that almost all major businesses, worldwide, will have to confront, sooner or later. This asks the question of whether you, as a business leader or a consumer of services, can see it clear enough. As a senior IT manager, do you feel or have you observed the strong industry pressures to transform? Or, do you feel the economic factors related to considering autonomic computing solutions and transformation activities for your enterprise?

Throughout this book, we have explored technical and strategic concepts that, in many cases go well beyond what those skilled in the traditional art of business operations have yet conceived or practiced. This new operational state of autonomic computing indeed requires a transformation, in many ways, inviting us all to continuously strive to achieve and maintain a new competitive edge. This includes tighter business partnerships intersecting with autonomic operations, new and innovative ways of thinking, and setting precedents for a new plateau of conducting business operations.

Consumers and Internet content providers are rapidly growing to expect more and more advanced services, when we want them—24/7—and exactly how we want them delivered. We also have a strong desire for more pervasive forms of conducting our daily lives utilizing a plurality of devices that are available in a multitude of form factors. We seem to desire to be continuously networked to these advanced services even with our appliances in our homes.

Conversely, global and in-country telecommunications firms delivering these services through "pipes" of a sort are working very diligently to bring the best and most advanced services to us. Likewise, business enterprises acting as service providers are striving to deliver the "killer applications" that we will all want to utilize in our everyday lives. Content providers are partnering with service providers to help them deliver the best possible forms of information to the general public. Technologies have become so complex that we are seeking a means for simplification. Autonomic computing is a state of achievement, not necessarily a plan of delivery.

Governments of the world and explorers of medicine, science, research, and academics are all trying to determine how best to leverage these types of powerful on demand services. As we have explored throughout the discussions in this book, some of the world's most powerful computing environments have been applied to the world's most difficult problems: cancer, smallpox, AIDS, and many more. As with any evolution, it is simply time itself that is required for us to see a whole New World of evolutionary business operations and cultural practices. Many of us see it now, and some of us have already achieved it, but this is not by any means a signal for us to become complacent.

The Internet continues to advance daily in the capabilities it provides our global societies. We are discovering ways in which to enhance our business positioning across the markets. Industries strive to increase time to markets and cut both operational and capital expenditures, while at the same time delivering enhanced forms of services. We are discovering ways in which to simplify

our daily lives, and even ways in which to increase our efficiencies in schools as students—
young and old alike. We now demand that all products and services deliver richer and more
robust features than ever imagined. Why? Simply, because it is possible to deliver vast amounts
of information—on demand.

Autonomic computing is an operational state of achievement, one that continues to refine itself
each and every day: A transformation. These perspectives on technology and strategy alone will
help to enable this new state of on demand operations. It is one that any business can ascertain,
once one understands the points of entry and the values yielded from such a transformation. And
so I pass the baton now to you, faithful reader of this book, and hope you will take the grand
challenge we discussed earlier and adopt and transform your enterprise by implementing autonomic computing solutions. Regrettably, there is not much alternative, for to continue on the
path of complexity will sentence us to a doomed future and ultimately chaos—which is unacceptable. Therefore, go forth and implement it!

One last thought:

> It's time to design and build computing systems capable of running themselves,
> adjusting to varying circumstances and preparing their resources to handle most effi-
> ciently the workloads we put upon them. These autonomic systems must anticipate
> needs and allow users to concentrate on what they want to accomplish rather than
> figuring out how to rig the computing systems to get them there.

Glossary of Autonomic Terms

his section contains definitions of Autonomic Computing terms, which are utilized in this book.

Analyze
The function of an autonomic manager that models complex situations.

Autonomic
Being accomplished without overt thought and action. An example is the human autonomic nervous system, which monitors and regulates temperature, pupil dilation, respiration, heart rate, digestion, etc.

Autonomic computing
An approach to self-managed computing systems with a minimum of human interference.

Autonomic manager
A part of an autonomic element that manages a managed element within the same autonomic element.

Data collection
Definitions for standard situational event formats in autonomic computing architecture (also called logging). This notion is one of the core technologies of autonomic computing.

Domain
A domain is a collection of resources that have been explicitly or implicitly grouped together for management purposes.

Effector
A way to change the state of a managed element.

Execute

The function of an autonomic manager that is responsible for interpreting plans and interacting with element effectors to insure that the appropriate actions occur.

Install (Installation)

Definitions for standard methods to describe software deployment and installation. This notion is one of the core technologies of autonomic computing.

Knowledge

The common information that the monitor, analyze, plan, and execute functions require in order to work in a coordinated manner.

Maturity Index

A graduated scale that expresses the level of maturity of autonomic computing, where level 1 is basic (completely manual), level 2 is managed, level 3 is predictive, level 4 is adaptive, and level 5 is completely autonomic.

OGSA (Open Grid Services Architecture)

A grid system architecture based on an integration of grid and Web services concepts and technologies.

Plan

The function of an autonomic manager that provides a way to coordinate interrelated actions over time.

Policy

A definite goal, course, or method of action to guide and determine future decisions. Policies are implemented or executed within a particular context. This is a set of behavioral constraints and preferences that influence decisions made by an autonomic manager. This notion of policy utilization is one of the core technologies of autonomic computing.

Policy-based management

A method of managing system behavior or resources by setting policies that the system interprets.

Self-configuring

An element setting itself up for operation.

Self-healing

An element repairing damage regarding its own integrity of operation.

Self-managing

An element directing and controlling itself. This is most often regarding self-configuring, self-optimizing, self-protecting, and self-healing operations.

Self-optimizing

An element tuning or improving its own performance.

Self-protecting
An element maintaining its own integrity of operation.

Sensor
A means to get information about a managed element.

Situations
Events that autonomic computing components report to the outside world. Situations vary in granularity and complexity, ranging from simple situations like the start of a component, to more complex situations like the failure of a disk subsystem.

Index

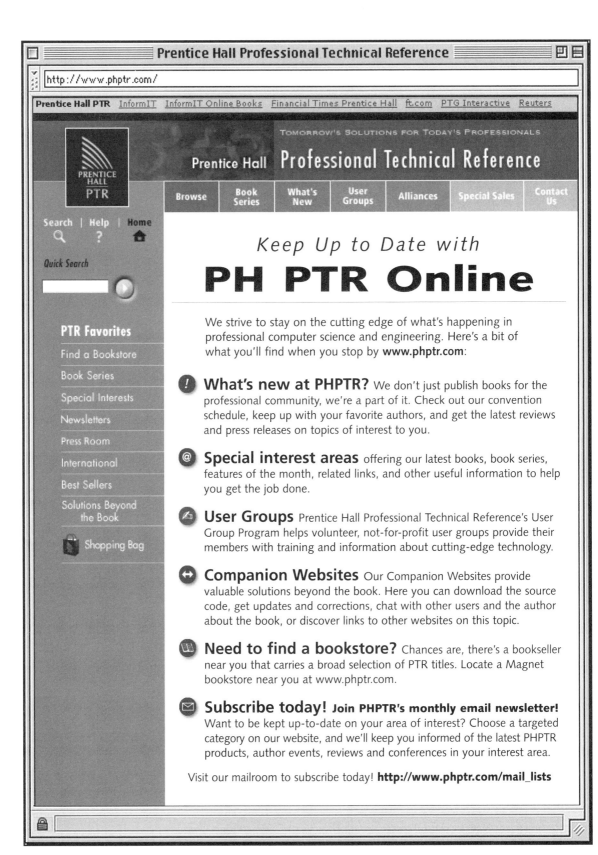